REQUIEM

for

AMERICAN

CRITICAL THINKING &
DEMOCRACY

GILLES M. K. DESMARAIS M.D.

PUBLISHED BY
Gilles M. K. Desmarais M. D.

Library of Congress Cataloging-in-Publication Data
Desmarais, Gilles M. K., M. D.

A Requiem for American Critical Thinking & Democracy

CONTENTS

PREFACE

After forty years in the practice of psychiatry, I've come to realize that we all suffer from blind spots. Even the best educated and terribly bright people suffer from these blind spots and are often very uninformed about significant areas of their lives. We tend to be highly emotional creatures, and our responses are often of the knee-jerk type. Slowing down our automatic responses, looking at things in a more logical light and using critical thinking is very important to individual and cultural lives. The human brain apparently has the choice of slowly using its intellectual functions and potentials, or simply putting it into high gear as quickly as possible. If we look at our cultural, political and economic surroundings we often find that we have just been swept along by the currents of our time. We may end up being very sorry that we did not help to navigate our own ship. This book is about the consequences that we are finding in our culture and our government. I did a good deal of research and found some "very interesting" information about the history of how the financial world and the powerful people evolved so that there is an ever-growing gap between the wealthy and the not so wealthy. The need for a radical change in our educational system is necessary to prevent the erosion of our personal freedoms and our national sovereignty. It has been a major enterprise. I have learned a good deal about why we are involved with socialism, globalization and major financial and international crises. I would urge you to read this book...so that you can use your own critical thinking in both criticizing this book and evaluating how you could help to deal with the major cultural problems that we face in the United States of America. Of course many of these issues are of concern to any earthly creature...wherever he is found.

VIII

INTRODUCTION

You will be meeting Izzy, otherwise known as Job Lost, a banker who has a mix of strengths and weaknesses. He ends up having quite a number of catastrophic events as a consequence of *Dame Fortune* and his own way of dealing with life. You will be exposed to some funny formulas and nonscientific ways of looking at science and life in general. You should have some fun reading this book. You'll see how a lack of "stopping to think" about what is going on around you leads to allowing others to run your life. The progress of wealth and power, and the influence wielded by their current inhabitants, will be openly discussed. You will be exposed to a good deal of material about how the financial world and the government really operate. It involves a lot of scary stuff. You will understand why emphasizing the need for a radical revamping of our educational system is a must. It does require all of us to do some thinking which, hopefully, will lead to some significant action.

PROLOGUE

You are about to be swept into a bewildering experience. Why should a fool ever write a book? Why is he talking about **European cave drawings** of thousands of years ago. Why is he talking about Social Security as a *giant Ponzi scheme* legitimized by Congress and the Supreme Court? Why is he looking at the world as an **upside down creature**, especially in education? Why are there no gyros controlling evolutionary trends, or are these gyros just really scary ones? Who is the thinker of the thought? Why is he talking about the **Assassins**? Why is he associating the **Rothschilds** with the **Khazar's**? Why are creativity and slave trading appearing in the same book? Is this fool using any critical thinking at all? Why? Why? Why? There are so many more questions. Is the fool only getting deeper and deeper into the quicksand? Has he stumbled into some very important stuff?

XIV

CRITICAL THINKING IN SEARCH OF WISDOM

Beware! A fool is writing this book. I told a friend that I was going to write a book about thinking, pick up some knowledge on the way and maybe stumble into some wisdom. He looked at me quizzically and said, "That's a laugh. You're the sort of guy who can dive into the deepest well of knowledge and come up bone dry." I think he was paraphrasing some well-known quotation. It sounds like something that Abraham Lincoln would've said. And it's not entirely fair since I'm pretty organized, except when I speak or act. I know that Abe did say, "better to remain silent and be thought a fool than to speak out and remove all doubt." Well, I'm going to go on with it anyway.

Let me get on with whatever nonsense I can come up with. Don't mind my *sintax*. I'll be introducing you a bit later to Izzy, who's no fool. This is a challenging century for *homo sapiens*, or should we call him *homo dyssapiens?* Human emotions interfere with objectivity. It'll become more complicated in the 21st century. I'm a very objective fellow and I've seen people avoid facing the truth about important issues. We all have biases acquired by our own observations and the influences of our friends and family. I'll give you a few examples.

We often say, "It logically follows," and jump to the wrong conclusions. That's a good example of not thinking logically. Fred and Ed are having a discussion about a budding romance, "I hear that Jeff is dating Cathy." "I can't believe that," says Ed. Ed simply does not believe that Jeff is handsome or smart enough to attract a beautiful and intelligent person like Cathy. Neither Fred nor Ed knows if Jeff has come into a large inheritance or if Cathy is looking for a stable guy following being dumped by the captain of the football team.

My security alarm was on the fritz, and would suddenly make alarming noises. Another terrible noise! I jumped up, grabbed my gun and told everyone to get into the cellar. I turned the lights off and called 911. The police patiently explained that there was no intruder and that I should call the maintenance company. After making a fool of myself I found that it was due to the smoke detector. It may be time to retool our thinking processes, certainly in my case.

The 20th century included two major world wars, a severe

depression, hard work and changes that came rather slowly. The 21st century is one in which people just want to have fun and things change very quickly. It's the age of *quick*. We are witnessing the transition from the mechanical to the digital age. It used to take 50 to 100 years for things to really change. Now we think in 6 to 12 month intervals.

It's the *nano* age. Think of a meter as about a yard. Bacteria are in the micrometer range, about a millionth of a yard or meter. The nanometer is a step down into the atomic range. We can visualize the atom using transmission electron microscopy and the scanning electron microscope. That last gadget is a scary looking instrument.

"Slow down, slow down, you're moving too fast!" That was part of a popular song awhile back. Diderot's *Encyclopedia* encompassed all knowledge in his work of 250 years ago. The equivalent amount of data is added to that every few weeks. Technology is ever so quick. There is the email, fax, cell phone, iphone, and all sorts of computer stuff. Millions of currencies are transferred in an instant. Hackers break into government and financial institutions and secrets and money disappear. Secrecy and privacy are sacrificed on the Internet as both information and fun are increased. Small price to pay! All you have to do is press the mouse on the left side, it will squeak and will give you information about things that occurred 3000 years ago.

My daughter is always scolding me about making too many commentaries. They certainly don't approach the quality of Caesar's *Commentaries* about the Gallic wars. She has no sense of humor. I'm always afraid of breaking a hip when I'm walking in the Forum Shops at Caesars in Las Vegas. Little people, heads down, walking very fast are heading straight at me. I have to jump out of the way. I know the paramedics are very good, but I'd rather have them demonstrate their skills on another person. Is the current human creature simply addicted to all this technology, with the need to get a quick fix of the latest update, as trivial as it might be?

I used to listen to the Boston Red Sox and Cleveland Indians baseball games. The score usually ended up 17 to 16. Ninety percent of any baseball game features inaction; the announcer had to fill in the time. He said that a study had shown that only 10% of college graduates had read a book a year out of college. That number, perhaps a poor statistic, impressed me a good deal.

2

Kids are naturally very inquisitive. The two and three year old boys around the house pester us constantly with "why's" and "how's" and "I wants." They get into everything and are constantly in trouble. Time outs are the *in* thing. They take everything apart. Amazingly they often put the parts back together in a workable order and rapidly learn how things works. The three year old is already facile with his tablet and his mother's laptop.

Where did all that energy go? Many students put a lot of that energy into barricades against learning anything. We all know people who hated school, tolerated it and stopped learning after they finished school. The caricature is one of the fellow who comes home from work, grabs a quick bite, pops a beer and becomes a couch potato in front of the TV. The pursuit of new information stops there. Of course that assumes that he has a job. Jobs are getting harder to find now. Young people are usually addicted to movies and music. Kids are now addicted to the computer, video games and the cell phones, so you have to add that to TVtropism.

But there is little in terms of intellectual development going on. **Critical thinking** is certainly not involved. If the lad is lucky enough to have a job he may be part of the ever-changing technological revolution. So he could be learning something new. But that exposure might be in a very narrow and select field. If he is not broadening his informational base, he may be allowing someone else to do his thinking. It's an age when it' s popular to talk about diversity. If your database is very small, very narrow, you may well need a diverse assortment of people to help you make any decision.

By now you are aware that a fool is writing this book about **thinking** and **logic**. A fool and his audience are soon parted. You may worry that, if you continue to read this book, you'll find some issues that intrigue you, offend you, issues that you really have been avoiding. This is a book filled with *thought redundancies* and *plagiarism*. It's filled with disclaimers. Rest assured, it isn't a book about you. It's about the other guy. You won't be offended. The good news is that this book is wonderful for insomniacs. This is better than any sleeping pill; and it will probably last you for a lifetime. Whatever the cost of this book, it will be recaptured many times over, especially at the price of medications these days.

People who know something about thinking and logic will certainly be flabbergasted by what is contained in this book. Of course

3

this fool would like to think, whatever that might be, that you are just not a victim of things that happen to you. Perhaps you could significantly influence your future, and the future of people around you.

This is a good time to scare you off with some real science. You probably don't remember the wisdom formula that you had to memorize in high school. We'll be using it as we go along:

W=K (B+F+E) x GJ (H+R+CS).

W = **WISDOM**
K = **KNOWLEDGE**
  B = **BASICS**
    1 - an individual's strengths and
      weaknesses such as intelligence
    2 - the fabric of the culture
  F = **FACTS AND INFORMATION**
    1 - academic schooling
    2 - positive things learned outside of school
  E = **EXPERIENCES**
    1 - personally involved
    2 - personally observed
    3 - diversity of experiences
GJ = **GOOD JUDGMENT**
  H = **HUMILITY**
    1 - insight into one's own biases and
      personal limitations
  R = **RATIONAL**
    1 - comprehensive and rational view of the
      issues
  CS = **COMMON SENSE**

At birth we face prejudice. We are compared to others in every way. Are we small? Are we pretty? We are born into an environment of prejudice, which is nothing more than a favorable or unfavorable comparison to something else. We inherit the biases of our culture, whether that is a preference for religion, structures, colors or sizes. Of course we are born with a certain type of personality and our coping skills are pretty well formed by the age of two. We've learned a good deal from our parents and our environment. We do a lot of things instinctively. Our actions are automatic, almost reflex. We do very little thinking, we just do things. Most of us stop at a red light and look on both sides of the road before crossing.

We hear and use a lot of terms on a daily basis which we may not fully understand. When I use the clothes dryer I always end up with some gray lint which I have to discard. No one seems to be able to explain why it is always gray. How should you cook a steak? Do you use a grill, an oven, a broiler or a frying pan? Should you combine these methods, and in what order? Sear it first before putting it in the oven? Some people have not a clue, others have very strong opinions. How do you get the breadcrumbs to stick to the chicken? What's the best glue? Do you need a refrigerator? People have been cooking for a few thousand years, yet everything seems to require reinvention.

We talk about broadband, balance of payments, radio waves, satellites in space, digital, electricity, fiberoptics, cameras, TVs. How do they work? How does a simple cash register work? Why is a hard square computer disk called a floppy disk, when an alternatively spelled disc is supposed to be a thin, circular thing-a-ma-jig. Someone else's been doing our thinking for us. My pet one is the balance of payments conundrum. We know that our imports exceed our exports by about $500 billion. We have heard that China loans us the money. But the importers have paid the full price. Where has this money gone? Seems like a simple enough question, but 99.99% of Americans haven't a clue. Your argument is valid, "I don't need to know this stuff."

Although we visualize or have heard about many activities, how many of us actually know much about any of them? What do you know about sailing, bowling, winemaking, cheesemaking, ice cream making, novels, the complexity of the camera, how to sew on a button, let alone what fabrics are included in your garments? I'll challenge you to give me a simple explanation about what is happened to the earth when you have seen the sun and the moon do their thing during the day. Okay, so you're a lot smarter than I am!

When asked by the grandchildren why gum sticks, I always reply, "because it's sticky." We also hear and say many things which we really don't understand. A good one is, "a pig in a poke." The customer was being ripped off in the Middle Ages. Having paid for a pig, he found a dog in a bag. We seldom devote a moment to an appreciation of how little we know about our world. Americans have seen a good deal about the English since the media has highlighted scandals, the Olympics and the elegant behaviors of Queen Elizabeth. So the British House of Windsor is familiar to us. I've asked a few friends where the name Windsor comes from. I'm going to have to look it up. I'll get back to you once I find out. It was Thomas Edison who said, "We don't know one millionth of one percent about anything."

We have moved from the mechanistic to the digital world, and now into the age of the nano. It was hard enough to find a good tool and die man. The math and science guys have taken over. It takes a pretty smart guy to be in those fields. One percent of the population is going to be doing our thinking.

We're also highly emotional creatures. We can get quite angry if our buttons are pushed. We also have many beliefs which we can't prove. We have learned the story of Adam and Eve from the Bible and our parents. There is more than one version. We also assume a lot of things in our lives without any question. That is not very important on an average day but it may become a pattern and that may lead us into what is called the **slippery slope**. When we do that we instantly stop thinking. We don't have to verify anything. We feel free to jump to conclusions.

Before we go too far in viewing our own responsibility for our own thinking and behaviors we should look at our culture. The 20th century has done a number on us. The radio never had the impact that television has. The television and movie people rapidly learned that sex and violence would draw a large audience. Saturation advertising would do the rest. Our children now spend six hours per day watching television, punching computer keys and playing video games. They spend only two hours per week doing some school homework. Educators are now worried that children are growing up without required social skills with their addiction to computer games. It appears that the participatory violence involved in these games translates into feeling comfortable inflicting violence on others. The news is filled with reports of mass murders in schools by young people. Could there be a connection? Of course the tech industry offers a different opinion.

We find that people voluntarily put a good deal of private information on the Internet. *Facebook,* Twitter and a myriad of other sites are said to enhance social interaction. With the advent of the mega everything, the mini person is a slave to the mega. The mega says that the mini is the better for it. The advertisers certainly have benefited from what they know about us. Facial recognition technology is about to revolutionize merchandising in department stores.

Let's go back a few thousand years. The first historians were both Greeks and lived in the fifth century B.C. The first was Herodotus and he wrote about the Persian wars. His accounts were not always factual and he tended to embellish. Thucydides wrote about the Peloponnesian war which involved Sparta and Athens. He reported the facts and is held in high regard. The mass media of the 20th century has been vulnerable to the **quick** syndrome. The news has to be reported immediately before anything can be verified. The first piece of information offered to a human being tends to stick. "Don't let the facts get in the way." So we are subjected to an instant distortion of history and our first impression presumably will leave a lasting impression. The commentators keep saying that it will take some time to get the facts or the numbers right, but the damage has been done.

Let me bore you with some statements or questions which we commonly hear. "This is the way it is. You don't need to think about it." That's a showstopper isn't it? That will certainly stop you in your tracks especially if the speaker is rather forceful and dominant. "Why are you asking that question?" is a neat way of not answering a question by forcing the other individual to justify why he is asking the question. "What do you think about that!" This often draws upon common opinions and is telling you not to think about it. "I hope that you're not going to do that!" "Why would you do that?" "Do you have any appetite for this?" There is a lot more behind those questions if you really think about it. But then these questions are mainly rhetorical and shut out discussion. Of course the listener might be capable of thinking a little. That changes the situation. **Thinking** is a bit more than being satisfied with the first statement, command or first impression. It has something to do with **analyzing** and **verifying**.

Let's look at some of our limitations. We're limited by our intelligence which has to do with our capacity to memorize things and analyze things. We may have limitations in either or both. We commonly use the term "intelligent" to mean someone who has received a lot of schooling and has acquired a lot of superficial knowledge. It is much more complex than that. Even when we think we have a good memory, we may be just kidding ourselves. A good memory is very useful if you're in school and taking exams. But our memory is not totally reliable. We tend to distort memories, especially as some time has elapsed. We tend to put in fillers. Observers report events quite differently. We are quite suggestible. The observations of court witnesses tend to be very unreliable.

7

Once we have heard something more than once, we tend to believe it. Marie Antoinette is reported to have said, "Let them eat cake." That sounds pretty bad. We're not even sure that she said that, and experts say that she was not referring to any form of dessert, but to a rather poor quality item in the bakery category. I'm sure you can think of better examples.

We get up every morning with an expectation of what the day is going to be like. Yet we are very poor at **probabilities** and **predictability**. So we have two strikes against us as soon as we get out of bed.

We are also terrible at numbers, especially big numbers. Let me see if I can find a good example. We are about 10 billion light years away from the most distant galaxies that we can see. Light travels 6 trillion miles in the course of a year. So let's multiply 10,000,000,000 x 6,000,000,000,000. The answer is 60,000,000,000,000,000,000,000, give or take a few zeros. You can always do it backwards with the nanometers. This can be a lot of fun. So who said that I was any good at math?

Let's get back to how our mind works. We tend to stick with the first piece of information that we receive. Then there is a thing called **pattern recognition**. This is based upon prior experiences and information that is easily accessible to us. Recent occurrences quickly come to mind. We instinctively sense that there is a high probability that something will or won't occur. **Pattern recognition** may be a genetic thing or it may be just taught. We are taught to do things in a repetitive fashion as we grow up, such as the placing of the tools that we eat with – – the knife and fork. Many things become habitual. Habits appear not to be born, but to be taught. But we have all been exposed to people who are ritualistic, whose habits are inflexible. They drive everybody crazy. They get very upset if "anything" disturbs their equilibrium, be it that the eggs are overcooked or the kid drops his spoon. You've guessed it, it's called being neurotic, a life of predictable **patterns**. That has to be genetic, it's so far out in left field.

We also tend to have many biases or preferences which affect our current judgment. We are rather stubborn. We tend to have fixed opinions even when we are privy to contradictory information. We may not even change our views or behaviors when dramatic events occur in our lives; we might if it is too catastrophic. We might take the money out of the bank if a conqueror is overrunning our town.

8

You know that we are quite judgmental people. We use the word *mistake* when we don't like the consequence of an action. We don't use the word *choice*. The *best choice* may not lead to the desired conclusion. It was not a *mistake*. We do tend to *blame others*, if things don't work out the way that we would like.

We are subject to the **feel-good** necessities. It's obvious that we feel more comfortable if we're in control of the situation. We need to protect ourselves almost at any cost, both for survival and self-esteem reasons. Denial and misrepresentation of the reality of the situation is easy to do.

I often hear the statement, "you be the judge." The bell shaped curve comes to mind. Some are very poor at this, and others are super. General Patton comes to mind. He was superb at the "art of war" but he made some bad personal judgments. You must've seen the movie. I'm sure that you recognize that you're good at certain things, and not so good at others. Very successful professionals are known to be duds when dealing with their spouses and children.

I should be dealing with the topic of **critical thinking**. That will come a little later. I'm just being *critical* about our natural way of thinking. I guess I'm going to have to say something about **heuristics.** It's a terrible word. Find a garbage can. It really means that we have knee-jerk ways of dealing with emergency situations. Little thought is needed. It helps people to evaluate issues quickly and make prompt decisions. Wikipedia gives examples such as "rule of thumb, educated guess, intuitive judgment, common sense and trial and error." The experts surmise that this evolves over time and that the caveman probably had a different set of responses. But the heuristic shortcut is prone to incorrect decisions. But we're human, and we don't like to admit mistakes. We look for facts or opinions that confirm our biases. "We should be able to find an argument that will support our point of view."

That ability to make prompt decisions reminds me of one of my own experiences. I had been encouraged to buy eight acres on the side of a monadnock, which is a small mountain. The landscape architect and I drove there late one afternoon. We crossed the road and looked up. "What you think," I asked? "Sell," came the instantaneous answer. He was a chatty sort of fellow, "I've been in analysis for four years. I finally finished. I'm still the same. I'm still the same son of a b......" I ended up with a very steep 800 foot driveway. It was a forest. I cut the trees. I learned that red oak is significantly denser than white oak. I would not be kind to myself if I admitted that I was a jerk. So there is a moral to my story, "you can always learn something for your mistake, I know that red oak is heavier than white oak."

So far we have discussed the fact that we rely on **pattern recognition, probability,** and **prior history.** We often shoot from the hip. Sometimes you're right and sometimes you're wrong. Sometimes emotions are good, sometimes they're bad.

The history of astronomy is filled with careful observations and calculations and a lot of guesswork. Ptolemy felt that the earth was the center of the universe. Wrong!, but it felt good and it made a lot of sense. Little did he envision that there would be billions of galaxies. It took a very long time before they figured out that the sun was the center of our solar system. I was going to say galaxy, but my engineer mentor told me that it was the solar system. He says the center of our galaxy is a black hole. He threatened me with a techno--hell of manipulated weaponized information driven into my easily seduced mind. There are many mysteries. Astrophysics has a plethora of them. Every mystery is replaced by an even more mysterious mystery. Mankind has been trying to understand the un-understood. The creator is either very disappointed by his offspring or having a good laugh.

Have you found someone to use that wisdom formula on? Let's look at somebody's behavior. I'm going to tell you the story of Job Lost. His first name is Job, like the character in the Bible. His friends call him Izzy. He's a bank manager at a small local branch of one of the large international banks.

Born in a small city, he was educated at a catholic school. His school had been desegregated and he experienced a good deal of bullying by the blacks. It was all verbal, there never was any physical confrontation. His mother was an elementary school teacher who loved painting, literature, cooking and movies. She loved to read the classic children's books to him, and forced him to go to some museums. She knew a lot about famous artists. He was bored, he was just too young to appreciate anything like that. She had a good sense of humor and was very laid-back except when it came to her religion. She was pretty permissive at home. She would often leave him at home while she went to the newer funny movies. She forced Izzy to learn to play the piano, which he hated. She let him play soccer and baseball.

His dad was a plumber and very short tempered. He was quite the disciplinarian and sometimes hit Izzy. He was always tired when he got home from work. He would watch some television and read the newspaper. He didn't spend much time with his son and never met any of his teachers, nor did he ever attend a school event. He would occasionally talk about some of the jobs that he was working on. He always showed Izzy how to fix things in the house. Izzy hated it. His father liked to go to the gym and did some fishing. He never took Izzy with him. He had a thing about the Jews, having been brought up in a Jewish neighborhood.

Izzy was forced to play the piano in the high school orchestra. He didn't play any sports. He was a bit of a loner and read detective novels. His mother didn't approve. He reluctantly had to learn the catechism and memorize it. He did have one good friend. They played baseball and football together, as well as the usual games. They played a lot of war games. His friend's father was a fireman who apparently recorded some rather gruesome experiences, such as seeing people who were burning alive.

He went to a local college and obtained a Masters in finance. He learned his computer skills while he was in school. He also had a friend who was in the Army reserves and had access to the most awful photos of war atrocities. Some nights Izzy had trouble going to sleep. Upon graduating from college, they both went to Europe for about six weeks. They did the usual backpack and hostel thing on a very tight budget. Izzy was lucky enough to always have a state job during the summer vacations. He saved up enough to pay for most of the vacation. His parents paid for the airfare. It was cheap at the time. Izzy was able to visit London and a good number of the larger European countries. He went as far as Russia and did cross over into Istanbul. A fellow who looked a lot like a Muslim stole his American Express checks and vanished into the crowd. That left Izzy with a lasting impression about that part of the world, even though he was able to replace the checks. With his provincial background, the newly experienced cultures left an indelible mark. Not like back home.

He started his banking career at a small local branch and ended up in one of the larger cities. He married soon after leaving school. His wife is a pleasant, trim and engaging person. She is a librarian and a good mother. They have two sons, the eight year old and is a good student and has several nice friends. Their fifteen year-old son does not do too well in school, is a bit rebellious and has a drug problem which his father does not know about. Izzy's irritated that they spent so much time watching TV and playing computer games. They are always asking him to go to the movies.

Izzy is a hard-working disciplinarian. He tends to explode at his kids. He talks about his wife with his few friends. He hates going to movies with his wife. He is emotional and appears to be prejudiced against the Jews and feels as if they are all wealthy, that they control the banking system and the financial world. He feels that he is underpaid. Izzy knows that people in charge don't listen, including his father, mother and his bosses. He does enjoy golfing, reading detective fiction, and vacationing with his wife. They usually try to go to San Francisco or New York and sometimes visit one of the historical places.

He has few close friends but he is generally liked. He is capable of holding pleasant but superficial conversations. He will talk about the baseball teams and their standings, but he doesn't know any of the players. He is too busy to watch baseball or football on TV and never listens to music. Izzy is a card counter but never goes to a casino. He drives a small car and keeps it very clean. He will dine out with his wife, but avoids dining out with other couples because he thinks that they are too boring.

He's having some problems with his boss at work. He has been instructed to be easy on home mortgages. He would often say, "I can just see something terrible happening." "Don't worry about it," was his boss's way of dealing with that issue. Izzy wasn't about to change his opinion. He's pretty stubborn. He keeps bringing up the issue even though he knows that his boss is irritated by his persistent repetition. He doesn't seem to appreciate that there could be some payback in the future.

He doesn' t like his work but feels trapped. He's a good branch manager, but he's a little too tough and demanding on his employees. Things are pretty predictable for him. He goes to work anticipating that he is going to have problems with his customers. He knows exactly what the customer is going to ask and do. He also knows exactly what to say to satisfy them. He has a lot of common sense. His judgment is pretty good and his solutions are usually acceptable. He sees his customers as rather stupid, demanding and unwilling to follow the rules. The Jews are too demanding and think they know everything. That is particularly true for the women. The blacks are always on their cell phones and can be rather rude. He does tend to be rather curt with both groups. "They just won't listen," is his way of dealing with this. He treats them all alike even when a customer is very nice, informed and very logical.

And there is always the potential for stress. One of his customers suffered a heart attack as she came through the doorway and his bank was robbed by three hoodlums during the day. They all had guns. Nobody got hurt, but he had to show compassion to his employees on that day. Internally he has a good deal of resentment towards his wife, his children, his boss, his employees and his customers. He hides it rather well at work, not so at home.

How much wisdom do you think that Izzy possesses? Let's look at that high school formula.

W=K (B+F+E) x GJ (H+R+CS).

W = **WISDOM**
K = **KNOWLEDGE**
    B = **BASICS**
        1 - an individual's strengths and weaknesses such as intelligence
        2 - the fabric of the culture
    F = **FACTS AND INFORMATION**
        1 - academic schooling
        2 - positive things learned outside of school
    E = **EXPERIENCES**
        1 - personally involved
        2 - personally observed
        3 - diversity of experiences
GJ = **GOOD JUDGMENT**
    H = **HUMILITY**
        1 - insight into one's own biases and personal limitations
    R = **RATIONAL**
        1 - comprehensive and rational view of the issues
    CS = **COMMON SENSE**

In the "knowledge" category we see that he has above-average intelligence and he has a Masters degree in finance. He does his job well, but he doesn't seem to be broadening his horizon.

He was brought up by parents who both worked. His mother was a teacher who exposed him to religion, music, painting, movies, soccer and baseball. He was forced to memorize the catechism. His father was a disciplinarian, prone to get angry. He showed very little interest in Izzy. He was prejudiced against the Jews. Izzy had some trouble with blacks at his school.

He had been exposed to the television and all the sex and violence that accompanied that. When in school he was exposed to photos of atrocities in another region of the world, traveled around Europe and had his travel checks stolen in Istanbul. Other than those experiences he seems to have had a rather parochial view of the world. He confidently handled a bank robbery and a heart attack at the bank.

His judgment seems to be fairly good in dealing with customers, but he is pretty emotional at home. His boss dismisses his concerns about the mortgage issue using his own heuristic denial, "don't worry about it."

He demonstrates a lot of **pattern recognition** and approaches every day with a lot of preconceptions. He has **prejudices** against customers, the blacks and the Jews. He also demonstrates his father's short temper at home, and similarly spends little time with his children and does not notice potential problems.

He seems to have a very simple way of dealing with life, and his reason does not control his biases and behaviors. He certainly does very little thinking about issues. He seems to be rather stubborn and does not change his opinions. Izzy is certainly a creature of habit. Izzy appears to be a fairly average guy but he's not scoring very high in the "wisdom" category.

So can we salvage something from our "embers of thinking," since we are so obviously governed by our flawed thinking and emotions? So how *should* we think? Let's leave the emotions behind and deal with **logic**. If you choose to continue reading his chapter, do so at your own peril since a foll is in charge of this investigation.

Warning! This is the only chapter which will remind you of school. After that it is really an easy read. It has some formulae, but you don't have to memorize them. You can just fold a corner of one of these pages and come back to it at your convenience. It is filled with a lot of specifics, but you can just skim the pages and get the general idea of what's important in **critical thinking.**

Critical thinking is about slowing down our thinking, not jumping to immediate conclusions and slowing our actions. The term "metacognition" means "thinking about thinking." I recall that my dad gave me a small book to read whose title was that very definition. Of course the experts have gotten a lot fancier with more precise, descriptive and complex models. It's part of human nature. We always have to change something, even if it doesn't lead to any improvement. Think of the size of the cover that our *IRS* tax code requires since it has to wrap around some 73,000 pages.

Critical thinking requires using logic while giving a serious look at the issue. Above all it requires that you do not have a conclusion in mind before you analyze the problem. Do not rationalize or plagiarize. You have to be a doubting Thomas and approach everything with good-natured skepticism. **Critical thinking** does not come naturally, *it has to be taught.*

The Greeks had three great philosophers in a row. Socrates didn't know how to write but he had a scribe named Plato, who was then followed by Aristotle in the fourth century B.C. Aristotle set the standard for logical thinking for the next 2000 years. Some say that it was improved in the 20th century, the computer facilitating that. Aristotle came up with a three part method of analyzing categorical premises. I never really could understand it. It's **syllogistic analysis**. It certainly explains why people avoid courses in math and logic in college, since humans are not naturally good at math and science.

The syllogism that is often quoted is, "all men are mortal, Socrates is a man, therefore Socrates is mortal." If two premises are affirmative, the conclusion has to be affirmative. If the two premises are negative, there is no conclusion. If one premise is negative, the conclusion is also negative. Of course if the premise is nonsense, the validity is nil. That's about as good as I can do, so let's just move on.

Logic has to do with **deductive reasoning**. If premises are shown to be true, then the conclusion also has to be true. **General** statements prove to be true in a specific example. You start with categories. **Inductive reasoning** starts with an observation and escalates to a **generalization** which may be invalid. The fact that science is based upon inductive reasoning doesn't seem to make any logical sense! Oh well, I told you that I didn't understand anything about logic.

Making a decision about things often requires some sort of gamble. Decision theory seems to make a lot of sense. You need to view the options, put them in order of probability and factor in value. Suppress the **I wish** and look at the facts. Make the decision. At least you tried.

Built into the human being are the concepts of justice and retribution. It doesn't always work out that way. But I have anecdotal hearsay evidence which shows how justice really works. There had been multiple strikes and the garbage was building up all over Boston. One of the striking unions blamed the sanitation contractors. The owner of a fleet of sanitation trucks operating out of Boston was driving through the tunnel from Logan airport when he came to a dead stop. His car took hours to reach a place where he was able to see that one of his own trucks had broken down and was blocking the traffic in both directions. The meeting with the unions had to be delayed. The unions didn't believe his story for a moment.

It appears that a lot of logical thinking has to do with *avoiding flawed thinking*. These examples are called **fallacies** and you would fall asleep if I listed them. I think that *Wikipedia* has over 25 different examples. We can look at a few of the common **fallacies** which we confront every day. There is actually a lot of overlap and some fallacies fall into several categories. You're familiar with the **post hoc** fallacy when you come up with some sort of argument to justify your conclusion. It is actually an abbreviation for the **post hoc ergo propter hoc.** A later event is presumed to have been caused by an earlier event. She died after she heard a clap of thunder. A clap of thunder obviously killed her. They later found out that she was poisoned.

I'm not sure if the following is an example of **post hoc** thinking. My daughter came into the room and told me that she had had the best time ever with her family, "we went to the soccer lesson, enjoyed the Native American dancing exhibition, went to two movies, ate at Chinese and Thai restaurants, drove around and ate all sorts of treats. You missed such a good time." I concluded that she had such a good time because I was not there.

Anchoring is one where there is a focus on only one aspect. After the Twin Towers fell on 9/11 you could hear people say, "what do you expect, he's a Muslim." Then there is the **correlation** fallacy, "he was driving too fast and that's why he died." He actually died of a heart attack.

There is the **slippery slope** fallacy, "if they ban assault weapons, it's just a matter of time before your hunting rifle is banned." Then there is the **ad hominem** when you focus on the man rather than the issue, "Hitler kills and plunders, therefore he could never give to charity." I'm not sure that I'm getting these right, but I'm trying. Another good example is the classy **reduction ad absurdum.** "The Pope is against abortions. Hitler thinks that abortions are okay, (if you are pro-abortion), then you have to vote for Hitler. I think this can also be put in the category of the **poison well**.

Remember the fellow who said, "he who is not with me is against me." That is a composite of two fallacies built into just one statement. That's a very good one. It's both an example of a **non sequitur** and a **reduction ad absurdum.** Two for the price of one.

Another fallacious argument is demonstrated when someone does not feel that he can prove his point; instead he asks people to prove that he's wrong. There is also the illogical deductive reasoning which implies that what is typical for a group also applies to an individual. We know that people jump to conclusions. They attribute a situation to a single cause when it may be due to a multiplicity of causes.

We also assume a conclusion to be right because it appears to be probable. We believe things to be right when they are wrong just because it **feels good**. A good example of this is the reporting by the *Wall Street Journal* that oily hair is due to overactivity of the sebaceous glands. The solution was to wash the hair more frequently. The reality is that the hair is being washed too frequently. Stop washing the hair and wait for the sebaceous glands to quiet down. There are many more examples of flawed thinking. We will cover some as we go along, and this book is just filled with **fallacious** thinking.

But before I leave this area, I am reminded of **Kripkean dogmatism.** This is when you are so certain that you are in possession of absolute truth that you reject any evidence to the contrary. One evening my roommate and I chanced to see professor Arthur Darby Nock walking in the Harvard Yard. I believe that he was the youngest man to become the "Frothingham Professor of the History of Religions" at Harvard. He was attired in an open long black coat, high waters and white socks with a bottle of wine protruding from his coat. Lecturing about religions, he would ask, "If I am in possession of absolute truth, what right do I have not to persecute?" It is a fallacious question, but the students had to put their logic cap on. He couldn't have been serious.

The caveman must've come up with the way that we naturally think. Then Aristotle introduced us to logic 2000 years ago. **Roger Bacon** may have been the inventor of the **scientific method** in the 13th century. No one person is really given the nod. But we do find *the method* to be most useful both in our everyday lives and in the scientific world.

Putting together a formula for **science** isn't easy. I think it's even tougher than studying math and science. So you're with me so far and demonstrating a lot of forbearance. **Science** is based upon **inductive reasoning**. It starts from guesswork or observation. The observation may have anything to do with any of our five or six senses such as taste, sight or hearing. It starts from something small, a particular, and becomes a generalization. What applies to one bird applies to all birds. That may pertain to this book, *for the birds*. **Science** ~ **inductive reasoning** is shortened to **IR.** So we start with the first part of this equation:

$$S \ (IR) \sim O + E = T.$$

S (science) ~ O (observation or guess) + E (experiments without presumptive conclusions) = T(conclusion-theory-generalization).

We then have to move on to the concepts of fallacy, probability, validity, verifiability and falsifiability. If you start with a premise that is **false,** your conclusion is going to be wrong. A probability value is known as a **P value.** It is a measure of the statistical probability that your conclusion is either positive or negative. A **valid** premise is supported by solid evidence leading to a solid conclusion. The conclusion must be **verified** by your experience or observation (let's call that empirical data). That empirical data itself must be subject to the risk of being proven **false** (**falsifiability**). So we have another formula. I'm sure that my use of the word formula is a misrepresentation of a concept which Spock would be heard to say, "it's illogical."

So **V (validity) = R (reliability) + F (falsifiability).** For a premise to be valid it must fulfill both criteria: **V = R + F**. Science won't work if the equation is **V = R/F**. So let's outline some of the concepts having to do with **scientific validity.**

 1 - A false premise leads to a wrong conclusion.
 2 - P value is a measure of the statistical probability that your conclusion is either positive or negative.
 3 - A valid (validity) premise is supported by solid evidence leading to a solid conclusion.
 4 - The conclusion must be verified (verifiability) by your experience or observation (let's call that empirical data).
 5 - That empirical data itself must be subject to the risk of being proven false (falsifiability).

V (validity) of a Premise = R (reliability) + F (falsifiability).
V = R + F.
IV(invalidity) of a Premise =
R (reliability)/F (falsifiability). IV = R/F.

This is certainly a complicated way of looking at things. It's really quite simple. After you make an observation, you slow down your emotional response, activate your informational and logical systems, and come to some conclusion. It's usual and customary for us to look at issues in a very superficial fashion and move on. Beneath that skin that we observe, there are layers of reasons why we are exposed to that superficial view of the skin. Think of an issue as an onion. Peel one layer, and you find another layer, etc. We need to peel away the heuristic initial response and look at the layer of logic that underlies it.

My friend suggested that I look at page 186 of Throgmorton Aloysius Malthus' book, *Don't Read this Book Tails from the Red Fox.* I can understand why. It seems to be a composite of our thinking processes. Here it is:

We shall start with saying that it is the *I that looks at things.*
We start with *a priori reasoning* concerning certain beliefs that we have.
We later use *a posteriori reasoning* after we see the outcome of things.
I may be the *subject* of a topic.
I may be the *object* of a topic.

19

I may use *observation*.
I may not be *allowed* to observe.
I may make a *correct observation*.
My observation may be *an illusion*.
I may desire to observe *an illusion*.
My *perception* may be affected by many variables.
There may be *errors* at any level.
There may be *confusion* at this level.
I may or may not like the *inductive method of reasoning*.
The *scientific method* may be avoided as being too tedious or mundane.
I may choose to view an *effect* and not believe in *cause and effect*.
I may just be *stubborn* and refuse to let the facts or beliefs get in the way.
I may already have a philosophical bent that *filters* anything I see you do.
I may see *evil* as an experiment that allows *good* to be perceived.

I think I've got it. You're simply saying that the perception of an illusion of a solution clears the confusion for some resolution.

He seems to have had some fun with this. I'm also trying to do the same thing. We know that various people have reiterated the idea that there were no new ideas. That is even contained in the Bible. We rely on science for new information. Science is really the foundation of critical thinking although it relies on induction. It must be factual, rigorous and systematic. Science involves skepticism, evolution and constant change as new facts are learned and new instruments become available. My engineer friend says, "everything I've learned is wrong!"

Even Freud was trying to figure out why people think and act the way they do. His ideas seem simple enough. Words like denial and rationalization appear to be simple concepts, but somebody has to come up with revolutionary simple concepts. He probably did more harm than good since he put the fields of psychology and psychiatry into the supernatural realms. That's what cocaine can do to you, or was he on some other drug?

Sometimes the big guys don't get it right. Aristotle thought that a heavier ball would fall faster than a lighter ball. It took 2000 years for Galileo to perform the experiment. They fell at the same rate. But the engineer says that that was also in error. Many additional factors had to be considered such as the shape of the object, wind resistance, etc.

Newtonian physics was revolutionary and fit the <u>big picture</u>. But when the scientists of the 20th century started to discover subatomic <u>particles</u> which acted in contradictory ways, quantum physics revolutionized the field. How could something be a particle and a wave at the same time? What is the **fallacy** here?

Science builds on the shoulders of others. Aristotle, Descartes and Galileo thought that the speed of light was instantaneous. In 1676 Ole Romer measured the speed of light, and he was off by about 25%. They were still having trouble measuring the distances in the galaxy. James Bradley came to a much closer approximation in 1729. Faraday's law of electromagnetism predicts how a magnetic field will interact with an electric current to produce voltage. That was in 1831. It was James Maxwell who demonstrated that electric and magnetic fields travel through space in the form of waves at the speed of light in 1865. The speed of light is 186,282 mi./s or 299,792,458 m/s. Then Albert Einstein came along and the special theory of relativity was born in 1905. He just plugged that number into his famous equation $E=mc2$.

You probably accidentally cracked this book to this page. I'll bet that you're still reading the first chapter. I told you this was as good as a sleeping pill. Go back to sleep. Let's see what's happening to Job Lost? *Bad things are happening to Job.* His parents died 2 years ago in a car accident. He took it pretty hard, especially since his mother had been very supportive. Then Izzy's wife died about a year ago from a brain hemorrhage. She died moments after they had a fight over his denial that his older son seemed to be having a lot of problems. He blamed himself for her death and has been overcome by grief. He really did not realize how much he really loved her and how dependent he was on her. That's not very unusual. He had not been doing a very good job raising his children. Izzy was brought up in a small city and is now living in a larger city. He was never close to any of his neighbors and has no support system.

This was followed by the death of his younger son following six months of suffering from acute leukemia. He was only ten years old. He was the favorite who was bright and motivated. During this period of time Izzy's financial world had been crumbling around him. Those bad mortgages caused a virtual collapse in the home and financial markets. He had been telling his boss that all along. His large bank decided to close several branches for economic reasons. His boss did find a job at another branch, but made no effort to find him a slot.

21

Izzy was let go.

Izzy did live a hand to mouth existence. He received only a month's termination pay and had no real savings. His mortgage payments were substantial and his own bank was foreclosing on him. He was applying for unemployment benefits but he was running into Clara, that beast who had given him so much trouble on the few occasions when he tried to help terminated employees who were filing for unemployment benefits. She informed him that his position at work did not qualify him for that benefit. Now he is running into the difficulties that are not uncommon. Denied benefits, it can take up to two months before you get a hearing, and it had taken those two months. He didn't seem to have any friends who could help him. He didn't have a job so he couldn't get a loan. He was living on his credit cards. It couldn't go on for much longer. He couldn't get over the death of his son and job opportunities were scarce. He was depressed and did not have the motivation to apply for any job. Eventually his home went into foreclosure and he and his son moved into a drab little apartment. The boy was getting into trouble at school and was hanging out with a bad crowd. He didn't listen to anything that Izzy said. Izzy was vaguely aware that his son was using drugs.

This stress took its toll. He had a heart attack. It didn't end there. While recuperating at home he received a call from an emergency room. The doctor said that he was very sorry, but his son had died of an overdose. "Is this really happening to me, am I a current day Job?," Izzy repeatedly asked himself. It didn't make a lot of sense. "God, why are you doing this to me?" He did not have a whole lot of faith in God, he never had. But he started going to church. He may have been aware of Pascal's view on the matter. Better to wager on God's help, it can't hurt. Would the current day Job experience a change in luck? So let's look at what's happening to Izzy after we review that fabulous formula.

W=K (B+F+E) x GJ (H+R+CS)

W = **WISDOM**
K = **KNOWLEDGE**
    B = **BASICS**
        1 - an individual's strengths and
             weaknesses such as intelligence
        2 - the fabric of the culture

F = FACTS AND INFORMATION
1 - academic schooling
2 - positive things learned outside of sc
E = EXPERIENCES
1 - personally involved
2 - personally observed
3 - diversity of experiences
GJ = GOOD JUDGMENT
H = HUMILITY
1 - insight into one's own biases and personal limitations
R = RATIONAL
1 - comprehensive and rational view of the issues
CS = COMMON SENSE

Izzy seems to be running into a lot of bad luck. He really did not think very much about his future. He didn't do a lot of planning considering that, as a banker, he was exposed to estate planning. His coping skills were certainly were poor. He experienced catastrophic experiences. He blamed himself for his wife's death since it followed an argument **(post hoc ergo proctor hoc)**. Rationally he should've made some adjustments. He apparently was mired in depression and he didn't have the energy or motivation to make changes. His favorite son died. His world was suddenly crumbling. He had been stuck in a job that he didn't like and had made no effort to review options. He simply was not thinking. He was also very stubborn and seems to have made little effort to please his boss. When the bank closed his boss made no effort to help him. His stubbornness was manifest in his daily life. He dealt with his world in a rigid way and wasn't inclined to change his mind. When he lost his job he ran into Clara whom he had managed to antagonize. She might have helped him get some unemployment benefits so that he would not have lost his home. There was **no critical thinking** involved in facing issues having to do with his older son. It might have been appropriate for Izzy to blame himself for his son's death. He had closed his eyes while his son was using drugs. But he didn't seem to do that, he blamed God.

Izzy certainly experienced some terrible things, but his coping skills were equally bad. He seemed incapable of making any decisions, and he stopped using any critical thinking or anything related to the scientific method. He turned to the supernatural. And we have not heard if that option worked. Izzy did have the benefits of good schooling and above-average intelligence. He and his father both were prejudiced. He left the important family stuff to his wife, so that he was ill-prepared to deal with raising his two sons when she died. His lack of involvement with his children allowed his older son to hide his drug abuse and his problems. His world was really a narrow one so that he was not surrounded by anyone who could help him. He was lacking in humility in that he had little insight into his own personal biases and personal limitations. He simply did not have the resources to help himself. He didn't reevaluate his situation and make whatever adjustments he might've been able to make.

Izzy has suffered some terrible tragedies all in close proximity. His passivity in the face of these awful events shows that he was no longer thinking. His judgment was obviously flawed and as we leave him with a history of not being a very wise man, he appears to be heading toward self-destruction.

II

EDUCATION IN THE AGE OF TERRORISM

We may have maxed out at this point. Maybe that is all that there is to this thing about thinking. After all it was Terence, a comic dramatist in the 2nd century B.C., who said, "in fact, nothing is said that has not been said before." From the Bible in Ecclesiastes, "is there anything whereof it may be said, see, this is new? It had been already of old time, which was before us." Mark Twain and Goethe said the same thing. A translation of Goethe goes something like this, "everything has been thought of before, but the problem is to think of it again."

That may not be totally true. A new idea has been born. We are genetically engineered! Science is going to improve our genetic structure! We recognize that very bright parents tend to have bright kids. Certain races are statured differently, have different bodily and facial contours that don't change easily. We know that certain deadly diseases are inherited. Some are pretty rare. Then there is the omnipresent diabetes.

So you come into the world with some level of intelligence, some level of physical strength, some level of stamina and some level of coordination. You may have a tendency to hyperactivity or have a tendency to be shy or bullied. If you have the right type of fibers in your muscles you may be able to compete with the Ethiopian and Kenyan marathon runners. So it goes, if you're lucky, your lucky. If you're not, you're not. Was it the musical *Kismet* in which we heard, "we go through life unguaranteed of right or good?"

We speak of intelligence, but there is a lot that goes into that. They routinely test for your IQ. Educators argue about the fairness of that standardized test. It's a pretty good indicator, but minority groups feel that there is a large prejudicial factor built into all of this. Then some people are just very good at tests. Some have really good memories and some are very creative. Some people are really good at numbers and can multiply rather complex fractions in their heads without effort. I used to walk by a lumber yard when I was in elementary school and a young fellow would actually come out and enjoy taunting me by asking me to multiply fractional numbers which he routinely did at work.

Then there was that rather shabbily dressed, unshaven fellow at the gas pump who overheard my friend talking about physics. He obviously hadn't spend a lot of time in school since his diction was rather poor. He said, "I've had a hankering to take some courses on that stuff. I really enjoy that wave and particle dilemma in quantum physics. It's really simple once you get into it. I hope that the supercollider doesn't break down again. I'm as anxious as they are about finding out more about what makes us tick. I've got to save up some money to take some of those math courses so that I can understand more about astrophysics." There are a lot of people out there with untapped potentials.

The researchers seem to feel that our personalities and coping skills are largely present at age two. Think about it. There is the laid-back guy, the bully, the saint, the worrier and the one who can't stand still. There are some groups which cause a lot of trouble to many people. One immediately thinks of politicians and criminals. Some say these are synonyms. Some pretty neutral personality characteristics can have significant impacts. The procrastinator and the person who keeps things to himself can be the engines of great train wrecks.

You've met people who are very self-centered and very neurotic. Every little thing seems to bother them. An inconvenience or something out of place is perceived as a catastrophe, and they instantaneously blame somebody for the incident. A procrastinating quality to this individual allows his companions to enjoy "the great train wreck."

The sociopath, who doesn't seem to have much of a conscience, may or may not do many evil things. My friend says, "just another closed-end biological mistake, an evolutionary cul-de-sac." Our television and computer age has increased the options for this individual. We see this happening to a minor extent with our adolescents who love to steal copyrighted things off the Internet and enjoy hacking into websites. The criminal mind tends to think that an average person or a situational encounter falls into the category of "something to be taken advantage of."

What do we know about the criminal? Back in 1870 Cesare Lombroso had a flash of creativity, "a flash of inspiration," and decided that a criminal was a separate entity, born as such and identifiable by his physical defects. He fell into some sort of subhuman category. Is that a flash of inductive reasoning? But what if criminality and/or homosexuality is or are God-given genetic traits? That does pose some issues, doesn't it? Are they to be judged by society and/or God, or both? Is it a question of predestination or personal responsibility, otherwise known as free will? Should there be consequences on earth and/or in an afterlife? I better quit. We don't want to get into the theological mysteries.

A criminal would be strongly advised to read this book so that he can better understand how the average mind works. Any additional information can be put to good use. I might use the Internet and see if I can sell this book to the criminals while they're enjoying a lot of free time to read in prison.

Some twins studies have compared the differences between identical and non-identical twins. If you find a criminal who has a twin, you will find the second identical twin to be a criminal 50% of the time, but only 25% of the time if the second twin is non-identical. Adopted children, reared apart from criminal parents, also have a much higher rate of criminality. Where you find a criminal, you'll find some alcohol in the next room. Genetics seems to play a role in criminality and alcoholism. The sociopath may reside within the walled community of his brain. Criminals are held responsible for their behaviors. No one has suggested that they suffer from a disease. However the psychiatric community has decided that alcoholism and drug addiction are diseases. Should they be considered, "not guilty by reason of alcoholism or drug addiction," for any of their negative behaviors? Since the negative behaviors are a product of mental illness one would expect the psychiatrists to be lobbying the government to make it so. Why haven't they done that? They are close to deciding that criminality is due to genetic inheritance. They can always quote from Cesare Lombroso. So if criminals are doomed to be criminals as a result of God-given genes, what right do you have not to find the criminal "not guilty by reason of criminalism." A reasonable fellow certainly should think in these terms. It's a great use of the **it naturally follows** argument. Do you see any **fallacy** in this argument?

You have just witnessed an excellent example of many **noncritical thinking** problems. Read that paragraph again. Can you find issues with any of these: **non sequitur, reductio ad absurdum, post hoc, slippery slope, judgment, illogicality, common sense, probability, Kripkean dogmatism, inductive reasoning** and **the scientific method?** There is a gold mine in that paragraph. I wish I would've thought of it. But the human mind has the capacity to distort issues to a series of **non sequiturs**, absurdities and incomprehensibilities.

But I'm reminded of what Throgmorton Aloysius Malthus had to say about this subject, "All men are created in God's image." That sets back any discussion about religion a few thousand years. We always thought that it was an example of **reductio ad absurdum**, but maybe it's not. Actually Man creates God in man's image. First there was a vengeful God, now it is a kindly forgiving God. God is whatever you wish her to be, she used to be a man, now she's a woman.

But I'm going to be a good guy here and give you a helping hand by reminding you of that fabulous formula: **W=K (B+F+E) x GJ (H+R+CS)**. You should be able to figure that out quite easily with the use of that formula.

This is the **Age of the Terrorist** in which there has been a tremendous perversion of the *Qur'anic* teachings. Mohammed was pretty much of a straight shooter and would have been appalled at what they have done to the interpretations of the *Hadith*. The Egyptian *Muslim Brotherhood* appears to have been the major fomenter of this crusade against the enemies of *Islam*. The Brotherhood has been the spiritual force behind much of the terrorism of the Middle East. Little wonder that Hosni Mubarak kept a lid on them while he was in power. A fellow by the name of Ayman Zawahiri apparently founded a splinter group about 30 years ago and was one of the founding fathers of the *Al Qaeda*. He apparently was one of the mentors of **Osama bin Laden**. I had to look up a few definitions to get this stuff straight. You've heard of the **jihad** which is a "struggle" against one's own nastiness to please God. That is obviously a pretty good thing. However the terrorists have interpreted this in a quite different way, "a struggle against the enemies of *Islam*."

Most of the local imams haven't been sent to one of the London universities for their education. They were taught at their local madrasahs by their predecessors who may have taught their own radical interpretation of the *Qur'an* and the *Hadith*. A 7th-century thinking imam is probably not going to influence his student to be a 21st-century imam. It's just not going to happen. The current **jihadists** may not be representing the finest minds of the seventh century.

The Muslims have the *Qur'an* which does not appear to have endured such an evolutionary history as we find in the Bible. Let's look

28

at that. There was no printing press when the originals of the *Old* and *New Testaments* came into being. I should say that the *New Testament* covers the time from 33 to 100 A.D. You have to be a glutton for punishment to be a research historian in the field of biblical studies. First of all you need to be able to read and really comprehend the Aramaic dialect, the Semitic language of Jesus.

Some of us have heard that the first Council of Nicaea in 325 A.D. had a lot to do with organizing the Bible. 1800 bishops were invited to meet in Turkey. 220 to 318 accepted the invitation. It's surprising that so few attended, since it was an all expenses paid trip with five companions. Of course there was no Hilton or Hyatt chains in operation at that time. Apparently there was a good deal of discussion about the material which was available pertaining to the *Gospels*, but they didn't reach any final decisions. They did decide that Jesus and God the father were made of the same stuff, but they avoided the issue of the Trinity.

At the Council of Rome in 382 A.D., Pope Damasus apparently commissioned St. Jerome, his personal secretary, to assemble a list of books for inclusion into the *Bible*. He was to translate them into Latin from the original Greek and Hebrew texts. Jerome's Latin Bible appears to have been translated between 390 and 405 A.D. It became known as the ***Latin Vulgate Bible.*** The Council of Carthage met in 397 A.D. and listed the acceptable books of the *New Testament,* although the final list was apparently put together in 419 A.D. I really couldn't figure out if these were the same lists. The earliest surviving manuscript of the ***Vulgate*** dates back to 750 A.D. Later surviving manuscripts show various changes. The Latin Bible didn't get printed by *Gutenberg* until 1456. The Council of Trent met from 1546 to 1564 at Trent in northern Italy. I include where these towns are located because I assume that we don't have any familiarity with these places. That council set the ***Latin Vulgate Bible*** in stone, essentially stating, if you dared to question anything about it, that you were a heretic.

It's hard to be sure about any of this. They had to cull through a lot of different *Gospels* to put the Bible together. Apparently the story of Mary Magdalene is a composite extraction from three different *Gospels*. And of course the Protestants have different interpretations. You always have splinter groups. Even the Jews have their problems. Back in the 17th century Thomas Hobbes and Baruch Spinoza both concluded that the portion of the *Torah* attributed to Moses could not have been entirely his.

So now we have a Pope, and there is canonical law. The
Council of Trent has set a lot of speculation into stone. And somewhere
along the line, the Pope became infallible. That is setting more doctrine
into stone. Moses broke some stone tablets, but that was in a different
context, and the Pope does not appear ready to break any of the stone
tablets. The Roman Catholics have little room for freedom of
interpretation.

But in Islam you have thousands of spiritual leaders, called
imams, who direct the thinking of their followers. The radical imams
interpret the "enemies of Islam" in various ways. Some don't allow
women to be educated or even show their faces. This is certainly not in
the *Qur'an*. The Muslims have the benefit of a *Qur'an* which has not
suffered all the permutations leading to the acceptable Bible. But they
have the *Hadith* which is based upon hearsay reported by Mohammed's
followers. This gives the imams a great deal of room for maneuvering.

Many Christians are in agreement with the Muslims that much
of the American culture should not be incorporated into any culture.
Sex, nudity and violence may be transformational, but enhancing the
quality of the culture? Certainly the impact of television and the
Internet on a closed and controlled society can open up many divisive
issues. I can see why many imams are trying to figure out how to help
their people resist these temptations. The non-Islamic world is trying to
figure out if license, not liberty, is enshrined in the *First Amendment of
the American Constitution.* Where do you set the limits? Is everything
okay? Is anarchy okay?

I looked up a few definitions, so I may as well share them with
you. You've heard that **Osama bin Laden** was part of the **mujahadeen**
in Afghanistan. You know what **jihad** means. It means "to struggle."
The person performing the jihad is a **mujahid** and the plural is
mujahadeen. The **Taliban** is a word for "students." Some students!

I've known about the **Tabligh** (to deliver the message) for
quite a while. It was founded in India about 1926 by Maulana
Mohammad Ilyas Kandhalvi. It translates into "Propagation of the
Muslim Faith." It didn't get any PR but the faithful went door to door
and country to country until they numbered over 70 million members
in 150 countries. That's pretty good proselytizing! It apparently was a
very positive movement. But good things can be used by bad people,
and apparently *Al Qaeda* has been using the organization for travel
documents, shelters and financial assistance. One can assume that

30

most of the people in the Tabligh are not aware of what is going on.

The founding fathers of the Jewish state were terrorists who judged that they could get the British out of there by so doing. I guess that the jihadists thought that they had a shot at taking over Mali, but they didn't bargain on the French resistance. This current jihad does not appear to have any positive objective. It spreads fear and many innocent women and children are their sacrificial lambs. You have to have a lot of anger and hatred to do something like that. Sociopaths and deranged people fit into that category. Many feel that they are a bunch of losers. Others feel that their feelings are too intense and that they take things to heart, especially when they strap a bomb to that heart. I admit that that was a bad one.

I am rambling on because I think it is important to deal with some of the facts that exist in our environment. Information gathering is part of making a good decision. There's a lot of bad stuff happening out there. I used to say, "considering how much bad stuff there is out there, very little happens." I sure have changed my opinion. We bear witness to tsunamis, floods, famine, millions of terrorized refugees and kids getting slaughtered in their classrooms. My engineer friend believes that only observation, along with information, leads to knowledge and wisdom. He told me, "if you're going to write a book, make sure that the people get their money's worth, after all they have spent a some bucks to read your book." He's right. By now you have concluded that much of what you're read is patently ridiculous. If you continue reading, using *post hoc* reasoning you will find many more arguments to bolster your position. You might not be able to tell which arguments have been inserted just to keep you on your toes. You have to admit that this disclaimer is a pretty good way of camouflaging my ongoing revelation of ignorance.

Let's continue with the theme of terrorism. Weapons of mass destruction are out there. Maybe we should be worried about "castor oil" since we are so worried about terrorism. The news media has covered a number of stories involving the poison, Ricin, which is found in the castor bean, anthrax and smallpox. It can be delivered to your doorstep in three different forms, powder, pellet or mist. You may be the next to get some anthrax by mail. It is a deadly poison that can cause respiratory failure, seizures, dehydration and death. You've heard of the attack on the Japanese subway in which Sarin was released as a gas. It is an extremely deadly nerve agent. It contracts all the muscles so that you can't breathe. The only way to relax is to die. There is a lot

31

of bad stuff out there. And if you really want to get even with your neighbor, then visit the Internet. There you will find a few sites which will give you instructions on how to make your home brew of either Ricin or Sarin. It's nice to have almost any information available at your fingertips. The secrets of the government and the financial world are better hidden, but you can always hire a top gun in the hacking business.

The emergence of worldwide terrorism in the 21st century is a new adventure which is ill understood by *the brightest and the best.* They certainly are ill-equipped to stomp on it and to stamp it out. What is wrong with the human brain? Why can't the experts figure things out? Is it that there are simply too many factors so that it is pure guesswork, a lot like betting in the lottery. Delving into a dark well looking for the key cause of terrorism is probably a prime example of entering Disneyland, a world of sheer fantasy. But Walt couldn't get away with such a fantasy of horror. Call it *Draculaland* or *Vladland.* You pick the right name for this.

The human brain is cursed with a tendency to view things in a polar opposite fashion. So the researchers', call them historians, brains are either infused with deductive or inductive reasoning. A good researcher should be an honest man with a pretty good idea about his own biases. He has to try to get as much information as he can, check if he has a diversity of facts and verify the facts. We know that hearsay evidence is unreliable, and **printed hearsay** also has to be approached with a great deal of trepidation. Cringe! The current researcher, building on the hearsay incorporated into a prior researcher's conclusions, has a lot of digging to do. He usually tries to bring all sorts of observations towards **one causative reason,** or he has an intuitive bias which allows him into the world of **generalizations**. Even the best of them can easily get their facts wrong. And if it is all about **multi-factorialism** then he may as well close the books, turn his cell phone off, shut off his computer and go to one of those horror movies. He may actually find something there that inspires him. The electric light bulb may suddenly be turned on.

After the World Trade Towers were destroyed, I went into Barnes & Noble looking for books on Islam and the Arab world. I found only one book. America was a great power and yet it's populace lacked any information about significant blocs in the world. An explosion of new books by experts in both fields ensued. Only one author mentioned anything about the **Tabligh,** a worldwide Islamic organization, and he got the founder's name completely wrong. If you look at the Internet now, you'll find a fair amount of information about that organization.

We are appalled by the global scope of the evil associated with terrorism. They now utilize cars and people as suicide bombers in mosques and shopping centers, killing innocent women and children. Perhaps this is a modest death toll in comparison to the millions of African and Asiatic peoples who are being massacred and forced to leave their homes, only to find themselves in squalid camps run by the UN.

A well-established fantasy, or should I say fallacy, is that terrorism is inspired by an Islamic hatred of American culture or Western religion. Some feel that the prime cause can be found in the US Middle Eastern foreign policy which is strongly supportive of the Jewish state of Israel. It blames the US for the Palestinian oppression and its militaristic destruction in the Islamic and Arab world. Another simplistic explanation is that the terrorists want to expunge the Western military and cultural influences from their country. Another very popular view is that this is all due to the poverty found in the Islamic world. If we could just send them enough money to build their infrastructure, educate the children, give them clean water and access to medical care, give them jobs and an adequate living wage, then all this terrorism would simply disappear!

We know that **Islam** was a powerful religious, military and cultural force in the 11th century. It all vanished. Apart from the miracle of finding oil under the sand, exports from the entire Arab world are in the range of what we find in Switzerland or some Scandinavian country. Many blame the rise of Sufism with its ultra-worldly focus. We can't even explain why the Chinese, with a vastly superior armada, didn't make the preemptive strike and colonize the world. The British Commonwealth might never have come into existence. Bring on the researchers.

The current researchers are trying to build a profile of what an *average* **Jihadist** is. They have been interviewing a lot of jihadists and looking into their backgrounds. They are also including a lot of dead jihadists which renders any conclusion more unreliable. Maybe I should correct that sentence. They have not been interviewing jihadists who are dead. They are finding that a good number of them were highly westernized, were not very religious, came from city backgrounds, were pretty well-educated, knew more than one language and have good computer skills. A good percentage ended up being converts to Islam. It's an entirely different picture in Afghanistan. As you might guess, some of the Western research tends to be skewed. One report is that 80% of the Afghanistan jihadists have physical and/or mental disabilities. The *New York Times* and the *Reuters* people feel that a lot of jihadists are interested in child pornography. That could be interpreted as a lack of commitment to religious beliefs. But child pornography and enslavement is not uncommonly found around the world, regardless of the practitioner's religious upbringing. Just a little flaw built into *homo sapiens.*

So where do we find the birth of terrorism? **Yasser Arafat** and Khalil al-Wazir founded *al Fatah* with the aim of using guerrilla warfare to get rid of Israel. The *PLO* (Palestinian Liberation Organization) was founded in 1964. The *PFLP* (Popular Front for the Liberation of Palestine), a revolutionary group, broke off from the PLO in 1967. Meanwhile **Nasser** was in the forefront of an anti-Western Arab revival movement which led to a coalition of Arab states attacking Israel in 1967. They have been in mortal combat with Israel ever since. The **Ayatollah Khomeini** led the Iranian revolution in 1979. He put his children soldiers in the front lines as Iran waged war with Iraq. It was a good military tactic. "Let the kids get killed, we'll save our good troops for the end." Of course we know that he loved kids and it was his way of insuring that they would be martyrs, and thus be lavishly rewarded by Allah. Many of the revolutionary leaders were scholars and highly educated men. *Hezbollah* pioneered the use of the suicide bomber. That certainly has been a welcome addition to guerrilla warfare. *Al Qaeda* came into this relatively late, around 1990.

We've been told by the Western media that the Muslim Brotherhood is a terrorist organization which has spread discord through all Islamic countries. Apparently we have viewed their history through a Weston prism. I was fortunate to meet a devout Muslim gentleman who has become quite a scholar in Middle Eastern history, Islamic history and the political history involved in this. He told me that I had gotten it all wrong. Each has ties me about the fact that I had no idea of the real name of the organization ... the *Al-lkhywan al-Muslimun.* He spoke quite openly about many issues and helped to clarify concepts and issues which we face today. Ah!, to think or not to think which makes such a calamity of my long life. It is so sad to be so wrong so often in just one generation!

Akhwan al-Muslimin is a Pan-Islamic, religious, political and social movement which was founded by the Islamic scholar Hassan al-Banna in 1928. It is known to Luz as the Muslim Brotherhood. It began as a religious organization which was socially oriented. It preach the Islamic faith, set up madrasas (schools) and hospitals and eventually became commercial and political and was involved in the overthrow of King Farouk.

The Brotherhood's website declares that its goal is the introduction of the Islamic Sharia as "the basis for controlling the affairs of state and society" and working to unify "Islamic countries and states, mainly among the Arab states and liberating them from foreign imperialism." The organization believes in reform, democracy, freedom of assembly and of the press. It is said that its founder calls for "a campaign against ostentation and dress and loose behavior," "segregation of male and female students," a separate curriculum for girls, and "the prohibition of dancing and other such pastimes ..." *Akhwan al-Muslimin* is said to strive for social justice eradication of poverty and corruption and political freedom to the extent allowed by the laws of Islam.

The Western media stresses the Brotherhood's involvement in so-called terrorist groups. My friend states that they have been involved in spreading their ideology to various political groups in the Middle East, the Islamic countries, but not in their activities. Their philosophy has been picked up by the *Islamic Action Front* in Jordan and *Hamas* in Gaza and the West Bank.

Akhwan al-Muslimin (Muslim Brotherhood) has carried its ideology into the *Jamate Islam* party in Pakistan, India and Bangladesh. Abul-ala-Moudodi was the founder of *Jamal-e-Islam* in India in 1935. Mohamadia was the founder of a similar party in Indonesia.

My new friend told me that the Quran expressly prohibited (*haram*) terrorism. He told me that the suicide bomber and terrorism were the creations of Hassan bin Sabah during the fourth Islamic caliphate, Fatimid Caliphate which lasted from 909 to 1171. Hassan was born in Iran around 1034. He came to believe that he was the incarnation of God. He founded the Nizari Ismailites, later known as Hashishins. They were later to be known as *Assassins.* Hassan founded a fortress high in the mountains of Qazwin which became known as the *Garden of Earthly Delights.* As the Valley was filled with exotic plants,

35

birds and animals from the then known world. There was sumptuous palaces with streams of wine and honey flowing through that garden of paradise. The initiates were offered hashish and provided with bountiful sexual pleasures which was only an introduction to a far more glorious afterlife. The culture was built on Sufism within the Shiite faith. They learned to kill by poison or dagger or both. They were initiated into the trade of being a secret agent. They learned several languages. These initiates became the *fidais,* committed themselves, to being *suicidal agents* who were willing to commit any act of terrorism demanded by the master. It is said that they were responsible for killing many good people whose faith was Sunni. They assassinated kings and generals. These *fidats* were guaranteed entrance into the *Garden of Heavenly Delights.* Not an easy reward to pass up

The *Assassins* became a formidable organization. They actually were intellectuals who understood how to use power and propaganda. But we again face the juxtaposition of the opposites. Hassan became a devout believer in the Ismaili faith and did not tolerate drinking or playing musical instruments in his castle. One son was executed for drinking. Hassan died in 1124 but the *Assassins* were finally defeated 100 years later. It is said that many of the Assassins' techniques were incorporated into the CIA manual and the name Hassan Sabbah is found in the document.

My scholar friend really has given me a lot of good information. So terrorism was invented 1000 years ago with their version of the suicide bomber. We of all been perplexed about this new era of **worldwide terrorism**. He gave me some chronological information so that one understands why the Taliban is alive and well. It all begins with the invasion of Afghanistan by the Russians in 1979 on their way to liberating some Pakistani ports thus giving them access to the Indian Ocean. They were to leave in 1989. It appears that the main reason for the invasion of Afghanistan was to secure access to the Indian ocean where they could become a major oil power. Apparently the CIA and other chaps did not want to let this happen. There was a strong appeal to Islamic countries to repeal the invasion of *infidels.* So soldiers were recruited from Arabic countries and many from Pakistan to repel these invaders. It became an Islamic Jihad. Billions of dollars, training and weaponry were poured in by the United Kingdom, United States, Saudi Arabia, Israel and Islamic countries the soldiers from Egypt, Libya, Pakistan and all the Islamic countries formed the *mujahideen.* Osama bin Laden was one of the *mujahideen.*

When the Russians left Afghanistan in 1989 the Western money dried up. Warlords took up the slack and controlled their individual regions of Afghanistan. Things were very chaotic and this is where Pakistan plays a major role. After the war the mujahideen were really well-educated and went back to the madrasas in Afghanistan, Pakistan and other Islamic countries. The warlords were creating problems. Pakistan took on the responsibility of stabilizing Afghanistan. General Hameed Gul, director of the ISI recruited these semiretired mujahideen. Osama bin Laden had relocated to the Sudan, but the United States was pressuring Sudan to turn him over. He fled to Afghanistan in the region of mullah Omar. The returning *mujahideen* systematically crushed warlord after warlord, centralizing a government which we now know as the Taliban. Taliban means student. It is a strongly Islamic fundamentalists political movement with the strict interpretation of Sharia law. They are known for their brutal treatment of women. The Taliban was supported by Al Qaeda, Saudi Arabia and fighters from Arab countries. They destroyed tens of thousands of homes and burnt thousands of fertile fields and no poppies grew.

General Pervez Musharraf provided the airbases and logistic support in Pakistan for the United States and the allies to invade Afghanistan in 2001. The professed reason for the invasion was to topple Osama bin Laden whom mullah Omar refused to hand over. The Taliban was overthrown and began its guerrilla warfare against the foreign forces and the Hamid Karzai government. His government promptly went back into the business of growing poppies and the lucrative drug trading business. And now Pakistan is paying the price for helping the Americans. The Taliban took refuge in the mountains of Afghanistan. A second faction of some 30 to 40,000 Taliban took refuge in the Northwest Frontier of Pakistan. This latter group is quite bitter about the Pakistani support of the American and NATO forces during the war in Afghanistan. Pakistan provided airfields for the bombers and the planes that brought provisions. Huge convoys of materials were shipped into Pakistan and found their way into Afghanistan via Charman, a border town of the province of Balochistan and Peshawar in the Northwest Frontier.

This second Taliban faction cannot be dislodged by the Pakistani army in the Hindu Kush mountains. They control that area and have been quite successful in infiltrating all of Pakistan. It is now known that 19,000 NATO supply carriers are missing, seized by the Taliban and terrorist groups. These trailers contained powerful military weaponry. So we find that the Americans are responsible for arming the Taliban which now offers its services as armed mercenaries to other terrorist groups in many other countries. They are in the process of blowing up Pakistani mosques and destroying its economy. America seems disinterested except for the fact that Pakistan has the atomic bomb. Before all of this started Pakistan was an economy which was enjoying considerable economic success and growth. Now the women are afraid to be on the streets late at night and no one is sure where and when the next bomb will explode.

This all appears to be a fine example of the *law of unintended consequences.* Saudi Arabia and the West created the mujahideen who successfully drove the Russians out of Afghanistan, who furthered their education in the madrasas of Pakistan and Afghanistan, then returned to Afghanistan to bolster a Taliban government only to be driven to the mountains of Afghanistan and Pakistan to become worldwide terrorists, soldiers of fortune, for hire. The conspiratorial theorists may even presume that this consequence was intended by America and the bankers of the world.

With all the disturbances in the Middle East we find that Morsi was elected president of Egypt in a democratic election. He quickly change things. He gave himself almost absolute powers and change the Constitution without input from the parliament. Great masses of people demonstrated in the streets and he eventually was deposed and detained by the Egyptian army. The Mubarak regime had tried to close the tunnels into Palestine. Morsi reopened them to supply the Palestinians with food and munitions. This led to legal actions against him and the Muslim Brotherhood was banned.

Now we have the **Arab Spring** which has turned into an **Arab Fall. Assad** is doing his best to treat the revolutionaries in Syria in the usual way. It appears that he thinks that the scorched earth policy will do the trick. I think architectural students are being exposed to a new form of *city planning.* Saddam Hussein was the violent, oppressive dictator in Iraq. He controlled the majority Shi'ites with a small group of Sunnis. Now that Saddam is no longer around both groups are free to return to tribal violence. **Bashar al-Assad** is the head of the *Alawites* who compose only 12% of the Syrian population. The Sunnis comprise over 60%. With the insurgency both groups are trying to exterminate one another. The Alawites have origins in both Syria and Iraq and were actually killing Muslims during the Crusades. They are not highly respected within the Muslim world, but have been, only recently, accepted as Muslims on the Shi'ite side.

Libya has a strong military presence and is not letting things get out of hand. In 1984 the assembly had passed a *Sharia* family code depriving women of many rights. There was the so-called **Algerian Spring** in the late 1980s with riots and strong militant groups such as *Hamas* and the *FIS (Islamic Salvation Front)*. Not to worry. When the *FIS* was well on the way to winning the election, the election was simply suspended and the military took control. The 1990's was a time of struggle between the military and Islamic Jihadists. Tens of thousands of Afghanistan war veterans joined the terrorist groups. During that period of time the holy month of Ramadan was used as a pretext for the terrorists to slaughter people. Some form of redemption! The different parties finally came to some sort of agreement. Algeria has had their *Al Qaeda* influence, but things are not getting out of hand. The *al-Jam'a* terrorists have few members. They have problems in the southern part of the country where a Tuareg separatist movement exists. No one has any idea of what is about to transpire in Tunisia and Egypt.

We keep hearing the term **Jihad**,which means struggle, a striving for individual spiritual self-perfection. Mohammed was into personal responsibility. **Terrorism** must be cloaked in the garb of something noble, something unassailable such as a religious duty. It is like **Lucifer** going to a masked ball dressed as Mary, mother of Jesus. The *Qur'an,* it may be argued, is a simplified form of the ethical teachings of the Jewish and Christian faiths. It's a small handbook of do's and don'ts. It should be required reading. You might disagree about a few issues, but the basics are there. The *Hadith* is an altogether different thing. It's hearsay evidence told by Mohammed's followers and interpreted by Islamic scholars.

So getting back to the researcher facing the precipice, "How do I safely get out of here and find the cause of terrorism?" Ain't going to be easy. Although we find the *Muslim Brotherhood* in charge in Egypt, the reasons have to do with a lot of individual perception and interpretations of being oppressed. People are jumping on the coattails of a group which is itself highly discontented. An awful lot of secular issues are in the soil of these hoped-for changes. Of course the oddsmakers in Las Vegas will give you great odds against anything really changing.

We keep thinking that changing a culture and its form of government into a democracy will be great. The revolting people think the same way as their so-called oppressors thought. They really have no frame of reference even if they read the classic self-help textbook on democracy, *Understanding Democracy.* You can't understand something unless you feel it emotionally. That's what being a human being is all about. Enjoy yourself, go to a movie, life is just too hard.

We've talked a bit about how we are limited by what we genetically come into the world with. We should say a few words about our environment. If you are born in Somalia or the Sudan you have quite different expectations than if you're born in the United States. If your parents are well-educated, you have a lot of their knowledge and experience imparted unto you. If your mother is a drug using, uneducated prostitute with a boyfriend who abuses you, your future could be very bleak. If your parents don't see any value in education, you probably will drop out of school. Your home may be in the slums and you may be surrounded by criminals and drug addicts. Your only protection may be to join a gang and become a part of the problem. You don't know another way unless you are exposed to another possible direction and someone is there to get you started. Otherwise your only hope is that you are that unusual *social genius* who is able to recognize how *meshugana* your environment is, and that you have to get out of it and make something of yourself.

Once upon a time a good education secured a prosperous future. But it now appears that our educators are letting us down. My good friend frequently says, "the only thing that interferes with my learning is my education." We'll find more examples where the brightest and the best led us in the wrong direction. It's not their fault, they're only human beings. The educators decided that everybody should go to college in the United States. They eliminated the trade schools which could get you a good job out of high school. The medical schools didn't teach their students how to take care of people, so they had to take four years of residency after they graduated from medical school. They made it even harder. Passing medical school didn't mean anything. The doctors had to take three other exams to be able to get into a specialty, such as family medicine. Then they had to take exams after they finished their training. The graduating lawyers had to take bar exams in every single state that they wished to practice in. And they didn't know how anything was done in the legal system, so they had to become apprentices to a legal firm.

At this point it makes some sense to interject some of the concerns that my friend has about education and its cost. Educators have been perpetrating a myth that a college graduate will earn $1 million more than the high school graduate. That just doesn't stand up to critical analysis. There is another way of looking at this. Take $100,000, multiply that by five and the answer is $500,000. That hundred thousand dollars invested over a forty year period will yield at least that amount. If you invest $400,000 in college and graduate studies, you should show it to be a good investment. You should have at least $2 million at retirement time. If your daddy is footing the bill, you don't have to worry. If you don't have a really good job, it's going to be very difficult to repay the loan. It might be far wiser for your daddy to have you go to work at Burger King and simply put that money into an investment so that you could retire with $2 million in the bank.

Bill Gates, Steve Jobs and Bill Ellison of Oracle are billionaires and never went to college. There are just a lot of non-college graduates who've worked very hard and been very successful. But if you have to work for somebody, then it's very important to get the training to be able to obtain a job. Some industries won't look at you unless you have that *diplomatic* diploma.

My friend furnished me with some statistics. 35% of student loan repayments are behind by 3 months. Since the mid-80s the tuition costs have risen by 500%. Only 1/3 of full-time students receive a college degree within 4 years. 48% of recent college graduates have not been able to find a job in their field. Only 56% of graduating lawyers are able to find a full-time job in the legal profession. Over 50% of college graduates were either unemployed or in part-time jobs. There are Internet sites whose theme is the "predatory loan practices" of the government, banks and institutions. Businesses, such as colleges and "institutes," need to keep the enrollment high and keep the money coming in. That's not surprising. "Let the buyer beware!" The *Wall Street Journal* said that 40% of out of school borrowers have defaulted. But you apparently can sign up for a program where the government will write off any debt after twenty-five years. So make sure that you can figure out how to get into that program.

Students are learning less because the courses are not as demanding and the students spend less than 10% of the time studying. The average college student is felt to be doing very well if he passes a basic algebra course. My friend sent me some information which he garnered over the Internet. Some of it covered how the standard for graduating from high school had so deteriorated that 50% of the kids entering college have to be enrolled, in college, in remedial education. Talk about waste and the duplication of effort. We know of the California high schools where the graduating students can't pass the graduating exam. They go on anyway. What is really scary is to appreciate that the eighth-grade students in the 19th century had passed very extensive and comprehensive exams which our college graduates can't do today. Do a little bit of reading about this if you have your doubts.

Another issue involves our new ethical standards in the US. Cheating is rampant even at the university level. Harvard college recently investigated 125 students for cheating. Over 50% of them were asked to leave for an "indefinite period." I would lay good odds that they'll soon be back in school. What happened to that "*good ole time religion?*"

My daughter went to one of those tough Eastern colleges. Between semesters she was at home and attended a course at the local college. They were given an assignment to read four chapters before the next lecture. The first thing that the teacher did at the next session was to ask what the students had actually read. The students indicated that they had only found time to read one chapter. The teacher set a new standard of reading: only one chapter a class. She couldn't flunk the students. She had to keep her job. So what if they got only a quarter of what they should've been learning? I can understand why many colleges and universities don't automatically transfer credits. Some of the poorer universities still have some strong departments. They are usually able to transfer those credits.

So the teacher has to figure out how to give every student at least a B. You can get a student to enroll in your class if it is known to be easy and funny. So the University of California at Irvine has a course entitled "Gaga for Gaga: Sex, Gender, and Identity." Columbia College offers "Zombies in Popular Media." At the State University of New York at Buffalo, they have to devote a huge auditorium to accommodate all the students enrolled in "Cyberporn and Society." The community college experiment has been a complete flop. 90% of the students never get any diploma. Perhaps we can justify that expense by putting it into the Parks and Recreation department.

My friend also sent me some stuff covering the fact that teachers are being given a bad rap as the perpetrators of **bad** education because they are forced to teach a government mandated curriculum which emphasizes rote memorization in just a few categories. I disagree with him on that issue. The government can be blamed for many different reasons. The overt reason for the mandate is the deterioration of student learning. It is like pouring more water on a drowning man.

The real cause is *the parent* who has abdicated the duty of doing what is necessary to educate his or her child. That parent also has found the way of excusing personal responsibility and finding an easy scapegoat. And we don't seem to have a pesticide to kill the disease that is killing the plant. I'll have to consult Monsanto and then surreptitiously either root out the plant or find a pesticide which no one can detect. It's not going to be easy.

The states have been happy to have some reimbursement of their taxes in the form of schools subsidies. That money may well have helped some of the really poor school systems by raising the standards. "I'll tell you what to do or you won't get any more money," came the steely federal voice, **the kiss of death**, the bureaucrat in charge. I have always been partial to dictators, they wear such pretty uniforms. It's part of the **slippery slope** picture. It's also an example of **guerrilla warfare** with its adjunct, **terrorism** which can only be appreciated as the **uncertainty principle** in disguise. As soon as you've identified the voice, it's gone, and no one knows where it's gone. And then there's another voice, in a sequence of **déjà vu** experiences. After awhile you come to appreciate that you're a character in a **Kafka** novel. I hope you can unravel the meaning in this scroll.

My friend later sent me something akin to the Actonian concept that "power corrupts absolutely." I'll just quote some of it, "centralization is the black hole that is destroying the nation's social and economic vigor. Decentralization, transparency, accountability, adaptability, social innovation, a community-based economy--these are the key features of a sustainable social order."

But is it fair to blame the teachers? We know that many teachers really don't understand the subject that they're teaching. A superb equestrian rider told his students to push their knees down really hard. Of course that catapulted them over the barrel. The swimming instructor, who had no idea about bone density, could not figure out why some students could not learn how to float. He told his friends that, "They are either lazy, afraid or just uncooperative. But then there is the natural born teacher who really understands his or her craft. I took one swing with my golf club, and my friend's father instantaneously showed me how to change my grip. My slice was gone and I had a controlled hook.

Some teachers are so bright in there respective fields that they seem to have bypassed learning the basics of their field. So they really don't cover the basics when they teach. You've got to be taught from the very beginning that you are in school *to learn how to do your own thinking.* There are a few simple rules which apply to "*how to teach.*" The first thing is to let the students know what they should learn in this course. I remember taking an organic chemistry course and looking at about forty molecular structures tied into and in the continuous circle with different things like -CH3 -NH3 -NO3 and -OH sticking out at all angles. Given the introduction of one reagent we were instructed to show how, in sequential form, the complex would break down. The entire course could have been summarized in the instruction to learn which bonds were the strongest and why. Of course the professor had never talked about the importance of bonding. A great final sendoff to the students as he went to Martha's Vineyard.

The second rule is to explain the basic concepts introduced in any discipline. As strange as this may seem, I remember a calculus teacher who always made a mistake on every calculus problem that he wrote on the blackboard. He put the letters in the equations on the board, but he never explain the differential concept or what dx/dy was all about. It's called *backwards learning* or writing Arabic in reverse. It is a great way of getting you to think. You can actually successfully pass a college course in calculus without understanding the fundamentals. Of course that means that it has been a total waste of understanding a thinking process. Of course the kid with a good mathematical mind understands all the stuff instinctively. So you'll hear him say, "It so simple, stupid, anyone can understand it."

That's not the sort of teacher who inspires anyone. This is where **randomness** plays a role in every person's life. Do you remember anyone who significantly affected you and perhaps altered your life course? A teacher can inspire you to be of significance to yourself and to the world. By now you have a clear understanding of why I never became a motivational speaker.

Our brains are not wired to understand logic, math or science. So you need to remember that the teachers who are teaching the students may have had trouble learning logic, math and science. They might even be teaching one of those courses. Scary? It's quite clear that our educational system needs to focus on those fields since the jobs are in the technological fields. The rest of the world will be burying us. We used to be the creators. The wave of our future is in dinosaur land. We are actually stifling creativity. The heads of college departments have fixed opinions about what people should be thinking about and what research is appropriate. If you expect to stay in that department you had better not be drawn to some creative cubicle.

We used to be farmers and we had a big bag of information and knowledge about how things worked. That's no longer the case. We are specialized individuals, and we like to have fun. Instead of teaching technological skills, we're teaching social skills. I wonder if that is why people are trying to socialize by dating people over the Internet? But I should try to stay on task. I should stay on task, but I won't. I just thought about something that I said years ago, "if you read a book a week for 25 weeks in different subjects you will find yourself to be among the top 5 % of the most informed people in the world. If you read 50 books, you'll be in the top 1%." Think about that. It's true. It's easy to self educate yourself if you have some intellectual stamina. And you can do it at your leisure in 6 to 12 months, if you so choose. You can even download those books onto your cell phone and you don't even have to read! If you're too tired to do the downloading yourself, ask your friend to do it.

I'm supposed to be focused on the process of **thinking**. Teachers should be honest and tell the kids that they are free to question things and not assume that whatever they are told has to be totally correct. Early on it could be in the form of some question-and-answer games. Just a few minutes a day could be spent on asking such questions as "why do you like that," "do you think that is right," "can you think of something different," "is that the only way of doing something?" You could get the kids thinking. The kids could learn to make new mistakes rather than just ape the mistakes of the adults. I'm sure a lot of teachers are already doing that, but I would feel a lot more comfortable if it was part of the curriculum. A small course entitled *"Are you thinking?"* I think the motto of the old Bridgewater State Teachers College was, "to act upon, and not to be acted upon."

We are in an era when **slow** needs to enter the arena and give battle to **quick**. Teachers instinctively understand that, but I have seen a principal throw her hands up in the air when that discussion comes up. Children watch a lot of television or are aware of what is going on with a lot of aspects of society, including a good number of their peers being slaughtered when they were at school. It's a good starting off point for the teachers to be able to discuss social morality. It can certainly be done in simple terms. We are all selfish and like to get our own way. We'd rather play than study. It can be pointed out that people whom we admire have worked very hard and have sacrificed a lot to be where they are. There are many sports heroes. We can also point out that kindness usually doesn't cost a lot and helps a lot of people. You also make a lot of friends that way. Being a bully, the toughest guy at school or on the street, a drug dealer, a gang banger does not lead to any long-term success. It's a good way to be a criminal and end up in jail. Examples of the advantages of being good readily come to mind.

We seem to leave the job of teaching social morality to religions and parents. That leaves a lot to chance. Religions are not known to do a great job. Many are too serious and doctrinaire and kids hate to go to church. Religion becomes an abstraction when children become young adults. The *Ten Commandments* recede into the shadows as coping with real life takes precedence. People just don't think in terms of being kind and fair towards people. It's not in the forefront of human existence. I know that religious leaders will disagree with that contention. People simply don't think about the consequences of their behaviors until it's too late. Teachers do have the power to substantially impact in this area by stressing a few rules of the road. They can make them up themselves. With constant reminder, in a pleasant way, the student will remind himself as he goes up the educational ladder. Repetition impacts on long-term memory. Is he getting an A, B, C , D or F in *social morality*?

There is a long history of manifest charity in all religions. Islam requires that 2 1/2% of one's income be given to charity. It's called *Zakah*, and additional voluntary charity is called *Sadagah*. We supplied $60 billion of materials to the Allies before entering World War II in December 1941. It was called the Lend-Lease Act. It required no repayment. Seriously, Americans have a long history of being a giving people. Great churches and universities were built on charitable contributions by both rich and poor. Who were John Harvard and Eli Yale? Have you heard of Henry Ford, Andrew Carnegie or any of those names that are now sponsoring PBS? Who is Bill Gates?

I've been impressed by the lack of practical examples that are offered to students in the math and science classes. Examples of how trigonometry and calculus are actually useful tools would pique the students interests, and it might even convert the "artsy craftsy" student into becoming a science major. It might even help them to develop their memories. Rote is so boring, and really doesn't translate well into long-term memory We know that the visual and practical experiences enhance our memory. Teaching kids to memorize numbers and dates is a real turn-off, especially if you haven't been taught any tricks about how to memorize numbers. So should we embrace an alternate definition of wisdom?

Wisdom = Skepticism towards formal education.

III

CREATIVITY AND THE CLASH OF CULTURES

This chapter defines *supercollider*. I've been tempted to hide while Western culture collides with the cultures of the Middle East and the East. The West is defined as Australia, the Americas and Europe. I'm not sure exactly where Russia fits in.

But I'm currently distracted. This opus is dedicated to clarifying **how we think**, how we should think and how to scale the mountain of **wisdom**. But I've just been told that an in-depth interview with the **prodigal son** has been found in the archives of the Alexandrian Museum. It apparently is not in good shape but the archivists are working at cleaning it up. It was originally found in the archives of the *Nazareth Times*. That interview probably encompasses all the wisdom of the world. End of chapter. End of book.

My friend says, "that can't be true, he had to be a *schmuck* to leave a cool place like that in the first place. He had it made in the shade." Maybe he's right. I guess I should just push on.

There are quite a few terms that we need to reference in this chapter. Let's make a list and go on.

prejudice	**emotional**
probability	**biases**
advertising	**first impression**
feel-good	**skepticism**
inductive reasoning	**post hoc ergo procter hoc**
ad hominem	**jump to conclusion**
non sequitur	**heuristic (reflex action)**
slippery slope	**predictability**
denial	**morality**
memory distortion	**judgment**
I wish	**generalization**
correlation	**reduction ad absurdum**
illogical	**a priori**
common sense	**pattern recognition**
anticipation	**responsibility**
quick	**deductive reasoning**
stubbornness	**critical thinking**

post hoc
anchor

poison well
Kripkean dogmatism
(I'm always right)

Time to press on. Does cultural thinking vary?

WEST		EAST
	industrial	
well-developed		underdeveloped-China & India progressing
	infrastructure	
extensive public services roads, schools, water		poor to marginal-some are evolving; many lack access to water and schools
	technology	
advanced, Internet		few phones or Internet
	wealth	
mostly prosperous		much poverty, Saudi Arabia & Indonesia prosper
	government	
many democracies		many dictatorships & autocracies
	indebtedness	
USA – excessive imports heavily indebted to China		colonialism, heavily indebted except China
	corruption	
some		prevalent
	races	
Caucasian		Orientals and Blacks
	education	
well-educated fine universities		fewer schools – women denied education
	pace	
rapid, quick		often quite slow
	philosophy	
doctrinaire-papal influence Moses, Jesus, Mohammed		emphasis on personal Confucius, Hindi, Buddha
	Kripkean dogmatism **(I'm always right)**	
omnipresent		common

rules

IRS, copyrights, laws, patents, permits, regulations	Patent & copyright infringement-arbitrary imprisonment

ethnic groups

emphasis on integration	tribal-genocidal-religious & ethnic persecutions

women

increasingly equal to men	many examples of brutality, denial of schooling and basic rights

invasions

Crusades, Iraq, Afghanistan colonialism, globalization	Al Qaeda, Islamic Jihad

personal focus

fun, personal satisfaction	survival (food, health & violence) for many

dependence

socialism, welfare programs, no jobs, unemployment benefits	foreign aid, NGOs, UN food and troops

personal liberty

democratic rights, police and army	despotic regimes, capricious decisions

thought control

corporate dollars, TV, politicians, advertising	imams, media control, propaganda

morals

TV-sex & violence, theft of movies and music, adolescents become crooks	Islamic clerics fear Internet & TV-sex, nudity, violence, social upheavals

civilization

the rights of man have been hard fought	rulers-slow to give up power necessary infrastructure is not developed

self-importance

product of prosperity	oppressed, people need to feel empowered

individual rights

ACLU tears down old values ? of retaining the culture	China & Africa sacrifice people for power or Western type prosperity

hegemony

the Roman Empire fell-
when will the USA fall?

China is moving in that
direction

Well that is a quick comparison of two cultures. We certainly know that prejudice is built into both cultures but it appears to be much harsher in the East. There are so many biases against races, nationalities and religions. It's clear that there is a lot of anticipation, pattern recognition, first impressions, heuristic responses built into all this probability and predictability These are very emotional issues and many of them lead to violence fueling ongoing hatred. In tribal areas the enmity goes on for generations. The West seems more forgiving. Think of the Marshall plan and how the West rebuilt Japan and Germany. The Germans killed off millions of Jews and the Japanese performed atrocity after atrocity. I remember a Dominican missionary priest who was in one of their prison camps. Since then I have not run into anyone who has expressed any hatred towards the Japanese. I think that is particularly strange and impressive. So there is some hope for the good in mankind to survive.

It seems pretty clear that the West is far ahead in terms of materialism. It always amazes me that the Islamic hegemony turned over and died in the 11th century. Now the jihadists are trying to make up for lost time. They should be mad at themselves, not at the West.

It's certainly true that cultures do evolve. Changes are going on at light speed nowadays. The United States is going from an agricultural economy to a service economy. Think about that. If you grew up on a farm you had to know about seeds, fertilizer, soil, machinery, electricity, plumbing, milking, slaughtering, preserving, cooking, sewing, carpentry, counting, reading and many other skills. You had to be a generalist. The generalist is gone, replaced by the specialist with little in the way of practical skills. You can understand why people who write about thinking emphasize that you need to get a lot of people together with a diversity of experience so that you can come to some conclusion and maybe even a solution. That's pretty sad.

It's quite clear that the average western citizen doesn't have a clue about how his rights and culture are being eroded. He's having too much fun. He doesn't do much thinking about any of this. The common man in the East is too busy trying to survive and perhaps trying to gain some freedom and power to engage in any of this Western thinking. And we all know that Lord Acton said, "power tends to corrupt, and absolute power corrupts absolutely." So the Middle Eastern powers are not about to give an inch. That's a good example of the slippery slope argument.

It's interesting to note that the West prides itself on valuing the rights of an individual, but it's philosophy is based upon the power of **one God**. Meanwhile the philosophers of the East emphasized personal development and responsibility only to find themselves oppressed by the power of **one man** or **one committee**. I wonder how that happened?

Meanwhile the West is pursuing **globalization** and is amazed by its reception in the East. Would you like to have your culture invaded by some foreigner's values, products and advertising? Would a male dominated culture with its veiled, powerless women enjoy the sex, nudity and violence found in the Western movies, TV and Internet?

My daughter reminds me that each culture is really quite parochial and quite tribal in nature. The power brokers of each culture are highly critical of the culture next-door, although its citizens may have considerably different views, especially with access to the Internet and the television. The Americans, Indians and the Indonesians have quite different values. Where is the wisdom in all of this? We all die and take it with us.

$$W=K (B+F+E) \times GJ (H+R+CS).$$

W = **WISDOM**
K = **KNOWLEDGE**

    B = **BASICS**
        1 - an individual's strengths and
            weaknesses such as intelligence
        2 - the fabric of the culture
    F = **FACTS AND INFORMATION**
        1 - academic schooling
        2 - positive things learned outside of school
    E = **EXPERIENCES**
        1 - personally involved
        2 - personally observed
        3 - diversity of experiences

GJ = GOOD JUDGMENT
H = HUMILITY
  1 - insight into one's own biases and
   personal limitations
R = RATIONAL
  1 - comprehensive and rational view of the
   issues
CS = COMMON SENSE

The West is certainly way ahead in the knowledge category at this point. It's infrastructure is a lot more advanced and its technological innovations are moving forward at lightning speed. Science is moving on. Meanwhile the prosperity of the individual citizen is falling. He is having more fun and doing less work. He seems to feel that he is entitled to all of these rewards; he's not being very realistic about the future. He scores poorly in the humility category and is not using his common sense; his judgment is obviously impaired. The Western culture now features trivia and superficiality at every turn. It is very corrosive to the infrastructure of a culture that was built on the effort and achievement of the individual. The culture obviously is built upon its citizenry, and does not benefit from a despotic top-down philosophy.

Meanwhile we are aware that China, India and Indonesia are catching up in the knowledge category. China is pouring money into its infrastructure. Their universities are growing at a rapid pace and they are becoming capitalists. They have a long way to go since most of their citizens are quite poor and are not benefiting from this cultural revolution. The average citizen is slowly gaining more influence, but he has to watch his step. He can be easily punished. If you believe that Western culture is the way to go, then you'd have to conclude that the decision makers are wise. They must have a good handle on their strengths and assets. They have a good game plan.

In Africa there are many corrupt regimes which are squandering their natural resources. The in-crowd is becoming very wealthy and doing virtually nothing for the people. The rulers have wealth, thus power which might be considered the product of personal wisdom. The nation itself suffers from crumbling infrastructure with ignorance, poverty, disease and hopelessness as a commonplace way of life. The people think only in terms of survival. The people who follow the present corrupt rulers will have learned how to be corrupt and the cycle will continue. For a nation to be wise, it needs its people to have some education and some skills. On the other hand you can learn some things quite easily without going to school, such as the art of corruption. But the Chinese are moving in and buying all sorts of stuff in Africa, so things might be changing.

I guess this is as good a place as any to chat about human behavior. It does appear to be a response to how we think. It makes sense that our personality has evolved, and that we are now influenced by our limited circle of friends and our culture. If some monkey learns something new, he can teach it to his friends. We monkeys are easily influenced to ape mannerisms and verbal expressions. I have one which hasn't caught on, "**tardy**." *Totally awesome rad dude.* You should leave the **y** out of **tardy** when you spell it. But **tard** just doesn't look right. Maybe that's why it didn't catch on.

The biochemists are hard at work trying to figure out how the brain works. They know that adrenaline and dopamine have a lot to do with our emotional responses. They've also figured out that we store our memories all over the place, so that at our level of scientific development, they've run into a dead end. We're very parochial and very myopic in our own vision of things. Visionaries are somewhat uncommon, and the creative genius is extremely rare. We know that we tend to stagnate after we finish school.

Historically observed, we are a passive and cowardly species preyed upon by a camouflaged subspecies. My eye caught sight of a very small black paperback at Barnes & Noble which had the **secret societies** in its title. It was the only copy, and it only cost me $2. I don't remember the name of the title or the author's name. It listed a few of the societies which are usually associated with the term. But most of the societies are not really very secret and, such as the ***Bohemian Club*** and the ***Bilderberg Group***. The ***Bohemian Club*** has been meeting for over 100 years and is attended by over 100 of the more powerful and talented people from around the world. They meet at the Bohemian Grove outside of San Francisco on 2700 acres. It's fairly private.

The ***Bilderberg Group***, named after a hotel in Holland, has been meeting since 1954. You'll find many of the same people who attend the ***Bohemian Club***. The same people can be found in other groups. Influential financial, political and intellectual figures attend these meetings. The name of **Kissinger** keeps popping up. Presumably they discuss issues and make plans that affect the common man. I don't see any conspiracy here, it is just the way you would expect the world to work. It just makes a lot of horse sense for them to meet together and try to figure out what to do about issues that are really important to them. But these 100 to 150 people are "very influential," and you might want to meet them. Perhaps you can have some influence about how the world turns. Many of the names are listed on the Internet. Not so secret for secret societies.

I hope that you don't think that I'm implying that those 100 to 150 people are part of the camouflaged subspecies. This might apply to some evil sociopaths, people behind the scenes who are manipulating political, financial or industrial machines; or even innovators in the technological bubble. Hopefully we'll stumble upon some of these members of the **camouflaged subspecies** as we go along.

We all know that we are in pursuit of pleasure. We prize instant gratification and we grab it anytime we can. Values change, young kids have frequent sex with different partners without much thought. They're entitled and there are tons of adults out there ready to bail them out. There is the free use of **Kripkean dogmatism** and **post hoc** rationalization.... "**I'm always right**" and "**I can blame somebody else**."

The **me generation** has given new meaning to selfishness. It is limited by the forbearance of the culture and to self-limiting guidelines. Loyalty to a person or to a cause enhances responsible behavior, at least as defined by the person or cause. We've seen that we use a lot of defense mechanisms to avoid seeing things as they are. We'll avoid facing the truth if it diminishes us in some way. Hence the saying, "let the truth go marching by." You don't have to fix a problem if you haven't even seen it. Let somebody else fix the problem. There has been an erosion of responsible behavior. The society, for all its pretension, actually fosters less reliance on the individual. The human creature relies on the government for its ever increasing demand for pleasures.

This social engineering fits in well with some Protestant predestination beliefs. We often delude ourselves into believing that we have been responsible for our good fortune. When you look for your first job, you are competing with a similar group of qualified people. Hopefully jobs are available. If that job market is good, you easily fill the slot. As you get older, the market has changed and you don't fit into the slot anymore. We waste a lot of money on retraining programs. Are the people just are too fat to fit into those narrow slots? If we're so wise, why has the God of "good fortune" abandoned us?

We've glossed over some of the passive and cowardly behavior of our species. We copy and plagiarize a lot. Are we doing that? Do we take charge of situations? Things might not work out even when you do your best. Robert McNamara was the brightest and the best, they thought. He was a top gun at Ford which led to his appointment as Secretary of Defense. He wrote several books explaining why his Vietnam War decisions led to the disastrous outcome. Compare that with Eisenhower who led the Allies to victory in World War II and was a successful American president. He graduated close to the bottom of his class at West Point.

We've been plodding along for awhile now. I can't think of any songs about plodders. We need to pick up the pace. I can think of the words, "when the Saints come marching in." That's got some vim to it. We need to talk about **creativity.** Our society selects a very small group of thinkers, innovators and creators for its survival or annihilation. As our technology moves more into the field of **artificial intelligence** and we become a more robotized culture, the need for those guys may vanish. We are certainly looking at cutting edge technology. You have to be very careful to walk on an edge like that and not slip.

When you start using a word like creativity you really get into the problem with the slippery slope. Words like innovate, create, invent, ingenuity and genius all seem to be used to define one another. At the top of that mountain of words is creator. God is freely interchanged at the top of that mountain. He certainly brought something new into existence. To create also means to produce something through the use of imagination or skills. That's not quite Godlike. That is more like the inventor. Ingenuity is defined as inventive talent. Genius is right next to God because that is defined as a person of extraordinary intellectual and creative powers. So much for being on the mark. All these terms are freely interchangeable when I speak of creativity in this book.

The 20th century came to think of diversity as creativity. The more minds you put together, the better chance you had at solving a problem or creating the atomic bomb. Remember the Manhattan project. Why does Los Alamos come to mind whenever I hear the term Manhattan project?

56

This area is wide open to discussion. We actually might start off with the concept of **deductive reasoning** which we are familiar with. We'll focus on the **deductive novel** which was a new art form invented by Edgar Allen Poe and developed by Sir Arthur Conan Doyle with the help of his illustrious detective, the unknighted Sherlock Holmes. Putting together a series of minor observations, Mr. Holmes would come to an ingenious conclusion (deductive reasoning). The emphasis was on the plot, the observations, the memory for details and the solution. The British continued using this formula in the Inspector Morse series, with an infusion of art, music and academic culture. There are just so many plots that one can think of, yet the TV comes up with some new ones every day and packs it with its main feature, **Violence!**

The United States was founded by a group of renegade visionaries. Their names are familiar to us. They put a good package together even though they expressed many a disagreement. History reveals a randomness to creative people joining forces for the **grand endeavor.** You never know when. In the 18th and early 19th centuries, the Brits had a group of their own. Adam Smith, Jeremy Bentham, Thomas Malthus, David Ricardo, James and John Stuart Mill were their names. They did a lot to push for free trade and liberty. When comes such another group of thinkers? They changed things.

The people of the United States think of themselves as being free, but this is not so. People who are no longer in a survival mode lose the distinction between what is important and what is truly unimportant. The people of the United States have moved into the quicksand of rules and regulations and the primacy of the *generic individual.* Everybody and everything has to be equal. Everything has to be controlled. You have to be educated and certified before you can do anything. There are many good things to be said about that, but it is certainly stifling. At age sixteen, I became an insurance broker. I read a small twenty page pamphlet and answered, in essay form, the questions that were printed on a letter-size piece of paper with crumpled corners. We functioned rather well knowing the basics. Now you can't even sit for the test without taking a whole bunch of financial courses. "That just makes a lot of sense, that's the way it should be," I can hear you saying that.

The people at the top really make it rather difficult for the young people coming up. You hear a lot of bitching. Nothing much changes. You hear that some students are given the choice of independent study in college, but few get involved in that. We've been trained to conform to routine patterns, and you can't be sure if you're going to find some static at the end of your studies. I know one lady who had a bad experience. Her mentor at Bryn Mawr suddenly vanished and the replacement did not like the outline and the topic. She put the kibosh on all that work. The student didn't have much choice, she had to start all over again. New mentor, new philosophy! My engineer friend has witnessed the frustration of several graduate students in science who were not allowed to follow their own creative juices. The programs were pretty rigid and the priority was to get the degree.

You say it can't be all that bad. The 20th century has witnessed the discoveries of a long string of geniuses in the particle field. True, but that was associated with a lot more independent thinking. But I'm not an expert, and I could be wrong. Remember to cringe when you hear the word **expert** (*time for a proskinesis*). He could be dead wrong. We have example after example of two experts, looking over the same data, coming to two quite different conclusions. Sometimes they are both wrong. Go with the one that seems to be founded on common sense. Or rely on **Occam's razor** or at least a version of it which states that "use the simplest means of arriving at the results and exclude everything not perceived by the senses."

The caveman, who noticed a rolling stone, was a keen observer. He became a genius when he managed to attach two of them to an axle and add a cart. Tradesmen learn their skills and perform them repetitively. **Thinking** has something to do with looking at a problem and trying to find some way of solving it or making something work. Many people are very good at learning a trade and repetitively doing the same thing quite skillfully. Creators are the geniuses who decide how to abandon an established routine and invent a new way of doing something which will hopefully benefit mankind in some small or large way. We confront inconvenient or difficult problems every day. Who is the genius who is going to figure out how to put a toilet in room so that it is convenient to use and convenient to fix. It's probably not going to be a graduate of Harvard, MIT or the Sorbonne.

Many a genius has his or her idea early in life. Einstein made his simple observation about time, space and motion when he was quite young but a unified theory evaded him. Pretty frustrating. He was excluded from the Manhattan project because they didn't trust him.

Ah!, The genius of understanding a simple observation. Sheer genius can lead to near annihilation of earthly creatures! Some people think that Sigmund Freud was a genius. He really just plodded along trying to make sense out of nonsense. Independent researchers think that he created more nonsense out of the nonsense. But he did invent some new terms which make a cocktail party a lot more interesting. I've mentioned that he also set the pseudoscience of psychiatry back about one hundred years.

Edison is credited with being the **archtype** of the inventor. He's the fellow who invented the lightbulb which flashes over your head when you have a really good idea. Humbly, he said that it was all trial and error. He tested hundreds of filaments before he came up with the right one. He also had an enormous lab and many people who worked with him.

What happens if two creators collide? Too poetic geniuses were not able to agree about the practical side of relationship and sexual needs. A tormented relationship with Ted Hughes, the poet Laureate of England, ended with Sylvia Plath's suicide.

We put a lot of emphasis on creativity but it may be entirely genetic. Science keeps finding new things. It has discovered something called the neuregulin 1 gene which is said to be associated with creativity and people with high intelligence. It's also said to be related to psychosis. Esthesia is a word meaning the capacity for sensation or feeling. Scientists have come up with a term called **synesthesia** which means that if one sensory or cognitive pathway is stimulated, then another pathway is automatically triggered. Associating a location with a number or a month of a year is an example of that. It tends to run in families and they've identified 60 types of synesthesias. Another definition is "when information between two senses are blended." **Synesthesia** is almost 10 times more frequent in artists and poets. That's why they're so good at imagery and symbolism. They have the immediate perception of several sensory pathways which allows the expression of shape or color or word that cries out, "behold that which you have not seen or heard!"

I've yet to be involved in any situation in which someone can't put a new spin on it. A friend said that **synesthesia** should be spelled in another way. He said that he couldn't think of a truly creative person who wasn't sexually liberated and using drugs. He said, "I would spell it **sin-esthesia**." I chuckled because my friend often says, "I can't believe that you just said that!" But I don't think that he is was saying that in any positive way. Oh well!

But if you want to get into the area of creativity and artwork you have to go back about 40,000 years and visit the caves of Spain and France. The El Castillo cave in Cantabria, Spain shows early hand prints that date back to 40,000 years ago. They've also found high-quality printing tools that go back to that same era. The Lascaux caves in France are about 20,000 years old and have over 2000 paintings of animals and people. The artists used mineral pigments. Some of these figures are incised. Many have three-dimensional forms with movement. We're familiar with the Egyptian art with those strange looking feet with the toes pointing at opposite ends of the paintings. The ornamental paintings of the medieval period didn't have as much action or three dimensionality. They also found some caves at Chauvet in France. They date back 35,000 years and it's five times larger than the caves at Lascaux. They have also found animal carvings and hunting tools that are truly creative together with symbolic pieces of artwork. Some experts in the field think that the artwork is as creative as the work of Picasso. So perhaps we can understand creative genius in a totally different way. We've thought of our ancestors as being very primitive. But their great minds and creations may well have surpassed our people's capacities. Perhaps there has been a dilution of the good stuff.

I need to digress a bit at this time. We've covered a little bit about creativity and inventing stuff, but the United States is rapidly losing its dominance in the scientific world. We need to get our young people focused on science. The best way is to hook the student up to a really good enthusiastic mentor. It's like anything else. Learning to play good tennis is hard and very boring. I forget the exact number of strokes that you have to learn, maybe 10. You have to hit the same stroke 6 to 8000 times before you become competent at that stroke. So you have to hit the ball 60 to 80,000 times before it gets to be fun. It's the same thing in science and with research. You have to have somebody looking over your shoulder and guiding you until you develop your own enthusiasm and enjoy being confident in your field. It may be dull work at first, especially in the research field, but a good teacher in that research lab will get you out of that rut. Setting obtainable short-term goals gets things rolling. You've heard of the *ladder* at the end of the tunnel, haven't you? Or was that a *light*?

I guess that brings us to an evaluation of how wise the government is. You'll say, "that's easy, it's dumb." That's pretty well what you hear from most people. Does it have validity? We're told that the first role of government, and the most important one, is to ensure the survival of the individual and the nation. We've seen empires come and go. There are no guarantees or easy solutions. 16 million people died in World War I and another 50 to 75,000,000 died in World War II. The A-bomb can get it done a lot faster. You've got a 90% chance of being killed if you're within a half-mile of where the bomb explodes, and only 30% chance within a mile. So if somebody tell you to, "get out of town," you'd better get cracking. The slower way of dying is to live in Somalia and die a very slow and painful death by famine. They lost a quarter of a million people there in the last couple of years. I wonder why I'm so negative, when I'm supposed to be talking about survival? I must be a pessimist.

It's apparent that you need to gain a lot of information, act on a lot of things, do a lot of thinking and analyzing on your way to achieving a reasonable level of wisdom on your way to making important decisions for yourself and your nation. The problem is that when you die you carry that wisdom with you. You've heard the quote, "if you don't know anything about history, you're doomed to repeat the mistakes of the past." It's more complicated than that. You have to feel the emotion associated with that experience for it to make any sense. That quote is sheer foolishness since you're doomed to make the same mistakes unless you really respect your mentor. That is why a dedicated teacher, friend or mentor is essential to the betterment of any human being and his tribe.

When we think of the American Revolution, names like Benjamin Franklin come to mind. Many great men, but a loser's name comes to mind. Thomas Paine was such a loser. His apprenticeships did not work out and he lost a lot of jobs. He was dismissed from his post as secretary of the "Committee on Foreign Affairs" in 1779. He was not courtmartialed. Robespierre imprisoned him in France in 1793 and there was a warrant for his arrest in England. He's remembered for *The Rights of Man* and *Common Sense*. He was a strong advocate for cutting the English umbilical cord, and proposed concepts now associated with *Social Security* and the *United Nations*. He and Jeremy Bentham shared some utilitarian values as they believed in maximizing good things for the most people. I should be such a loser.

Contrast that with Machiavellian ideas and with the Lord Acton's insights, "power tends to corrupt, and absolute power corrupts absolutely." Where am I headed? Survival, national independence, personal freedom and happiness need to be wary of the chopping block both from without and within. I'll repeat Abraham Lincoln's warning, "America will never be destroyed from the outside. If we falter and lose our freedoms, it will be because we destroyed ourselves."

Democracy is a niche form of government on a chessboard with the usual Kings, Queens, Knights, Bishops, Rooks and Pawns. There are many examples of Kings and Queens which are quite autocratic. Let's not delude ourselves, the word democracy does not imply a peace loving people. They'll attack you as well. I would assume that Iraq and Afghanistan would feel that way towards the United States. I wonder if the folks at the *Oxford English Dictionary* are considering a revision of the definition of national sovereignty? Democracy involves a delicate balancing act between power and protection. Let's not kid ourselves, the little man has need for self-esteem and power. It's a delicate balance, don't let him have too much or else you'll be sorry. That falls into that slippery slope argument, if you give a little you'll end up losing it all. Powerful people tend to suppress the people who are on their way up.

The papacy was the temporal controlling agent which had to be forced to give up those powers. Remember that the Crusades had the papal seal of approval. The Pope is very reluctant to give up any power and makes decrees that have nothing to do with religion. The church is losing its power in Europe and in the United States and is having to move to Africa and South America.

Have you ever read *The Brothers Karamazov*? Ivan tells his brother Alyosha the fable of Christ's second coming in Seville. Jesus is picked up and put in jail and interrogated by the Grand Inquisitor. The Grand Inquisitor apparently can't or won't put up with Jesus kissing him. He lets him go in the dead of night with the threat that "he better not come back." Literary and religious experts have interpreted that fable in several ways. Just an aside, what does it mean to you?

With the inception of any new religion, the followers are exposed to many versions and interpretations of its birth. I heard a bit of news which may relate to Dostoevsky's fable. Some strangers don't get off so easily. I'm told that a stranger came into a Russian town and was invited to spend some time in jail. He possessed a "suspicious character quality" which was validated by the fact that he spent time with criminals while he was in jail. He was sent to prison for a bit longer. I ask you, "is there a logical fallacy here?" I don't see one.

If the two stories are related, it may shed some light upon the differences between czarist and 21st century Russia. If this is the 3rd coming, or the 2nd Russian coming, you certainly have to revise your thinking about what Russian thinking was back in the 19th century. Well I won't belabor this vein, since I have been known to make many a vain attempt to find gold in many a vein.

Fyodor Dostoevsky joined a group which discussed literary and political matters. It was called the Mikhail Petrashevsky circle which was sentenced to a firing squad in 1849. The Czar commuted the sentence to hard labor in Siberia. Released in 1854, he was forced to be a soldier for an additional five years in Siberia. His philosophy matured into that of finding redemption through suffering and faith. He suffered through the death of close family members and financial ruin through his gambling. There appears to be elements of self-fulfilling prophecies here. It will you will you what I think, is an and in and in and will and in a good night Alexander will will is is is is is is will lucky to have survived with his incursion into that religious fable. Many Islamic radicals put out contracts when they deem that the prophet Mohammed's name has been sullied or caricatured in some way. They call it a "fatwa." The Iranian Ayatollah Khomeini called for one on Salman Rushdie for his alleged blasphemy. That was in the true spirit of the 7th century. This may not be related, but Voltaire urges the common man to accept responsibility for his actions and not to rely on the concept of God or nature bailing him out.

This not a chapter about the consequences of bad government. We can look at that in another chapter, if that seems to be the case. Most of what I have to say pertains to the American government. We all know that confidence in any government is always in question, and conspiracy theories make people nervous.

"Follow the money," is a very insightful statement. It has become a very powerful tool in controlling the people who get elected to the government. It takes an awful lot of money to get elected, and in one generation we have seen the evolution from an elected individual to a *professional politician*. The professional politician has to do what his party tells him to do, otherwise the purse for the reelection campaign is found to have a large hole in it. And the lobbyists,

representing the military-industrial complex and the insurance and financial institutions, have their offices the next street over in Washington. You can be out in the open when you possess absolute power.

Of course a good candidate is capable of persuasive speech, even when it is quite clear that there is little substance to his statements or arguments. You can refer back to the chapter on logic. It appears that logical fallacies abound in the armamentarium of the politician. They focus only on one aspect of an issue, they appeal to the majority, they focus on something having to do with the opponent rather than on the issue, etc. etc. There is a lot of marketing research and a lot of very expensive advertising in the media. And we accuse other countries of propaganda!

We are experiencing the erosion of protectionism on the part of the United States, with the subsequent loss of jobs and manufacturing industries. 50% of college graduates can't find a job. We'd have to buy our steel from the invading armies to be able to protect ourselves. Lucre has moved us into globalization at light speed. Changes occur so quickly that there is no time for adjustment or correction. **Quick** is on the go.

We've been conquered without knowing it. The average per capita federal debt is $45,000. You thought the cost of the medical expenses for bringing the child into the world was way too expensive! *"Honi pense qui mal y pense,"* you just brought your kid into the world with a $45,000 debt. It's French for, *"shamed be he who thinks evil of it."* I was discussing this with my friend whose wife wants to have children. He said, "I'm going to have to tell my wife that our family can save 90,000 bucks by not having those two kids."

An individual has to live on the money that's available to him. It's called a budget. Who has decided that you don't have to live within a budget when you are a nation? Wyoming lives within a budget. If the revenue doesn't come in, they curtail expenses. I think that Islam has the right idea when they have a requirement that you give 2 1/2% of your income to charity. It is called Zakah. Foreign aid and international catastrophic aid should fall into that category of charity. I think it would be fair to allocate up to 5% of our GNP to that cause. It doesn't make much sense to give a lot of money to charity if you're way over your head in debt.

With ten millions of people moving to refugee camps rather than being slaughtered, the call goes out for contributions. Nations pledge a lot but don't cough up. I've often wondered what happens to all those people incarcerated in those camps. Most of them don't have many skills and are probably hard to relocate. They say that three million Syrians will be refugees very shortly. Many had jobs and skills and have a better chance of being allowed to immigrate into an industrial nation. But there is nothing for them to return to in Syria. A good example of that is the fellow who owned an orchard which was destroyed in the bombing. Orchards probably take somewhere between five and thirteen years to regrow.

I think that a good chunk of that debt is due to our imports. Everyone's so happy buying those luxury items from Europe and those really cheap items from China. I remember that I used to drive by a large American car manufacturing plant and I'd remark, "what are all those Japanese cars doing in the parking lot?" People would just laugh when I raised that issue in casual conversation. They were privately thinking, "he must be a kook." They were right then, and they still are.

The capitalist system is built upon the concept that individuals and private companies create jobs. *Laissez-faire* means that the government is supposed to be in the background. Both the citizen and the government are to be policed by a free press. Free Press!, that's a joke, the *New York Times* costs $400 and the *Wall Street Journal* costs $200. But the bureaucracy of the government has grown so large that it functions like the Mafia, taking large chunks of personal income. The government calls this sequestration taxes, the Mafia has a different name for it.

We are happy to have our government providing services and seeing to it that we have clean water and good health measures. Theodore Roosevelt understood some of those responsibilities quite well. He was responsible for the *Pure Food and Drug Act* and he was responsible for the creation of 5 national parks, 18 national monuments and 51 wildlife refuges. In addition he added 150 national forests increasing the total acreage to 172 million. He went after J.P. Morgan's Northern Securities Company and the Supreme Court ordered it dismantled.

It's a obvious that the government can enhance its citizens' quality-of-life. It can also make it much more difficult to simply function. People can't imagine that the government can think up more regulations, but they are wrong. The thinkers always come up with something new. But they are not anticipatory thinkers. They wait until something bad happens, and then they punish the innocents for the sins of the few. The government found some pension fund frauds and implemented regulations that were so costly that fifty percent of the pension funds had to be terminated. It goes on and on, but I'm going to give you a break and stop.

IV

CONCENTRATION OF WEALTH

Let's look at Adam Smith' s concept of the *wisdom of the marketplace,* **W=K (B+F+E) x GJ (H+R+CS). W= KNOWLEDGE x GOOD JUDGMENT.** Capitalism has been built since the 18th century upon a *laissez-faire* model which is supposed to create, in an equitable manner, the W*ealth of the Nation.* It has had its dips, commonly referred to as recessions and depressions. The public sector was there mainly to provide public services, not monetary services and job creation. This seems to have changed rather dramatically with the great crash of 1929. Part of our definition of knowledge includes having enough information to be able to judge things appropriately. I'm going to have to include a lot of facts to be able to have a clearer view of what's happening to us.

The twenties was a time of great prosperity in the radio, auto and airplane industries. There was widespread speculation and everybody seemed to be buying stocks on margin. The stock market rose by 400% from 1926 to 1929. The United States was exporting a lot and demanding payment in gold bullion. The tree no longer produced the golden fruit and our exports went down. Some financial historians disagree with that. But they agree that everyone became a "speculator." Undercapitalized banks opened every day, and they even loaned money on the hyperinflated stocks as collateral. They were also using the savings of their depositors to invest in the stock market. The exploding bubble precipitated bank failures, unemployment and great poverty. **Hoover**'s name is remembered for "Black Tuesday" and Hoover Dam.

We need a little history here. Our nation did not have a central bank until 1913 when Woodrow Wilson gave birth to the *Federal Reserve* which decided on a headquarters in Washington D.C. with twelve branches around the country. It truly is an independent, decentralized central bank. It really pays lip service to Congress. If there was a check and balance system in place, Congress could pay for a granite headstone in a Washington cemetery with the inscription "here lyeth an independent mistaken idol." It was envisaged as a tool to control the interest rate, to regulate the money supply and to control inflation. "So let it be said, so let it be done!"

The Fed issued stock to thousands of banks, paid them 6% interest and required them to invest 3% of their capital in the Federal Reserve. You'll see that it gets more interesting as we go along. So we get into the 1920s and the stock market is growing at a 15% clip per year and the Feds are printing money and lending it out to the commercial banks for about 4%. You'd have to be a fool not to borrow something at 4% and make a 300-400% profit on that transaction. Even better, you didn't have to come up with all the money that you needed to purchase a security. You could buy it on margin, and that could be a small percentage of the cost of the security. You borrow the rest from your broker or bank.

So the scenario is set. People are prosperous, they are buying more, more money is needed to buy these goods, the Fed prints more money. It is requiring more and more soapsuds for this giant bubble. Belatedly the Fed raises the discount rate to 6%. The people who make their living in the stock market, and understand it, see the writing on the wall. They start selling. The market gets a little shaky and the average person gets a little panicky and starts selling. Crash! And what happened to all those banks? In 1929 there were 25,000 banks. In 1933 there were 14,000 banks.

So let's look at the *wisdom of the marketplace.* **W=K (B+F+E) x GJ (H+R+CS). W= KNOWLEDGE x GOOD JUDGMENT.** Golly, Gee! The bankers are intelligent people and probably have been fairly well schooled. They've studied the banking crises of the 19th century. They know that central banking will be able to take care of the business cycle. They are making money. They are keeping the interest rate low, increasing the money supply, loaning money on margin as the inflation rate is rising. In retrospect monetary people say, if you have inflation, raise the interest rate; if you're in a recession you keep the interest rate low. The Fed did the opposite. They certainly fell down in the rational and common sense categories. This certainly was not a comprehensive and rational view of the issues at the time. They let it get out of hand and then they raised the discount rate. It's the way of the world. You naturally get on the bandwagon. It's never **The Age of Moderation.**

FDR immediately went off the gold standard, and after consultation with **Sir John Maynard Keynes,** embraced **Keynesian** economics. There is a simplistic way of looking at this. If the government spends money, it puts money in someone's pocket. That money, spent either by that someone or by a pickpocket, puts money in someone else's pocket, who in turn spends that, etc. So the theory was put into practice. The **New Deal** was just getting started. The public sector became the dominant force in the American economy. A lot of the money was spent on infrastructure, employment and the maintenance of our cultural heritage. Many government agencies were established. Many endure. You've heard of the *FHA, FDIC, WPA, TVA* and *Social Security*. Many feel that our government expenditure during World War II really gave us the boost that made us the major world economic power.

Friedrich Engels, Karl Marx and Joseph Stalin had different ideas about economics and government. You don't always get it right. The *laissez-faire* system broke down in America. The financial world is still pushing the doctrine. President **Obama** is a Keynesian but his bailout wasn't spent on any infrastructure. He bailed out the financial institutions.

But back to the thirties. A very important piece of legislation was passed in 1933. It is known as the *Glass-Steagall Act* which prohibited commercial banks from participating with investment banks and brokerage houses. That would have protected us from the crisis that occurred in 2008. You have to watch the financial world. A lot of very smart people are very devious in that industry. Citicorp and Travelers merged into **Citigroup** in 1998. It was illegal but the *Federal Reserve* said it was okay. The following year the *Graham-Leach, Bliley Act of 1999* was passed which allowed commercial banks, investment banks, securities firms and insurance companies to consolidate. It took less to than a decade to lead to all sorts of scandals. **Lehman Brothers** seems to have led the charge in packaging poor quality mortgages into bundles for quick sale and quick profits. This has led to millions of foreclosures.

Standard & Poor's, Moody's and Fitch have the lock on the investment rating business. They were duplicitous in giving the best ratings for these junk mortgages. They charged a premium. The government is now suing S&P. There is no mention of the other two right now, but if they end up paying one of the usual fines, the money will probably end up in the government's pocket, and not to the fellow who lost his or her home. So it goes. There is so much greed and fraud going on that it would take several books to give an overview. **HSBC** is paying close to $2 billion for its money laundering, even with Iran. You've heard of **Libor,** the London interbank offering rate. Several banks are getting sued because they fixed that rate. This global interest rate affects $500 trillion worth of investments. I think we're getting close to the speed of light and the global transfer of funds is going faster than the speed of light. There are many more infractions and outright fraud. Names like **Barclays, Deutsche, Flagstar, ING, UBS** show up on a list of the big guys with current problems.

Anyone with any common sense clearly understands that the banking industry is no friend of the common man. We know that power corrupts absolutely. The banks are too large and wield too much power. Then we are told that they are too large to collapse and that the individual, the victim of banking, has to shore them up. What utter nonsense! The banks do whatever they want to do. I was talking to a friend who discussed why Americans were so indebted. The plastic credit card came in as a convenience factor. Your expense records were clearly delineated. American Express expected you to pay all of the bill at the end of the mouth. Then suddenly the concept was expanded to allow for large individual credit loans which were called "credit card limits." The amount of debt carried by the average credit cardholder is astronomical. I certainly won't go into the numbers with you.

The government is going through some window dressing at this point asking for greater reserves and regulations and actually imposing large numerical fines on these banks. But that large numerical figure is but a tiny fraction of the gross profit. Always leave the plebeians a few crumbs ... that is my motto.

It's obvious that *some statesman* needs to appear and ring the chapel bell alerting the citizens to the terrible power that these banks control. Something certainly should be done about this. This is probably time for me to discuss an alternate banking philosophy that is present in the world today. It's called *Islamic Interest-free Banking* which is based on an entirely different philosophy. Western banking is based upon a capital base market philosophy. Islamic banking is much more akin to the America Utopia socialist model which we shall briefly discuss in the chapter on socialism.

The Islamic banking system is based on the concept of profit and loss sharing. Modern-day application of this concept has only been around for about the last fifty years, but there are over 300 Islamic banks worldwide. Islamic banking must adhere to Sharia law ensuring fair play. Western banking is based upon protecting the bank and is called risk-transfer. Islamic banking is based upon risk-sharing. There are several ways in which a home mortgage transaction can be made, including leasing, rental and partnership arrangements. With a partnership arrangement if the property loses 70% of its value the bank absorbs that proportion of loss. The person who is purchasing the property is not the one left holding the bag, as is the way with Western banking. The banking system was truly responsible for the economic collapse suffered around the world. That would never have happened under Islamic banking rules and people would not have lost their homes.

The Islamic banks are also expected to have a very high reserve. Much of the commercial banking involves both banker and borrower entering into a contract arrangement in which both profit or lose according to a specified percentage. It certainly is innovative and a lot fairer than what we have been used to. Since interest is considered usury, it certainly puts a cramp on the credit card business and forces the individual to think with more frugal terms.

There's a lot of scary stuff going on worldwide. **Globalization** and the Internet are tearing down all of our borders and our national fabric. Now **ICE** (Intercontinental Exchange) is buying out the **NYSE** which controls **Liffe**, Europe's second largest derivatives market. I didn't have the time to look this up, but apparently this puts **Deutsche Boerse** in control of the world's third-largest derivatives market. America is giving the store away. What if it's true, that were moving in the direction of a one world order? I'm not a conspiracy theorist, but it could be part of the **natural order.**

A lot of people feel that the United States is way in over its head in terms of its commitments around the world. We need to go back to *Bretton Woods* in New Hampshire in the year 1944. I believe that over 40 countries were represented at that conference. It established the rules by which commercial and financial transactions would be made between nations. The names may have changed somewhat but the *IMF (International Monetary Fund)* and the *World Bank* came into existence. The monetary policy of maintaining an exchange rate was set by tying national currencies to the US dollar. By 1971 the US dollar was the reserve currency. The stage was set for *GATT (General Agreement on Tariffs and Trade)* and the *IBRD (International Bank for Reconstruction and Development)*. The *IBRD* borrows money on the world market and apparently has a good history.

This is probably as good a time as any to reflect on the wisdom of Adam Smith. It has gotten us into murky waters and our ship may have already run aground. The philosophy of **free trade** has been around for a few centuries now. It's a great idea. It's a great idea amongst equals, and certainly benefits individual and corporate interests. A few centuries appears to be ample time to reevaluate any philosophy. The United States has seen the benefits of buying cheap products from countries, such as China and Mexico, which pay their workers as little as 10% of what an American worker earns. This has led to the closure of American manufactures and the loss of middle-class American jobs. The middle class is vital to the American economy.

Free trade worked very well when we were the manufacturing country of the world and exported our products. The cheap labor abroad is associated with poverty and terrible working conditions. The concept of humanity is but a vapor. Those national governments close their eyes to dangerous working conditions, poor education, malnutrition and an absence of medical care.

The concept of **free trade** implies that each nation does what it does best, and thus all nations benefit. The overview after two centuries is that the playing field should be fairly level. It requires some equality between nations. If your employees are slaves, you have a great competitive advantage. There are two choices if you wish to compete. You can turn Americans into slaves or you can impose tariffs limiting the imports from the slavers in other nations.

Don't get me wrong, **free trade** is a great idea if it is done slowly and the individuals of all countries come to gradually reach some level of equality. The level playing field then exists. Each nation can do what it does best.

It is another example of where *quick* can destroy *slow*. It is also an example of where you always have to question *the brightest and the best*. The *free-trade advocates* are simply following the precepts of their learned mentors. Very well trained economists don't seem to be able to revise the philosophies that they have been taught... they simply *press on*. Very few people revise an established *Way* unless they recognize that they are in a state of ignorance.

That is why *instant globalization* is so dangerous. It gives you no time to readjust. Individuals and corporations clearly benefit but the *individuals within the nation* are the ones who are at risk. ***Tariffs*** with the gradual lowering of protectionism is really a wise way to go. It gives one the time to readjust and to protect the individuals...which a nation's government is supposed to serve.

Let's return to the financial world that was created for us after the second world war. The ***World Bank*** and the ***IMF*** have a bad record. 38 of the world's poorest countries were given loans, followed by additional loans to cover the repayment and interest on the bad loans. They finally decided in 2005 to just write off $50 billion worth of loans. We all know that a lot of that money went into Swiss bank accounts. The industrial nations are contributing about $10 billion per year to the ***IMF*** and ***World Bank***.

Then there is the ***African Development Bank,*** which has 78 members. 60% are African nations and the other 40% are non-continental ***donors***. The United States certainly is a heavy contributor. This bank has an excellent credit rating because the donors keep increasing their contributions. I guess this high rating must come from S&P and Moody's.

I wonder what the definition of "financial responsibility" is in the corrupt third world? China is one of the donor nations, but I wonder if their land and asset purchases in Africa are counted as donations? But let's look at how the financial world has helped the average man over the last generation. The individual investor is essentially a thing of the past. Mutual funds have existed since the late 19th century. Some smart people came along in the 1960s and started marketing them so that by 1970 there were close to 400 funds with $48 billion in assets. By 2011 the number of mutual funds had grown to 14,000 with an asset worth of $13 trillion with 600 to 1500 billion stocks traded daily.

There was a period from 1982 to 1987 when the market soared. The crash is known as "Black Monday." The Dow lost over 20% in a single day. As an aside we have experienced approximately 13 Black Mondays since the 13th century. It was a period of hostile takeovers, leveraged buyouts and merger mania. **Michael Milliken**'s junk-bond expertise was all over the *Wall Street Journal* during that period of time. I think the *Wall Street Journal* is prescient and regularly lists the names of many criminals before they are indicted. I think his conviction was for securities fraud and he had to spend a few years in jail. That is in the past and he is a very wealthy man who is very philanthropic.

73

Then there was the **Dot-com bubble** which saw the *NASDAQ* fall from 5000 to 1000. It lost 4000 points from 2000 to 2002. **Quick** was the name of the game. I had a friend who became an overnight multimillionaire, a very intelligent fellow who did not have the wisdom to get out at a reasonable time. The stockbrokers were on the verge of losing their best customers. They had been taught in finance school to diversify the portfolio and to expect an 8% yearly return. Don't put too much into the *get rich* stocks. "What's wrong with you, my partner doubled his money this last year!" So the stockbroker had to abandon everything he learned in school, steer into risky waters and go along with what the customer wanted.

There was also the *Savings and Loan Association (S&L)* debacle in the 1980s and 1990s. Over 700 of those associations were permanently closed. They specialized in using your savings to grant mortgage loans. It was an inflationary period and they were doing okay. They borrowed short-term money from the feds at a low interest rate and made money on the long-term mortgage rate. They probably should have anticipated that the Fed chairman, Paul Volcker, would raise the interest rate. He raised it a lot. Let's say they were committed to a 3% mortgage. They had borrowed at 2% and were making a 50% profit every year. Suddenly the discount rate went up. Then they had to borrow their short-term money at 4%. So they were on the wrong side by 1% (I'm not good at calculating percentages, but that looks like they were actually losing 25% every year). No one wants to admit that their business is failing. So they used creative accounting schemes. The actuaries finally had to divulge that. Very few people ended up having any sort of criminal accountability pursued. Such is the way of the financial world.

I'm going to have to use some brevity, which I don't do very well. The money industry is so large and so complicated that it is hard to be succinct. Like any other industry, it tends to hide behind some fancy words. They use the term **derivative** a lot now. When I was a boy they use the term **options**. An acceptable definition of the word derivative is "a financial instrument which derives its value from assets, indices, interest rates, etc."

These options have, like Janus, two faces. The first involves risk management, sort of an insurance policy. It's called a **hedge.** Hedge funds have been having problems lately. You've heard of *OTC,* the "over-the-counter" contracts between private parties. The *ETD* refers to the "exchange traded derivatives." $600 trillion worth of these options were traded on the **ETD** in a single quarter. Multiply that by four and you're into the quadrillion range. Maybe I'm mispronouncing quadrillion and you think that I'm talking about the **cotillion** ballroom dance for debutantes. But let's remember that **Libor** oversees $500 trillion. I really don't feel comfortable with all these big numbers.

Let's stop a moment and **think**. We should be analyzing some of this. There is some **heuristic** thinking here. Two opposing camps have stopped thinking. The *laissez-faire* vs the *socialist/communist* ideologies. There is no middle ground, no rethinking, no reanalysis. The first group points out that if you redistribute the wealth of the chap living in the castle at the top of the hill, that it will only give a few shekels to everyone at the bottom. They will have lost theirs stable source of survival. The central idea is that the man on the hill can be counted on to invest in such a way that the poor are better off. The reality is that the gap between the poor and the rich is ever widening.

I'm looking at some charts about wealth distribution. Worldwide 10% of the population controls 49% of the wealth, 90% control 51% of the wealth. One can say that the poor people, hence, are wealthier than the rich people. Is there some problem with the logic being used here? The figures for the US are a little old, but they give the general idea. 5% of the population controls 62% of the wealth, and the top 10% control 75% of the wealth of the nation. There has been more concentration, but that does give you a pretty good idea.

There is a global argument that capitalism provides the wealth that is needed to generate jobs and prosperity for the common man. Things are supposed to be improving for the little guy. Then you see those millions of starving Africans, and the new statistics that 250,000 people in Somalia have died of famine. Do you think that a capitalist economy for that continent would change anything? Improving the health and wealth of the underclass is a lot more complicated than some economic system.

The *socialist/communist* block does not have a stellar record. See what happened to China under **Mao** and to Cuba under **Castro**. They are semi-pure examples of communism. The **socialist** nations of Europe have a somewhat better record. Some of the Scandinavian countries rank at the top of the most desired places to live. The taxes are rather high, but there are a lot of free services. The poverty rate is said to be about 5% compared to 17% in the US. The unemployed are paid about 60% of their usual income. Over 80% of the cost of medical care is covered and there is a lot of social assistance. Education at the university level is heavily subsidized and may even be free. Every retiree is given a pension.

Overall taxation is 50% of the GDP. The corporate income taxes 30%. A personal income under $40,000 is taxed at a 30% rate, above that the rate is 60%. There are really no deductions. The capital gains rate is 30%, but there are some loopholes. If the company is unlisted, it doesn't have to pay the capital gains tax. The company has to contribute 33% toward Social Security, the individual paying 7%. There are federal, state, municipal, county and even church taxes. I don't understand that last tax. Are they promoting godlessness?

The US has faster growth, a higher per capita GDP and more disposable income. Less taxes, more disposable income. So should you be moving to a Scandinavian country? Is this an example of **slow**? There are a lot of social benefits, but the trade-off is that wage earners have less to spend on material items and fun stuff. The lower 10% of both economies still have it rather rough.

The figures about **wealth** are astounding. The top 10% in the US has 75% of the wealth, compared to 83% in Scandinavia. *A socialist model does not close the gap between the poor and the rich.* It would appear that raising taxes does nothing to the fellow living in the castle on the hill. There is something wrong with the basic thinking of both economic models. Is this an example of a natural force which is inexplicable? It's just the way it is? *In the beginning were the poor, and so shall it be.* So the capitalist and socialist models coexist. The Communist model has been disastrous. We think of the 18th century and the poverty of those people depicted in the Dickensonian novels. There's certainly appeared to be a lot of poor people during the colonial days.

It's all coming to me now. The **financial/economic/governmental models**, which we have been looking at, have nothing to do with this. It was the **Industrial Revolution** which allowed our societies to evolve into more prosperous positions. Whatever form of government in existence, be it King, Queen, Parliament, Prime Minister, President or simply tyrant, has always had its pecking order. The people in power gather the wealth and the poor try to get some piece of it. There may be some grand names associated with that effort such as the *Magna Carta.* **John Locke** struggled with that issue. At one point he thought that the government should try to equalize the wealth, but I believe that he eventually conceded that wealth was okay. Some of the scholars felt that he got mixed up with philosophical and religious concepts. If your wealth was based upon perishable goods which could be wasted, then it was felt to be a bad thing. But it was okay if you owned gold or durable goods. Values tend to change over time, and the later generations always say that they don't know how people could have thought that way.

So there must be some **natural selection** to this process of the *inevitability of the concentration of wealth*. It's just common sense. You have to be a fool not to understand that there is a **natural order** to all of this. No matter how you try to get the guy in the castle at the top of the hill, you won't succeed. He's out of there, he's building another castle on some other hill. Just think of Belise and the Cayman Islands. If you're not taxing the rich because you think that he won't have the money to invest in new job creation, don't kid yourself! If money is needed for the development of something, the financial world or the government will always find some way of creating that. It's inevitable. Remember that over 80% of stocks are the property of 10% of the population. And the really wealthy people have good advisors. Don't worry about them. They're looking to the future and they make sure that their wealth is well represented in areas of raw materials, food supplies, energy, communications and other essentials.

It's comparable to the inventing process. Individuals and governments keep stealing things with the intention of getting the upper hand. They never really do. In the recent years the Americans had all the research labs and the Japanese and Chinese took those ideas, developed them and marketed the products. But my engineer friend says that it doesn't matter, "our research is always ahead of their own."

You've got me, you've found me **guilty** of abusing **inductive reasoning**. I've taken a few percentages and two nations and come to sweeping generalizations. There are many other facts and variables that I have not taken account of. My conclusions could be completely wrong. We might conclude with a fuller understanding that there are so many variables that the validity of any predictability is controlled by variability. You might've been thinking of going to see the psychiatrist. This will either precipitate the visit or lead to a complete cure.

So the **Industrial Revolution** improved the lot of the common man and probably was responsible for the widening gap between rich and poor. Not to worry, put your money on our technological revolution. Bet on nanotechnology. Maybe, just maybe, it will improve the lot of the poor. The middle class is currently suffering. If *only* the superbright and the already wealthy are included in this revolution, the rest of us won't be too happy. We may have to redefine the class structure. The British are in the process of doing that. So is the **middle class** renamed the **observing class?**

We probably will have to redefine the concept of wisdom when we're discussing the financial black hole. Wisdom seems to be defined mainly in the short term in the financial world. You do whatever you have to do to maximize profits in the short term. To hell with the future even if that affects the kids. I guess you could call this a slight variation of Adam Smith's concept of the self-correcting marketplace. Let's keep that quiet. It's not good for business.

Financial Wisdom = MSTP (*Maximization of Short Term Profits*).

V

COMPLEX SOLUTIONS TO WORLD PROBLEMS

Our daily thinking processes appear to be quite disorganized. But in our last chapter we stumbled upon the "fact" that historically the **distribution of wealth** seemed to follow a *natural order.* A natural order to the *wealth gap?* Are we trying to find disorder in order, or order in disorder? Could we be dealing with pure chaos? Is our thinking merely a reflection of a disorganized world, or even of a disorganized universe? Of a disorganized God? The astrophysicists sense that they are discovering more order in the universe.

Einstein was looking for a unified theory, and the philosophers who preceded him were trying to study the **nature** of things. Some of their languages were different from mine, and I frequently didn't understand their concepts. "Incomprehensible" was the word that I frequently used. Some of **Alfred Lord Whitehead's** writings seem to be truly psychotic. But then they tell me that he was a genius, so that made me, at the very best, an "ungenius." That's a polite term for idiot.

John Locke was looking for the same sort of thing when he had issues with man's **natural rights**, liberty and wealth distribution. He really didn't get into our tendencies to be petty, gossipy, peevish and to blame others for our own failures. So maybe there is a **natural order** to how governments work, how they evolve, how the economy works; we know that the stock market is cyclical. If all this stuff is predestined, then we are just a bunch of fools running around trying to put out *illusionary fires*, when there is really no fire to put out. My engineer friend says that everything is really an illusion. He points to the marble countertop and says, "there's nothing there, just a bunch of molecules making you think that everything is very hard." He also says, "your book is a thinking man's nightmare."

So this book is perhaps about the *illusion of thinking* and we're stumbling into a quagmire of confusion with much inappropriate behavior. We belong to a species which doesn't think ahead and claims to be the best species on earth. The lion has concentrated on a few essentials and goals and seems to do a pretty good job. He seems to understand the limits of his brainpower; we do not. We have overextended ourselves. "A man's got to know his limits."

We're a reactive species. People invent things and then start thinking about the possible uses of the invention. They put the **I wish** to work to make it worthwhile and profitable. The unexpected consequences and the possible peripheral damages don't even come to mind. The criminal mind will put it to use if it's at all possible, a nd we tend to put criminals into a moronic subspecies with little capacity for creativity. Sherlock Holmes found professor Moriarty to be very much his equal.

We certainly are a bunch of complainers. We naturally notice all the so-called bad things that occur both in our personal lives and around the world. The media knows that we enjoy that so that is what news is all about. But we're not noticing the natural world doing its usual stuff probably with a preponderance of good. The usual stuff may have a lot of stuff which is not to my liking. We individuals have our natural preferences. You probably are quite irritated by what I have chosen to discuss.

I can think of an example about complaining and not thinking ahead. We complain about the **Islamic jihadists** and their worldwide terrorism. But we have given them the technology and the Internet to facilitate their goals. Even our banking system facilitates that. We've created the Internet without thinking about the evolution and some of its scary consequences. Privacy is gone, vast sums of money are stolen, and the Chinese are stealing governmental and technological secrets. So we are a thinking species?

Rousseau's noble savages were said to be basically good before they combined into a community. Someone was hoping that the sum of all these savages would be greater than the sum of its parts. But it's pure guesswork when you enter into the **natural order.** You have probably forgotten a lot of these platitudes. It helps to relearn things, and you don't tend to forget those remembered memories. The more times that you remember memories, that is to say, you remember remembered memories, the better they stick. My English teacher used to say, "grammar ain't easy to learn."

In the next few chapters we may find that **there are no solutions.** If there is a **natural order** controlling all things, then the effect of thinking is inconsequential. So let's keep an open mind about the natural order, the way we naturally think and whether critical thinking has any impact. Remember that if it's all an illusion, the short-term benefits of critical thinking may have no impact. It may just make us **feel good,** "vengeance proud" it was said of Coriolanus in Shakespeare's play. After all your empire may win many battles and even wars, but it may eventually vanish. The Romans and the Third Reich both thought that they might last a thousand years, they didn't.

This book is supposed to be about doing some thinking so that we can have some positive impact upon our lives or the lives of others. So as we identify issues, why don't **you**, and sometimes **me**, do some of this thinking as we go along. When we come to the issue of democracy, we could ask, somewhat reluctantly, some questions, "Do you like your democracy? What do you like about it? How could you protect it? How could you improve it?" If you don't like your democracy, then you could ask a series of different questions, " What don't you like about it? What are the problems? What solutions can you think of? Can you find more information? Which is the best solution? Which has the best chance of working?"

We've spoken about how natural it is to be filled with prejudice. Relating to cultures, "genocides" may be the norm. I'll try to bore you just a bit. **Genghis Khan's** birth name was Temujin. He was born in 1155 and he and his Mongols destroyed the Turkish Khwarizm dynasty, slaughtering as many of their people and animals as he could. He had as many as 200,000 soldiers. It was a state of the art army with bow and arrows, shields, daggers, lassos, swords, javelins, body armor, battle axes, maces and lances with hooks to pull the opposing riders off their horses. The Khwarezmids moved on after this onslaught; they burned and slew all in front of them until they reached Jerusalem. But that is another story.

Vlad, "The Impaler," lived in the 15th century. He was a nice guy and a strong family man. He told good jokes, and everyone had a good belly laugh. Not too long ago Yugoslavia fell apart after **President Josip Tito** died in 1980. He had managed to keep Serbs, Croats, Muslims Slavs, Slovenes, Albanians, Macedonians, Montenegrins and Hungarians together in peace. It finally exploded as the Bosnian Serbs killed 8000 Bosnian Muslims. The civilized city of Belgrade lost its orchestra and its civilization.

We've heard of the Turkish/Ottoman slaughter of the Armenians in 1915, the Kurdish genocide and the ongoing slaughter of many ethnic and religious groups in Africa and Asia, using weapons that are a few thousand years old, such as machetes and swords, capable of multiple beheadings. *Tribalism* is certainly highlighted in both the Middle East and in Africa. In the past the Ottomans were truly an enlightened people. They accepted the tribalism of the people they conquered, while they simply expected them to pay taxes. The old definition of tribalism refers to small pockets of people who have the same cultural identity. However the new, enlarged and improved definition states that it is a strong cultural or ethnic identity which separates one group from another, but without any national boundaries.

We know that this has been the way of the world. Even today small tribes attack one another and do horrible things to one another. They may do this in the name of color, race or religion or whatever. Prejudice and bias are part of the **natural order.** "When will it ever end, the answer is written in the wind." There was no reference to natural order in that song.

There is a lot of prejudice and biases addressed towards the Jews. This has been going on for a few millennia. The experts are really not sure what this is all about, because it does not make a lot of sense in many situations. Let's do a quick rundown. We seem to be able to comprehend the concept of conquering nations. King David attacked the Jebusites and conquered Jerusalem three thousand years before Christ. There is frequent mention that David conquered the Philistines. But apparently the Philistines were not involved in that conflict at all. We're all familiar with the David and Goliath myth and Goliath was a Philistine. The Philistines were a coastal group southwest of of Israel and apparently clashed with the Hebrews on and off but were only in prominence around 1000 years before Christ. There appears to be a lot of confusion in this area. One can easily understand that, since there is little in the way of written material available and few scholars are familiar with the languages of the time. If you enjoy frustration, do a little reading about this period of history. Biblical history is "inerrant." I thought I'd toss in that word. I had to look it up. It means infallible. **Yasir Arafat** claimed that the Palestinians were descended from the Jebusites. "We got there before the Jews, so we have a legal claim to the land," said the scholarly **Arafat.**

Jerusalem was part of Israel, which was in the north, and Judea was in the south. The Assyrians conquered Israel in 722 B.C. and the Babylonians conquered Judea in 586 B.C. The Persians came in 530 B.C., followed by Alexander in 331 B.C., or thereabouts. The Maccabeans revolted in 167 B.C. and eventually came under the protection of the Romans. The Byzantines came and many Jews fled. The caliphate showed up around 638 A.D. You know about the

Crusades. The Manulukes took over from 1250 A.D. to 1500 A.D. The Ottomans came along and conquered the area, followed by Napoleon around 1798 A.D. which led to a terrible amount of turbulence. The Jews fled again.

You know the Russian word **pogrom** which means destruction, murder, rape and any other vile thing that you can think of. There were three Russian pogroms from 1881 to 1921. This was also happening in Germany, Austria, Romania, Morocco, Algeria, Persia and the Balkan countries. The German-Polish collaboration from 1939 to 1945 saw hundreds of thousands of Polish Jews, whom living in Warsaw, sent to the extermination camp in Treblinka. The ones living in the ghetto of Kraków soon experienced a sudden decline in their quality of life, as they were sent to the network of Auschwitz concentration and extermination camps.

The Jews just do not seem to have been able to shed this imagined cloak of evil tribalism. Perhaps there is simply a case of *tribalotropism* attracting hatred. You hear the accusation that they control the money and that they isolate themselves. They even have been persecuted for their control of money when they were dirt poor. I've heard people telling me about some of the hearsay stories told by their parents and grandparents, who were themselves told hearsay stories about previous generations. The **hearsay biases** weapon has been used against individuals and cultures for a long time, even when you personally have no reason to raise that weapon.

Meanwhile Iran has been threatening to wipe Israel off the face of the earth. They have been moving towards developing an atomic bomb. They are tooling up for this way underground. The US and Israel know where the action is. It may well be that will have to use a **MOP**. This is no ordinary mop. It can penetrate anything. It's a 30,000 ton bomb called a massive ordinance penetrator. The Jews don't want to leave the homeland again.

They Jews do play significant roles in banking, the arts and certainly in the movie world of the United States. They're trying to keep their history and culture alive, but that's hard to do since there is so much integration in the American culture. Don't think that tribalism has vanished in America. I don't believe that it ever will. But there is a different quality to tribalism in most of America. The French, Italians and Irish were pretty bitter competitive foes for one hundred years, but they moved on.

Let's move away from this and discuss what is going on with our young people. We have identified that they are moving in the **quick** mode. They have moved away from the Neanderthal Age when work, morality, and responsibility were in vogue. They are into fun things and do less than two hours of school work per week. They are facile with electronic gadgets and their social interfaces are primarily with Facebook and Twitter. This happens dozens of times a day. The pros clock in at about one hundred per day. My daughter tells me that this is all about narcissism, making themselves feel important. It's all about self deception. I thought that it was an insightful interpretation.

We've been told that humans have a herd instinct, well, this is the herd. Advertising plays a significant role in the American culture, and they and their peers are *going with the flow*. Of course they are under the influence of their parents, who hopefully can rein in some of this runaway behavior. It ain't easy, as any decent parent can tell you. Of course there are many children who have poor to terrible parents. Some children possess a good internal regulator, and know what they have to do to accomplish something, be that in some athletic or academic subject. The kid who is born in the culture of poverty, ignorance and drugs doesn't have much of a chance.

A lot of people are making decisions for us as we grow up. Our parents, our teachers, our friends, our employers and the mass media. It's probably time to recite the *Ode to the Brainwashed.* Our addiction to the Internet, the TV and the cell phone has made slaves of us all. Then the government comes in with all the laws, rules and regulations that enclose us into a very small cell, which of course has bars, but allows us to see what is going on outside of the windows. We have no reason to look through those bars since we are constantly twittering and using all those fun apps.

Is this really what we would call freedom? It has a **Kafka** like quality. America is thought of as the land of the free, but it has the most controls of any nation on earth. Think of it, our government knows everything about us and we can even be arrested for jaywalking on the street. There is a natural progression of ever increasing control when a society is no longer worried about its survival, and the lambs are not calling their attorneys to find out what's going on in the slaughterhouse up ahead.

We know that teachers say that they can't teach if there is no discipline in the classroom. That discipline starts at home. Successful students usually do a lot of homework. There has been a breakdown in the parenting skills in America. Part of that is cultural. The emphasis on materialism requires that both parents go to work. And the single-parent family has come into being. That parent, usually a woman, has to be a heroine to be able to wake the kid up, feed him, get him to school, go to work, pick up the kid, prepare the supper, spend a little quality time, ask about school, check any homework, get him to bed, prepare lunch, wash the dishes, do the essentials, get the clothes ready for tomorrow, put on the TV and at least watch the news before going to bed. WOW!

The Israelis have accommodated themselves to some of these problems. They have the "kibbutz" which is a relatively small community where the children have day care and a lot of individual attention in classes with small numbers of students. The children have supervised activities and do live with their parents. This is obviously impractical for the major urban centers of America. Supervising the children both at school and at their social activities must be implemented if you want to build good character in the 21st century student. We are a reactive species, so why not react? We've created the problem, seen the problem and now a thinking society needs to take charge. "You solve it," I say, "but I'm going to criticize you every step of the way." There is definitely a a path to solving that social problem I'll address that in a later chapter. "Another chapter, when will this ever end?"

This is a chapter about **no solutions**. Well, you can't solve anything if you don't make any effort. And we don't want to try the **heuristic trial and error** solution. We need a perfect answer. That guarantees **no solution**. I keep hearing people say that the world is all too complicated. There are so many issues. I hear my teachers saying, "take one issue is time." But that is a very difficult thing to do if everything is intertwined.

Let's start with the issue of **crime** and gangs. Of course we are just a bunch of amateurs if we compare ourselves with the Mafia and the Mexican cartels. There's always somebody better than you. The Mafia is much more civilized. We know that civilization arbitrarily defines what a criminal is. The government makes rules and the police enforce the rules. We characterize their behaviors as: #1 acquiring property, #2 violence, #3 cruelty. The Mexicans seem to enjoy practicing #3 with rape and mutilation being a common practice.

The **American blacks** form a disproportionate percentage of the people housed in prisons. A lot of that has to do with very poor parenting, little education, an atmosphere of drugs, lack of exposure to work and the wish to enjoy the fruits of somebody else's labor. It would appear that there needs to be an internal push by the blacks themselves to clean this up. I heard a discussion by people who are experts in this field and by educators. The colleges are just waiting for the blacks to come up, but they are poorly motivated to become educated, so the schools are left with a lot of open spots.

There are always solutions to problems, and they may be distasteful or even illegal. The cream of the blacks has already risen to the top. There are many reasons to explain why a hard-core is a hard-core. The larger group is passive, uneducated and uninformed. The children of that group need to be exposed to successful and/or educated members of their own race, Big Brothers and Big Sisters. This group needs to be protected from the gang members. What I'm talking about is also true for the Latinos. This large group needs to be protected from their own ethnic criminal group.

The gang member problem can be dealt with in a tough way. The society can figure out what it costs in public services to deal with the gangs. It can allocate that money to a special fund. The police can really help here. They know who the toughest guy is on each block and can proceed to negotiate with him to be **the enforcer.** He can feel free to handle the drug and violence problems in any way that he has to. In the old days it might have been possible to round up all these gang members, buy a small African country, and send them off. Another Liberian adventure? The kids could be severely punished for breaking any of **the enforcer's** rules. And social workers would be empowered to go after the parents using the usual stick and carrot routine. Some control over the welfare purse string has the potential of having some positive impact. The children would be forced to go to school, and at the very least, to learn a trade. The auto trade would be a very popular one. And they certainly could be kept busy learning to play sports and watch comedic movies, as well as those fascinating naturalist and cosmic movies. Once the process gets going, it would be self replicating. It is of course very important for **the enforcer** to be extremely well-paid.

The drug problem has an obvious solution which is still in the discussion stage. If the drug business was made legal, much of the evil would disappear. The government would impose a hefty sales tax leading to money in the coffers, safer streets and much lower police costs. There was a significant issue with opium at the turn of the 20th century. That took care of itself. The me generation would certainly feel deprived and entitled and would probably continue using drugs for a while. The government certainly would still be more prosperous. Contrary to the popular opinion that interventional measures can solve the problem, there are only two measures that have any impact. The first is the loss of a significant personal relationship and the second is the loss of a job. And obviously that doesn't always work, especially if people don't mean anything to you and you don't have a job. But the wasteful course of the rehabilitation effort would be curtailed. The insurance companies certainly would be happier, and they could make tax-deductible contributions to the enforcer. Let's move on to another category of disasters.

The area of natural disasters is certainly being studied. Are there no solutions there? Global warming has been highlighted for quite a while now and nations are slow to react. Many experts feel that the thinking of the majority of scientists in the field is a good example of a post hoc fallacy. A prior happening may not be the cause. After all, do we know what caused the Ice Age? We are a reactive species and none of us is currently dying. Nothing is being done about all the people who are dying in Africa. We do know where the carbon dioxide emissions are coming from. 40% comes from transportation and the rest of the emissions are equally caused by the utilities, industry and residences. A revolution in the technology of fueling the transportation industry would be required. Instead we see a trickling of change in that sector. Many people point the finger at the oil industry for blocking any change. The truth is that the industry has the money to change the technology if it would be profitable. But the average citizen and the average transportation contractor does not want to see any change for a variety of reasons. So it's a cultural problem.

It will take a long time for people to be dying from the heat. Remember that *homo sapiens* survived in the harshest of temperatures. There are bacteria and shrimp thriving in the holes of the ocean floors where the volcanic gases extrude at thousands of degrees by any scale. You think that you can't live without air conditioning. It will take a long time before you're dying from the blazing heat of the sun. Then you can blame your ancestors. Coal fired furnaces are continuing to be built and hey there is really not much going on with the the windmills and with the solar paneling at this point.

Waste management and recycling are currently popular issues. We hear millions of people talking about this, mostly demanding that other people do something about all this. It really feels as if mankind is just putting that mythical big toe into the water just to see how cold it is. Surprise!, It's pretty cold. But for the last fifty years some very effective recycling projects have been implemented. I guess that Sweden started all of this in 1961 with an underground waste collection process. They have large vacuum tubes which bring waste, including human waste, to collection stations where it's all compacted in sealed containers and sent to plants where it can be used as composting material for the fields or burned to generate electricity and heat for homes and industry. They actually have to import waste from other countries. How about that!

Roosevelt Island in New York is the only location in the United States where this technology is being used. Nobody seems to remember New York City under siege by the trash collectors when colossal amounts of trash simply piled up on the streets as a sort of decor. People always have choices. They can avoid the ravages of critical thinking by simply driving very fast. That's certainly a logical way of thinking.

We recognize that we are running short of **water** in the world. We are very slow to react with conservation measures and certainly with the building of desalination plants. We have built extensive electric grid systems to distribute the energy across the United States as needed. We have a lot of water coming down from those mountains, we have a lot of floods, we have a lot of rain which could be captured and routed around the country. Water pipelines? We do that with gas and oil, don't we? Cost? Not practical? I have a question, "is water more important than oil?" I could add a lot of numbers and percentages here, but I think I've bored you enough with numbers and percentages. People talk a great deal about issues which are really important, but the door seldom opens to the laboratory and the production rooms. Don't get me wrong, I know there's a lot of research being done, but the results don't have enough nudity and violence involved to be newsworthy.

Then we have the issues of volcanoes, hurricanes, cyclones, tsunamis, tidal waves, floods and lightning. Science is hard at work trying to predict some of these events. We know it costs a lot to do anything. The cost of doing nothing is incredibly high. People put things off. A good example is the recent flooding of New Orleans. It is a city built below the oceanic water level. The politicians deferred necessary improvements and used the money for something else. Perhaps they had a very large siphon. Venice and the Netherlands both have long histories of jousting against the **Knights of the Water.** They would be happy to offer some advice. The Army Corps of Engineers still has a lot of work to do. The catastrophe brought into focus the corruption and the quagmire of criminality in New Orleans. The mayor, Ray Nagin, went to prison. The New Orleans' French Quarter and its jazz image has been badly tarnished, but the Mardi Gras festivities have returned.

The intertwined problems of poverty, famine, disease, the deaths of millions of children and corruption seem unsurmountable. The Africans and the Chinese know a great deal about this. The Chinese seem to be doing something. The Chinese are very busy people, but it's hard to figure out what "the something" is. Meanwhile they freely sacrifice millions of their people. The short-term costs are acceptable as they are looking towards their horizon. Many African rulers have no vision of the future at all. Their foreign aid income is deposited directly into protected containers in several foreign countries. Charitable institutions donate tons of food and medical supplies. Once they reach the country, the donors and the goods are not allowed access to the starving and disease people. "People should do things the way I want them to be done," is a statement that has endured the test of time. It is in the **nature of man** as he becomes powerful and corrupt.

The planners think that mother Earth will have 9 or 10 billion citizens by the end of the 21st century. Where is all this food going to come from? Monsanto and a lot of other companies are hard at work engineering new seeds that are highly resistant to insects and produce a high yield. Newer insecticides will be coming on the market. The West has learned a great deal about how to maximize productivity with basic research in the earth sciences, together with those huge tractors and combines. The teaching of proper agricultural techniques can make a huge African landmass into a source of pride for its inhabitants. Small groups of people are trying to teach them how to make their own wells. It's that primitive. It's pretty obvious that they can produce a whole heck of a lot more agricultural products if they are given the know-how and somebody with deep pockets is willing to mechanize them. China appears to have made that commitment.

We now have satellites taking pictures of every rice paddy and diagnosing what the problems are associated with each plot of land. Maybe it's the type of plant, the wrong soil, the need for fertilizer or whatever. There are alternate sources of food which are not currently being used. Some experts have noticed that those tasty termites, locusts, beetles and grasshoppers have very high nutritional value and should be incorporated in the menus at McDonald's and Burger King. It's a challenge, but people already eat them if they're chocolate coated. Some say that seaweed is the way to go. They have started to make artificial hamburger from cow stem cells. The sea with its plankton and algae can be turned into delicacies. The culinary delights of the sea will require the development of entirely new schools of *haute cuisine.*

People are pretty lazy and it's hard to sell them on the idea that they should be growing their own gardens. It's harder to do in the brownstones of New York, but we know that it can be done, especially on the rooftop. Newer construction can allow gardens to be grown indoors. Large vats can be built into the walls to allow for fisheries. The experts have to be positive, but their confidence meter is not very exuberant. The answer may come from another source such as pestilence or global wars.

A major cause of the poverty, famine and disease is the entrenched corruption of the endemic populations. In Pakistan one of their leaders is known as **Mr. 10%**. In Africa many of the leaders are known as **Mr. 90%**. The junior member has only 10% to work with, but he takes 90% of that 10%. It keeps going down the line in the same way. I think it is a wonderful example of the "mathematical fractal." Many think that Einstein was referring to national corruption when he offered his "theory of relativity." The degree, type and extent of corruption varies a good deal from culture to culture and from nation to nation. In some countries it is the only source of income and of survival. We should always have appreciation for that necessity when we judge other people's behaviors.

How do you change a culture of poverty and corruption? With great difficulty. I fear that it will require a fearless inspirational martyr capable of solving the conundrum of the Gordian knot. We can discuss the fact that the arable land in China is being flooded so that dams can be built to furnish hydroelectric power. You've heard of eminent domain. It's called stealing the land. You pay peanuts for it. Some of the governors involved in this behavior are now being removed. This is happening at a time when the prosperous Chinese are eating more beef.

It takes a lot of vegetation to feed the cow. So with the reduction of arable land coupled with the green production being used for beef production, we find that the sum of the parts is in the negative range. Besides that China is really running out of water. The Yellow River is now dry 90% of the time. China is buying a lot of land in Africa and going into the agriculture business there. They now have their first aircraft carrier and are devoting a higher percentage of their GNP to military expenditures. They may have to invade their southern neighbors.

Then we come to a very big problem in America which appears to have **no solution.** It's the one where you live beyond your means. We've already covered the fact that the American government has accumulated a $16 trillion debt with a per capita debt is $45,000. "Don't worry about it, things will even out in the end," is a favorite politician's saying. Any fool will tell you that this just can't go on and should never have happened.

The drunken government gambler is steadily losing and increasing his bets at the American roulette wheel. The casino loves to have him come in and gives him the presidential suite and all the perks. He is surrounded by armed protection. These bodyguards prevent him from any assault by *Gamblers Anonymous*. It's so obvious that a national debt increasing at the rate of $1 trillion per year will lead to national bankruptcy. My banking friend says, "not to worry, all the US has to do is to say that it's wiping out the debt. So we start from scratch. Everybody needs our business. We do that with the Africans all the time, so why can't we get away with the same thing? You've just got to be creative." Well I guess that's the way the financial world thinks. It's really irresponsible and this is an area where you should expect responsibility. "Greed trumps all honesty," is a rather famous quotation, but is it associated with Mae West? Our higher government officials are lackeys to the moneyed empire.

Leadership is conspicuously absent in the American version of democracy. The concept of the courageous leader has been lost, and has been replaced by that of the "fawning publican." Substitute the term **professional politician,** he who has lost touch with his duties and his empathy for his hard-working friends. Enter the political ring and the man becomes a robot. But everyone aspires to be that robot. It gives him a lot of power and he no longer has heard of Lord Acton. There may be a new Watergate about to unfold. During Obama's second term it has been noted that the *IRS* has targeted conservative and religious groups which tend to contribute significantly to the Republican party. What is wrong with people? It's so obvious that term limits and voting the politician out of office are powerful weapons against this. The electorate had a chance to do that recently, and reelected 95% of the members of Congress who were up for election. The citizen is brainwashed and returns the royalty to office. Where is the **critical thinking** in this? "Who made him dead to rapture and despair... whose breath blew out the light within this brain?"

We know that we must get rid of the professionally honed politician with a lifetime appointment. It only takes a few people to organize small groups in each state, who can in turn put smaller groups together in each city. These people can talk to a lot of people and raise some money. They really can put great pressure on their representatives and senators. Only elect the candidate who agrees to a one term limit and agrees to vote that into law. All you need is a few good people.

We already know that the politicians are entrenched because big money puts them there and keeps them there. We skimmed over the issue that the problems of the world involve many issues that are all intertwined. If we look at our government, we realize that we can break down the issues into several understandable categories. You have a lot to choose from. Pick an issue whether it has to do with corruption, political power, banking abuse, the federal debt, the credit debt ceiling or abandonment of space exploration.

Our balance of trade is $5 or 600 billion on the short side every year. I've heard someone say that we'll grow ourselves out of this. He may have been referring to something else. After all it is just hearsay. The US has been pushing to abolish protectionism at the global level. With just an iota of sense, it's quite clear that the policy should be implemented very slowly. The French continue an agricultural subsidy policy of about 40%. Our headlong plunge into this has rid us of our steel industry and a good deal of our manufactures. In a six-month period 750 furniture manufacturing plants closed in North Carolina. This must be the *New Age of Enlightenment.* Slow down, you're moving too fast. Perhaps it's the *New Age of Unreason.*

Our economy has made that giant leap into making its living as a service industry. This country no longer operates out of the executive office. It can be found in the basement, in the maintenance department. It has made the transition to an information led economy which is supposed to be knowledge-based. How does this knowledge fit into that formula on wisdom? It has a lot to do with the Internet, the digital revolution, the so-called high-tech companies, expanding financial institutions, globalization and competition. Our traditional economy was based on agriculture, construction, manufacturing, and on wholesale and retail marketing. This is a lot like an uneducated immigrant finding his way in a new country without even knowing the language. We' re witnessing ourselves going downhill so rapidly because we never hit the brakes. It's possible that China may also suffer the consequences of trying to get somewhere too quickly. Let's encourage them to slow down. We don't want to be annihilated too soon.

George Soros has been one of the central actors in this *Age of Globalization.* We used to say that a half-wit could see the problems in a picture like this. Now it only takes a quarter-wit to be worried about what is going on. There are extreme cases. I remember reading about one corporation which bought over 200 companies in one year. Do you have any idea of what goes into analyzing a company before you're going to buy it? What is the financial picture, what does it owe, what is the management like, how does it operate, where are the manufacturing plants located, what are the unions like, what do the customers expect, what are the short and long-term marketing expectations, etc.?

I met a CEO on a Singapore Airlines flight a few years ago. His company was in the computer chip manufacturing industry and they had six plants located in different countries. He laughed at the idea of buying several companies at the same time. He listed the stringent evaluation of each sector of a company which they were thinking of acquiring. If it seemed pretty solid, they would then send their seasoned sector specialists for 6 to 12 months, to make sure the company was doing quite well. He was sitting in coach. He said they regularly rewarded the employees for competent work and for longevity, with a Rolex. By the way, coach is pretty comfortable on Singapore Airlines and the food is good.

We have come to recognize that cultures can destroy themselves without the need of invading forces. You remember that Lincoln quotation warning people that the only way that the United States would be destroyed would be from within? This appears to be happening in the United States. The *ACLU* is undermining our basic fabric by making a mockery of what *the protection of individual rights* is supposed to protect. But if **slow** is a desirable quality in our national evolution, then our legal system and our *ecology preservers* should be getting *summa cum laude* degrees. They might even be invited to my acceptance of the *Arthur D. Simpleton Chair of Inversional Thinking.*

The US currently enjoys a **hegemonic** position which has lasted over 70 years. A hegemon is defined as a nation which manifests leadership and predominant influence over other nations. But our resources are being stretched very thin. What are our priorities? There is an exponential increase in our indebtedness. Why do we still have 40,000 troops in Germany? We're downsizing the military at a time when more and more shadows are appearing. How many aircraft carriers do we need? Why are three of them anchored at Pearl Harbor while North Korea is threatening to bomb the US? How much of a cat and mouse game should we participate in with the likes of Iran and North Korea? We have learned that invading tribal nations without a scorched-earth policy has little impact.

China has us on a short leash since they are heavily underwriting the US debt. They are heavily investing in the land, commodities and infrastructures of many African countries. They commissioned their first aircraft carrier, and their defense budget is increasing. Two hegemons will be contending for supremacy in the 21st century. China has shown a remarkable capacity to move from a disastrous communistic economy into a rapidly emerging capitalist one.

The Chinese really don't value human life. Millions have been sacrificed in the name of the betterment of the nation. They've taken a few lessons from the Russian censorship of the Cold War. They crack down on dissidents and the press. People start getting upset if the oppression lasts too long. So they ease up for a while. Then they suddenly crack down again. People are always uneasy and are constantly looking over their shoulder. The Russians, and now the Chinese, have to spend a lot of time looking over their shoulders. **Censorship** is certainly not a new thing. I'm just old enough to be able to remember the Inquisition and the Council which declared the *Vulgate Latin Bible* infallible and anathematized any questionners. "Power to the people." That's a good one!

Let's remember that democracy is just a fancy kind of government which survives alongside many competing frameworks. It is far from perfect. It incorporates several myths such as "people are equal" and that Americans are entitled to the good life. It is inevitable that it will evolve. But some things don't seem to evolve. The world is filled with dictators and poor people who are being oppressed. If we look back at the early conquerors there was a lot of cruelty. The Western world still is involved in it to some extent but says that it doesn't believe in it anymore. Meanwhile we see it going on at a grand scale all over the world. We talk about national integrity but we justify repeated invasions and incursions into the concept of national sovereignty. Remember Iraq and Afghanistan and the drones in Pakistan. Now we're being squeamish about going into Syria. We're trying to get other nations to do the work now. China is certainly avoiding doing the dirty work. I think that I've mentioned that a new course is being offered to architectural students. The main course work is covered in a book recently published by **Assad** about city planning and redevelopment. It's called _Creative Architectural Concepts._

The Muslim world began as a tribal world and hasn't changed that much. The concept of integration never took hold. We need to accept the idea that the cultures of the West can't be fused with tribalism. That probably will not change for many thousands of years.

The immigration issue is really one of our lesser problems, at least in the short term. Many citizens of the Third World want to move to more prosperous countries with the hope of bettering their lives. Some find that they are treated as chattel. Many European countries are aware that the influx of Islamic cultures is rapidly leading to national cultural identity crises. Big business has encouraged the Mexican migrants because of the benefits of cheap labor, and Americans don't want to dirty their hands anymore. This will also lead to a cultural shift, but not as rapidly as in Europe. It's clear that the people in power are not dealing with the issue directly. The political rhetoric keeps the American voter happy and keeps the political contributions coming. A long time ago President McKinley strongly recommended that immigrants should bring skills which would enhance the culture of the United States. I think he was assassinated.

We probably should summarize some of our concerns now. We have a huge debt and no one is willing to do much about that. The balance of payment issue is not being addressed and the citizens don't want to curtail the luxury imports. **Globalization** has taken a huge toll and the Americans seem intent on repeating "*The Charge of the Light Brigade*" with this wild ride into "the jaws of death." A total global financial collapse or a devastating global war would allow us to consider the values of some isolation and protectionism, together with the wisdom of having a startup manufacturing sector.

Cutting our defense industry is not the answer. We need to shore up our educational system, rev up our R&D by subsidizing industrial research and resume our commitment to space exploration. One always has to salvage oneself when one's tails is on fire. We need to run faster.

I was looking at the short list of sites of terrorism on earth. The names of Algeria, Djibouti, Egypt, Ethiopia, Kenya, Libya, Mauritania, Morocco, Nigeria, Niger, Chad, South Africa, Sudan, Tanzania, Uganda, Zimbabwe, Eritrea, Syria, Lebanon and Mali are on my incomplete list. I don't think that I've put a definition to terrorism out to view, but it is essentially violence or threat of violence which is used to cause fear. Sometimes there is no perceived goal.

Meanwhile the intelligence community has been thwarting hundreds of terrorist plots, arresting hundreds of terrorists and convicting many of them. They really are not given much media coverage and credit for all of that silent work. But they are crucified when something bad happens. Why aren't they perfect? The results of our intelligence community efforts is far less than the sum of its parts. It appears rather embarrassing when you see the regimes of Algeria, Morocco, Egypt and Syria unraveling. Everyone acts surprised, then they say, "it was just a matter of time." A lot of **post hoc** reasoning. Maybe the sacking of Saddam Hussein caused a domino effect. People just simply started thinking and talking and twittering. It can be clearly understood by the statement, "sometimes you're right, sometimes you're wrong and sometimes you don't have a clue."

There is the *American dream* which justifies the way we think in our expectation that the rest of the world will want to be like as, and eventually will become like us. The US acts as if it feels responsible for the rest of the world. We are faced with worldwide issues involving brutality, starvation, war and corruption. Is it our duty to fix the world? The Western world certainly does not understand the tribal countries and does not understand their cultures. So how are we going to fix all those things?

I've come up with a *utopian dream*. The mentality of taking pride in being a donor nation has to stop. If an industrial nation took one developing African nation under its wing, it would have greater impact. If you were to work with the governing entity, paid with largesse, had control of the purse strings, built up the infrastructure, educated the population, focused on health issues and job creation and put some controls on the endemic corruption of the nation..... you would have a chance of really helping the people of that nation. That would be the best type of foreign aid that we could furnish, and we could obtain our recompense by investing in the industries of the nation. It's more like being an "enlightened" donor nation than being a "sucker" donor nation.

My engineer friend keeps repeating that wisdom is simply based upon experience. I think it's a lot more complicated than that. But I think we have to go beyond the wisdom of the individual and see how he impacts on the wisdom of the culture. We keep coming back to the idea that 1 - the *individual* is the key element in any society and 2 - improving the infrastructure would make him stronger and better and 3 - enhance that society's survival and success. Maybe that's all an illusion. The <u>alternate</u> is to think of the individual as a **Pawn**, Wealth as the King, the Queen's Wall Street, the Bishops are the politicians, the Knights are the military-industrial complex and the Rooks are the CIA and the Armed Services.

I'm not much of a chess player, but I don't think that there are usually any pawns left at checkmate time. It's only in checkers that any piece has a good chance of getting through all the obstacles, and gain a lot of power. Chess is considered a highbrow game, requiring a good deal of intelligence and critical thinking. Chess seems to represent the **natural order** in which **the Royals** always control the board. Checkers just keeps the lowbrows busy, but it does give a piece the chance to disrupt the **natural order.**

Are we going to end this book with the conclusion that there is really *no solution?* I'm going to devote a little time to education shortly, but I'd like to look at a few examples of mankind's effort to move ahead. Sometimes the best of us still stumble and simply fall down.

Let's start with a very successful architect by the name of **Minoru Yamasaki.** He helped to design the Tulsa Performing Arts Center, the World Trade Center and many other highly praised structures. He was responsible for building the Pruitt-Igoe housing development in St. Louis, Missouri in 1954. It was a 33 building complex which was abandoned 15 years later and demolished in the

1970s. It was highly praised when built. Few people really came to live there. There was significant segregation issues at the time and it was extremely dangerous to live there. People were mugged on a regular basis and their checks and possessions stolen. He was later blamed for not understanding the sociology of the people at that time. There are accolades for the *World Trade Center.* But then many architects were very critical of the structural design after the terrorists flew two passenger planes into those towers on September 11, 2001. Who would've guessed that anything like that would occur in the near future? Now the Arabs are building their towers of Babel, only to have people belatedly asking how the firemen are going to get hoses up there if there is a fire. So even if you use the best minds and have lots of money, you can still make mistakes or simply have Providence against you.

Shanghai is in the process of building a skyscraper which is supposed to be the answer to a crowded city. It is supposed to have everything that a city has within it, including parks. I hope they're not going to incorporate gangs into the city. The ghost of Pruitt-Igoe lurks in the shadows. They're going to have to make sure that they put responsible people into that utopian city. People have been talking for years about downtown renewal projects or expanding communities with green belts. We'll just have to wait and see. Perhaps nobody will want to move in, and the unexpected is to be expected.

I'm having too much fun, so I'll be moving on with this boring thing having to do with education. We already know that the problem with our educational system is a parental problem. Nobody really wants to emphasize that problem. That's not a politically savvy thing to do. So there's **no solution.** "Make the parents responsible!, don't even think about it," was heard from a very soft voice coming from somewhere in the wilderness. You may have noticed that I have been avoiding any reference to the formula on wisdom. The individual and cultural scores seem to be embarrassingly low.

While our standards in the legal and medical specialties go up and up, and it gets harder and harder to get into the Ivy League schools, our high school graduates can't pass a low grade graduating exam. It must be like a Chinese food conveyor belt with no one removing any of the bad apples. They don't study, they don't know anything, let's overlook the problem, make them feel good and graduate them without knowledge or skills. An educational friend said that he would like to strangle the imbecile who decided to eliminate vocational, so-called technical schools. He had pointed to a youngster outside of the restaurant who was just hanging around. "I know that kid, he had the brains to learn how to run those auto diagnostic machines and earn $100,000 per year. He had no interest in the type of schooling that he was offered, and he just dropped out. He's just another casualty of our educational system. It's a shame." The teachers seem to be trying hard, although their own personal standards have steadily been going downhill for years. Their superiors, the educators, seem to be in that **ivory tower** which I've never been able to locate. I think that fits into the **common sense** category in our wisdom definition.

Meanwhile there is a mandatory federal education program which is supposed to guarantee that people can read, write and do some arithmetic. The teachers think that it is a complete failure and that it stifles thinking and creativity. It is based upon rote memory. But this is all absurd. Why is everybody worried about this educational process? There are inconceivable technological advances which make basic math prehistoric. The angstrom unit, 10 nanometers, is now a unit which everybody feels comfortable with, sort of like an ounce. I think that I've mentioned that I quit learning anything about science when I had to conceptualize how small an angstrom unit was years ago.

I'm going to come back to the so-called insoluble problem of educational stagnation. There really has been no significant changes in the educational evolution for the past 150 years. The computer and the Internet could facilitate a major revolution. I'll get to that later on. Meanwhile I'll refer you to Sellig M. K. Siaramsed's famous book, *The Sense of Nonsense*, about the evolution of the educational process. He gives the chronology of the progression of educational insights into teaching. I'll include it at this time:

1- The 3R's go back 2500 years
2- Molding good conduct and character also goes back 2500 years
3- Socratic wisdom warred against political skills back 2500 years
4- Aristotle wanted state-controlled education
5- Athletics was important 2500 years ago; few people were educated
6- 900 years ago schools to educate the clergy were licensed
7- 900 years ago teachers were licensed by examination
8- 600 years ago the first liberal treatise was written
9- 500 years ago Luther pushed for peasant education

10- 500 years ago the grading system was born
11- 500 years ago the need for better pay for teachers was recognized
12- 500 years ago the need for more student freedom was noted
13- 500 years ago tutoring and individual attention were promoted
14- 500 years ago Puritans establish a fundamentalist theocracy
15- 400 years ago American schools stressed ancient language and literature
16- 300 years ago Franklin urged useful teaching in the schools
17- 200 years ago discipline and rote memory prevailed
18- 200 years ago the individual needs of the child were noted
19- 200 years ago the kindergarden was founded
20- 200 years ago Massachusetts set up a board of education
21- 150 years ago Vassar, a female college was founded
22- 150 years ago schools for teachers were founded
23- 150 years ago experimental schools allowed students to self-teach

But at this point let's talk more about what we have learned about the thinking of the individual. I know that repetition is boring, but it's necessary to keep the information in your long-term memory. So here is a synopsis about what we have learned about *homo sapiens.* He doesn't do a lot of thinking. He is highly emotional, biased, does not seek out valid information and is poor at math, science and statistics. He has a very myopic view, is very self-centered, seeks immediate gratification, doesn't believe in hard work, goes along with the herd instinct. He does no thinking about what is going on around him or what he is doing, and can be easily manipulated. It's only when he really begins to suffer that he thinks about changing something. The American is too soft.

We need good parents, and we need a culture which strongly encourages positive behaviors. It needs to encourage the individual to be responsible. The individual needs to learn as much as he can and to stay informed. He should seek out reliable information. He must verify the information, and seek opposing views. After all that is what validity is all about, and thinking has to allow for falsifiability. The individual must be taught to be skeptical and to use **critical thinking.** Apparently that is counter intuitive, so it is difficult to teach. Since his only view is an imperfect view, he must seek the comfort of diverse opinions. A consensus view will probably be the best for decision-making purposes. This goal is the stuff having to do with scientific validity.

So as we close this dialogue let's refresh our memory about some of the things that we thought were important in this area. Let's once again review the concepts of fallacy, probability, validity, verifiability and falsifiability. If you start with a premise that is **false,** your conclusion is going to be wrong. A probability value is known as a **P value.** It is a measure of the statistical probability that your conclusion is either positive or negative. A **valid** premise is supported by solid evidence leading to a solid conclusion. The conclusion must be **verified** by your experience or observation (let's call that empirical data). That empirical data itself must be subject to the risk of being proven **false (falsifiability).** So we have another formula. I'm sure that my use of the word formula is a misrepresentation of a concept which Spock would be heard to say, "it's illogical."

So **V (validity) = R (reliability) + F (falsifiability).** For a premise to be valid it must fulfill both criteria: **V = R + F.** Science won't work if the equation is **V = R/F.** So let's outline some of the concepts having to do with **scientific validity.**

1 - A false premise leads to a wrong conclusion.
2 - P value is a measure of the statistical probability that your conclusion is either positive or negative.
3 - A valid (validity) premise is supported by solid evidence leading to a solid conclusion.
4 - The conclusion must be verified (verifiability) by your experience or observation (let's call that empirical data).
5 - That empirical data itself must be subject to the risk of being proven false (falsifiability).

**V (validity) of a Premise = R (reliability) + F (falsifiability).
V = R + F.
IV(invalidity) of a Premise =
R (reliability)/F (falsifiability). IV = R/F.**

I'm never sure what people mean when they say, "you only go around once." I've always seen it more as a linear function. We're not in a time machine, we can never redo something that has been done. We do come to forks in the road, and perhaps we may be given a chance to modify our direction. It's much better to make a positive and correct decision right from the very beginning and **critical thinking** should help you to make that decision.

The good thinking citizen usually has to balance a lot of things in his life, including having good ethical values. Predicting the future is very inexact; the validity formula is hard to apply. But you're going to have to know the rules of the game if you expect to put any of those balls into the net. In short *the rational mind uses critical thinking and the scientific method, with skepticism.* All conclusions are tentative. You may not be able to do much about the natural order, but you sure can give it a try.

We might as well review what goes into **logical thinking**, so-called **critical thinking.** *Don't Read this Book* The *Tails from the Red Fox* might be useful here as an example of plagiarism:

Absolute truth is found in mathematics.
All constants are constantly being revised.
Absolute truth is found in religions.
Each religion believes in a different truth.
Pieces of truth are found everywhere.
They should be placed on a large space to solve the puzzle.
Some truths are truer than other truths.
Some truths have high odds.
Honest men give better odds.
Some truths have lower odds.
Politicians give lower odds.
Some truths are regional such as eternal darkness.
Some truths are cyclical.
Summer is Summer 25% of the time.
Daytime is present 50% of the time.
Some truths are unpredictable.
Your wife is virtuous.
Some truths are unexplainable.
A magic show or a house of mirrors.
Some truths are not reported.
Your wife was not virtuous.
Some truths have four faces.
Rashomon had a samurai, a wife, a thief and a forester with four versions.
Some observed truths have filters.
An English play with an audience of a blind man, a deaf man, a mute man from Nepal.

I hope this has been a useful exercise in stimulating the repetition of memories leaving you with a hard-core memory. We'll be moving on in the next chapter with some suggestions about implementing some basic changes in our educational system. Before that I'm going to raise some issues and questions for you to ponder..

As Americans we thank our founding fathers for their wisdom, courage and the birth of a great nation with a protective Constitution. Are we invincible? I was impressed by what has happened in Turkey recently. Protesters showed up saying they did not want a mall to replace a park. To protest such an issue appeared reasonable. Nobody mentioned that the park was hardly used because it was very dangerous. Suddenly all sorts of protesters showed up with issues that had nothing to do with the park. Many of the issues were rather bizarre. And protests for protest sake gained momentum and spread to dozens of cities in Turkey. There is a possibility that the government will fall and lead to further turbulence. The United States seems less vulnerable to this sort of scenario at the moment. But let's say that the United States really falls on hard times and poverty and unrest spread. There could easily be a coup d'état. Don't kid yourself, it could happen. The military could take over. What makes you think that we are above that sort of thing? The *twitterers* are now potentially a potent force for the demolition of democracy.

I was thinking that much of this book is focused on improving an individual's critical thinking with the idea that it would be to everyone's benefit. There is the implied hope that our nation would have a better and more secure future. But this presupposes that the American individual is really a noble savage, not in a bad sense. The colonies had a lot less people, presumably people knew one another and kept one another in line. The myth of equality was just that, a myth, something to be attained. I think that the average person wasn't as wrapped up in self-importance as he is today. My daughter's observation that Facebook and Twitter have a lot to do with narcissism, the thumping of one's chest, is probably correct. Rumors and inane opinions can spread like wildfire. Terrible passions can be aroused by faceless people whom you certainly would not want to meet face-to-face. I shudder to think that crazy people like that could incite people to riot and even silence the voice of reason. Of course the *Twitter generation* says that the social media allows more transparency of the government actions and allows the individual more freedom of expression. That sounds really good doesn't it.

103

Of course there is always the humorous side. The social media people in London *twitter* their coterie to meet at the square X to protest something or other. They then call the TV station to tell them to be there. The police come. The game is on. The *twitter* group is called to go to square Y. They are enjoying themselves *twittering* from one place to another, making fun of the police and causing an adolescent public nuisance.

Sir Berners-Lee still feels that his creation, the *World Wide Web*, has positive potential for spreading information. He admits that it is not being used the way that he thought that it would develop. He and Robert Cailliau put the www together around 1990 while they were working for the *European Organization for Nuclear Research (CERN)*. We think of the www as the Internet, but it's actually an informational service using the Internet. He of course is a brilliant guy. I guess the Internet was turned off at least on one occasion. He warns that nations have to be wary of this potential.

I can read your mind, "he introduced himself as a fool at the beginning of this book, and he's proving it now." But let's remember that the great civilizations of Greece and Rome vanished and were followed by the Dark Ages. Some of that was salvaged by the Islamic scholars. As this book unfolds it appears that it is the responsibility of the individual to evolve, and to band together with the collective will to improve the infrastructure of the nation. It must come from the individual, since we have seen such failure in our government. Hopefully there is some genetic material left by the founding fathers to bring together thinkers and implementers capable of making the needed changes in this 21st century.

We are probably governed by the **natural order**. There's no point in beating our heads against a cement wall. We all know that everyone is prejudiced to some degree. It's a waste of time to make everyone a blank duplicate, and it suppresses any ember of creativity. Wars, slaughters and famine will continue. Revolutionaries will continue the practices of their oppressors. Waste is to be expected. We find a lot of that in the academic and research areas as well as at the buffet tables in Las Vegas. Perfection is never going to happen and it's a waste of resources trying to make that happen. **Critical thinking** is about **reasonable thinking**. That's what this whole book is about.

I've highlighted the fact that the history of mankind has involved a lot of really bad and cruel events and even the religions that preach good have been involved in terrible things. We are now worried about whether people are offended by the perception of inappropriate cultural, ethnic, racial or sexual comments. Some of the comments are really funny and they are widely used. Many of the individuals, to whom the comments are directed, actually find them not to be offensive. There is a big difference between joking around and walking up to somebody and trying to insult him or her. We "sophisticated people" approach things on a higher plane. We should expect everyone to treat us as royalty, after all it's the American way. There is always humor in the absurd. The French apparently are going to prosecute Abercrombie and Fitch for not having enough ugly salespeople. There is rabid discrimination going on. They hire pretty people! We have to root out this ***oppressive Evil***.

But you may have an issue with all of that. That's very natural. We all have issues. Everyone thinks somebody else's issue is not worth a penny's worth of thought. Our intelligentsia and our rulers make a big thing about "our national heritage." We have magnificent museums which contains thousands of relics of other cultures. There is much discussion about the legal or moral obligation to return Egyptian relics to Egypt, etc. Yet the US went into Baghdad and made absolutely no effort to preserve the Iraqi Museum. Thousands of artifacts were looted. Was it a matter of priorities? Didn't anyone from West Point ever hear about museums and artwork?

In the old days the Macedonians and the Romans conquered, and looted to pay the troops. The conquered had to pay taxes and serve the conquerors. They also had to pay for the garrisons. Now we find ourselves invading Iraq and Afghanistan, spending billions of dollars, being criticized for not doing enough. How times have changed! Now there is an *apologia* for being successful, "what have you done for me lately?" **Spock** would certainly agree with me that there is **little critical thinking** going on here. What are the options? This is a topic worthy of some discussion, without prejudice.

Should there be some open discussion about the **sovereignty of a nation**? Everyone gives lip service to that, but they break the rules continuously. Do we secretly believe that the *United Nations* should be in charge of implementing that **One World Order** which we hear so much about? Let's take a look at the **Arab Spring & Fall** in **Egypt**. A fellow named **Morsi** was elected president and immediately moved from democracy to establishing an *Islamic fundamentalist state* led by the *Muslim Brotherhood*. He quickly changed the Constitution. People rioted, the military moved in to reestablish order. We all know that the *Muslim Brotherhood* leadership is composed of terrorists who have been responsible for much of the *terrorist jihadist* behaviors in the Middle East. The *Muslim Brotherhood* has 3 to 400,000 people who are terrorists. The rest are simple folk who are given services by the *Muslim Brotherhood* and who now are part of a loyal group. It's a lot like Americans who listen to all the propaganda of the American media and don't know that they are carbon copies of loyalists in the *Muslim Brotherhood.*

The Western media decided that a democratically elected president had been unjustly deposed by the military, and called it a *coup*. The Egyptian military had been confronting the *Muslim Brotherhood* terrorists for years. The West, including Obama, criticized the army and wanted **Morsi** to be put back as president. Meanwhile the *Muslim Brotherhood* had people shooting at the Army, forcing the army to shoot into the crowds. *The Muslim Brotherhood* understood the concept of public relations when dealing with the Western news media. The **BBC** finally had one person who pointed out that the West was now supportive of a *terrorist jihadist regime*.

The common citizen of the Western world does not want *jihadist terrorists* taking over any country. Yet their representatives are such a timid group of people that they hear offending anyone, and operate a *why can't we all love one another* foreign policy. I do try to avoid using the word *stupid*, but it just slipped out. The American people certainly should get involved in an open dialogue about what their president should be doing. I don't hear much open discussion. Is that a reference to *The Silence of the Lambs?* The *United Nations* certainly has had *zero* influence. If you look at **Syria** they can't even get their people into evaluate whether **Sarin** was used.

Egypt was a much calmer place when **Hosni Mubarak** was in charge. Iraq was a much calmer place when **Saddam Hussein** was around. Syria had some citizens living in Syria before **Assad's** regime was assailed. Very strong leadership appears to be a requirement for stability in the Middle East. The terrorism of tribalism surfaces very quickly. What would the **New World Order** led by the *United Nations* change about the human nature of man?

All of this certainly raises questions about America's role in the world. We are in need of the input of our citizens who should be able to find a few statesmen who have been afraid to come out of the closet. Our *leadership* appears to be *rudderless*. You can see that there are so many issues to be clearly discussed so that there are competent navigators to help the captain at the helm. We need to get **reason** and **critical thinking** back into the government.

That's a long *aside* which is really of fundamental importance. I should just get back to the topics of **conspiracy theory** and the **New World Order.** The aroma of **conspiracy theory** has been in the air for a good number of years now. The theory is probably bogus. The **New World Order** is probably one of the way stations along the way of the **natural order.** Everything in the world is getting closer and quicker and national leaders with thousands of miles separating them are speaking and looking at one another on **Skype.** It's so natural to form alliances and business relationships. The *Bilderberg* and *Bohemian* groups just naturally jump aboard. **Globalization** is just part of the process. My main fear is that it is going so quickly that it causes too much collateral damage. The best that we can probably hope for is to have things **slow** down.

Throughout this book we've been invited to be cinema goers viewing many events and movements of a parallel universe. "How could all of these things be happening," we say as we watch the drama unfold. We certainly can't say that historical records have shown any evidence of plateauing. We know that Alexander the Great tried to pursue the conquest of the world. The Roman Empire also believed in the **One World Order.** The caliphate did pretty well for a while in the Ottoman Empire which understood what was workable in a **One World Order.** We also know that Hitler was a great advocate of it.

Woodrow Wilson proposed 14 points in his proposal for world peace. It included the concepts of free trade, no secret agreements, democracy and self determination for minorities who were being oppressed. He proposed a world organization to provide for collective security for all nations. The *League of Nations* was indeed formed, but the American Senate never ratified it. It was fairly ineffective but it did last until 1946. The United States chose a period of isolation. Woodrow Wilson asked Walter Lippmann to assemble a bunch of young scholars to put together his proposals. They regrouped and formed the *Council on Foreign Relations* in 1921. They have over 4000 members who were involved in government, scholarly, business, legal and media affairs. Large groups of them are part of a great number of committees that come and go in Washington. You can guess how much influence they have. The Council also publishes the

"Journal of Foreign Affairs," which appears to have a lot of quality to it.

The *League* wanted retribution and forced the Germans to pay heavy compensation. It was a fertile turf in which to nurture a Hitler. But then came World War II and the allies came together to form a *United Nations* and the financial and political tools which we've covered. The communication barrier, namely the sea, is gone and everybody is interconnected. We know that it is going to be about 3 billion years before the Earth is incinerated by the sun. So we do have a lot of time to make counter moves. We just need to slow down the troops of the **natural order.** We need to continue believing in our democracy, and the rights of man, and liberty and focus on our own survival. We need to neutralize the effects of corruption, dictatorship, poverty, famine and internecine wars on ourselves.

So we can stop thinking about the conspiracy theory, and simply recognize that greed in all forms is jumping on the bandwagon of the **One World Order.** You can already see that the flotilla moving in that direction is having problems in the *European Union*.

When I started this book about **critical thinking** I had no idea that it would be like hurling a flat stone onto the water and watching it bouncing and skimming and suggesting so many issues that we should be thinking about. I wish I were brighter and could've unraveled the poignant core of these earthly issues. I'll probably add a few more things for you to think about before this book is finished.

VI

PURSUIT OF WEALTH
KHAZARS TO SECRET SOCIETIES

I've already done a lot of work on the final chapter having to do with a revision of our entire educational system. I've tried to add some funny stuff into that chapter, but I'm dissatisfied with my own **critical thinking.** I went back and looked at another chapter in which I found myself saying, "are we going to end this book with the conclusion that there is really **no solution?**"

Then I looked at the following paragraph, "We are probably governed by the **natural order.** There is no point to beating our heads against a cement wall. We all know that everyone is prejudiced to some degree. It's a waste of time to make everyone a blank duplicate of one another, and it suppresses any ember of creativity. Wars, slaughters and famine will continue. Revolutionaries will continue the practices of their oppressors. Waste is to be expected. We find a lot of that in the academic and research areas as well as at the buffet tables in Las Vegas. Perfection is never going to happen and it's a waste of resources trying to make that happen. **Critical thinking** is about **reasonable thinking.** That's what this whole book is about."

A lot of my thinking has been inductive in this book, and I'm supposed to be pushing deductive reasoning and critical thinking. I've come to the realization that *this is no time for acceptance.* Since you have come so far with me on this journey towards wisdom, I should have you look at some underlying history which we can't find in the proffered textbooks found in our schools. I owe you this. I think you would like to know the antecedents of a culture which appears to have us on the road to a rather sticky web, with predators awakened to a gourmet morsel. These "predators" may actually be *worker bees* who are simply doing their duty. I'm going to **jump to the conclusion** that we need to add a **Secretary of Ethics and Cultural Philosophy** to the cabinet in Washington. You're sure to say, "what is this fool up to?"

We'll be looking at how *Socialism* and *merchant bankers* have warped the mettle of our governmental institutions. It has taken a good deal of effort to put this together. Much contradictory and imagined evidence is found mostly in the financial area. I've tried to give you a lot of information and I've attempted to verify the data that I have gleaned. It can be tedious going at times. You will find that I give you blocs of names of people and businesses that are in several organizations so that you can cross reference them in other organizations. You can just skim through those lists, and come back to them later on, as the need arises. Just bend the corners of those pages. See if you have a better understanding of what you are exposed to in everyday life. We all have opinions, see if yours are confirmed.

We need to look at the relationship between *the government and the citizen,* as well as the distribution of **federal and state rights**. Both are good examples of a **slippery slope**. These smaller particles may actually be victims of an avalanche. The federal government is imposing ever-increasing rules with serious penalties for showing displeasure, even if the displeasure is only verbal. There could be many a chapter written about this, but I'm sure you're familiar with this general argument. The U.S. Constitution was built upon the concept of protecting the liberty and the rights of the common man.

It appears that **King George** is making a comeback. The president brings us to **war** in the Middle East without it being authorized by Congress. The citizens, and more importantly, their elected representatives in Congress, just let it happen. But there is an even more pernicious behavior on the part of the president of the United States. I haven't read the Constitution in years, but I doubt that there is a provision for **Executive Orders** which allow the president to put these together, even bundling them. This is extremely dangerous since they can't be reviewed by Congress for 6 months after they have been implemented. **Enlightened Despotism?**

We've identified that **wealth** and **liberty** and **power** are of great importance to the common man. We need to find out if the emergence of wealth, power, and socialism is leading towards an insidious movement called a **New World Order.** We are observers of flowering plants and crops being overrun by pernicious weeds. We know that it takes a lot of care to keep the flowers and crops growing. I think that we've learned that sound husbandry requires that we find out how the plants are first seeded and what their roots are like. We've learned that many a root system is very deep and/or invasive. Hence the term to *"root them out."*

Where did all this wealth and government power came from? It's essential that we uncover that, but it won't be easy. "Absolute power corrupts absolutely," and it likes to keep its secrets quite private.

Many examples of the federal government preempting the rights of the state come to mind. Education is now in the hands of the federal government, which is actually mandating *socially appropriate jargon* ... sheer nonsense. The culture has changed, the technology has changed and the goals should be changing. The states have done a poor job of defending their own rights.

I'm reminded of one of Cicero's speeches. I've been reading a book about this man and I'm truly impressed. In 43 B.C. Cicero Marcus Tullius spake thus, "a nation can survive its fools, and even the ambitious. But it cannot survive treason from within. An enemy at the gates is less formidable, for he is known and carries his banner openly. But the traitor moves amongst those within the gate freely, his sly whispers rustling through all the alleys, heard in the very halls of government itself. For the traitor appears not a traitor; he speaks in accents familiar to his victims, and he wears their face and their arguments, he appeals the baseness that lies deep in the hearts of all men. He rots the soul of a nation, he works secretly and unknown in the night to undermine the pillars of the city, he infects the public body so that it can no longer resist. A matter is less to fear. The traitor is the plague."

I have to put in my own disclaimer at this time. Most of us have a vague idea about all these conspiratorial theories and confront them with healthy skepticism. Believing in conspiratorial theories involves some level of paranoia. One fellow explained that it had to do with the fallacy which connects two independent events without proof of a connection. I think that's as good an explanation as I can come up with. But if you do any *any looking into,* called research, any aspect of historical or political events, you'll find it cloaked in mystery and "obfuscation." I particularly like that word obfuscation because there is a good deal of secrecy built into any culture. We are currently using the noun *transparency* with the hope that we can find some glimmer of truth as to how the real world works.

There are people who have devoted their lives to studying the occult, cults, religions, symbols and whatever. The mere mention of the *Statue of Freedom* at the top of the U.S. Capitol building in Washington brings you into the so-called, symbols, secret societies and most notably *Freemasonry.* It's like trying to study the Bible's history. Many researchers, *men looking into the past,* have worked very hard to understand how things have evolved. Most won't admit that they don't understand why or how events have occurred, or why organizations have been formed. Honest effort should lead to some reward and you have to be a fool to document your own ignorance.

In studying some of these organizations, I found it difficult to separate one from another. This is particularly true of the **secret societies,** known to you, and to me, as the **SS.** That would imbue **SS** with both the **anchor fallacy** and **pattern recognition.** Even well-known organizations such as the *UN*, the *Federal Reserve* and the *World Bank* are cloaked in a great deal of secrecy. For the sake of a concise use of words and letters in this chapter I shall refer to them as *NGOs*. *NGOs* may mean "nongovernmental organizations" to you. For this chapter we shall abandon the usual meaning and refer to all organizations as *no good organizations.* So let's go with *NGOs*.

Since things are so secret, I'm going to have to whisper. I stumbled upon a **Global 2000 Report** which was prepared for Jimmy Carter at the request of Cyrus Vance, the Secretary of State. **Kissinger** is a member of the **Club of Rome** which believes in depopulation, and is said to have asked Cyrus Vance to push its agenda. The **Club of Rome** is influenced by the **Black Nobility.** Don't worry about these names, I'll discuss them further a bit later. The report emphasized that the world population was exploding and that the Earth's natural resources would be inadequate to meet the energy needs, leading to an inadequate food supply, lack of available shelter and loss of jobs. One billion living people are subsisting on less than one dollar per day. My abbreviation for **conspiracy theorist** is simple, it's **CT.** I have not read the report but the **CTs** feel that it was recommending a mass genocide to eliminate two billion people in the Third World. They go on to say that the AIDS virus was genetically engineered at the United States Army Medical Research Institute located at Fort Detrick in Maryland. They also believe that the AIDS virus was spread by the UN smallpox vaccination program in Central African nations.

It's impossible to verify this kind of information. We don't know much about the infectious disease research labs. We do know about the US Public Health study which followed syphilitic black males, who were not treated, from 1932 to 1972. Some cholera epidemics are said to have been have been deliberately introduced. The **CTs** also cite the sterilization of about 50% of the American Indian women of childbearing age during the 60s and 70s. There are many other examples. It's known that vibratory cycles vary from virus to virus, and they can kill the viruses. They can also kill off cancer cells. The **CTs** think that this is being overlooked as a courtesy to the pharmaceutical lobby. I really don't know anything about this, but it is an interesting appendage to the list of things that you can or cannot do to control population growth. This is good conspiratorial stuff.

I did look into some data about the problem with the world running out of food. Only 22% of the land on earth can be used to grow crops. There are only 82,000,000,000 acres available; half is being used for cultivation and the other half for grazing. 98% of the food that we eat comes from farmland. Rice, wheat and corn supply 50% of all human energy requirements. The acreage is going down as erosion, urbanization and deforestation takes place. There are but three ready choices that are both positive and easily come to mind. They are population control, preservation of arable land and increasing the yields from the land.

The changes in the world feeding habits also play a role. As India, China and other Third World countries become wealthier, their citizens start to eat more meat. Cattle are fed on grain. If you place the cattle between the grain on the ground and the human consumer you lose 90% of the calories. That's a pretty scary statistic.

We have about 7 billion people on earth now. The projections are exponential. The statisticians figure that if you limit the birth rate to one per person that it would take 40 years to stabilize. We lose two million per year to HIV, 4 million to cancer and 20 million to abortions. We lose millions to famine and disease especially in Africa. And we don't want to overlook that the terrorists' contributions to population control all over the world. The population keeps going up.

Most scientists agree that there is such a thing as global warming. There are many very competent scientists who don't. We hear that carbon dioxide is the main greenhouse gas that blocks the transmission of low-frequency heat radiation back into space. I think that we've covered this before and that it comes mostly from transportation.

We hear a lot about having a hole in our ozone layer that protects us from the **ultraviolet-B (UV-B)** which causes cancer and impairs the growth of crops and forests. **Ozone** is O_3 and it absorbs almost 100% of the high-frequency ultraviolet light. The ozone layer is situated in the lower portion of the stratosphere, known as the troposphere, and it varies from 8 to 30 miles above Earth's surface. It is measured by the "Dobson unit." It is an interesting process. Apparently

UV splits the normally occurring oxygen atoms (O2) into individual atoms (O) which then go on to combine with other oxygen (O2) to form O3, another Ozone. Ozone (O3) is also unstable and breaks down. It's a continuous process. Apparently 50% of the Ozone is produced in the tropics.

Chlorofluorocarbons (CFC) do a substantial amount of the damage to the ozone layer. CFC is found in aerosols, refrigeration equipment and solvents commonly used in homes. You would've known it as Freon. I Ozone depletion is due primarily to chlorine and bromine contained in industrial chemicals. It takes 10 years for the chemicals to migrate from mother Earth to the stratosphere. The scary part is that the CFCs upon arrival have 75 to 110 years to work their ozone depleting reaction magic. Is that worth some time to do some thinking about this subject?

This is where it gets interesting. At ground level ozone is formed primarily by **nitrogen oxides** reacting with **volatile hydrocarbons** in sunlight. The gas from the automobiles, the coal from the power plants and forest fires are great sources of **nitrogen oxides**. The **volatile hydrocarbons** also come from factories, trees and other vegetations. The scientists don't seem to be too clear about how much damage is done to vegetation by the ozone at ground level.

Funny thing, that is the stuff that the global warming people want to ban. They have to get all this stuff straight. Then we could watch a great fight – – the title match for **Heavyweight Global Savior.**

But let me get back to the trail of the **SS.** The ancestors of the current British Royal family apparently went by the names of Brunswick, **Guelph** and Hanover. The **House of Windsor** springs from the marriage of Queen Victoria to Prince Albert in 1840. He was the son of the **Duke of Saxe-Coburg-Gotha** in Germany and his name became the one used by the British Royal family. Saxe-Coburg-Gotha turned out not to be his real surname, which was **Wettin.** Prince Albert was called **Prince Albert of Saxe-Coburg-Gotha.** After careful studies they apparently recognized that the correct lineage name was Wettin.There appeared to be several links to the house of Wettin. The Reformation was led by Martin Luther and was funded by Frederick III of Saxony, of the house of **Wettin.**

But King George V suddenly changed the name to **Windsor** on July 17, 1917. **The Gotha G.IV** was a German aircraft bomber which was bombing London during World War I. The name Gotha was despised. Hence the name changed. The British Royal family has its official residence at Windsor Castle in the borough of Windsor.

The name of the royal house is Windsor, but the surname of the Queen and the Duke of Edinburgh (Prince Philip) should be Mountbatten-Windsor. Not so by Royal decree. The Duke is also from the house of Schleswig-Holstein-Sonderburg-Glucksburg and so, arguably are his heirs.

The Germanic background of British Royal family led to the house of **Guelph** which was one of the oldest and most powerful families in **Venice**. The oligarchs of Venice and Genoa had a monopoly on trading rights in the 12th-century. The **Guelphs** were part of this group. They had originally emigrated from the Middle East. They were the **Khazars** who had blended through intermarriage with the **Canaanites**. They initially called themselves **Sepharvaims** when they moved to northern Italy.

We're leading into the **Black Nobility,** but before I can do that we actually have to get into the subject of religion, ethnicity and ancestry. This gets to be rather complex and confusing, but rather enlightening. The peoples of Russia and the Middle East would be the founding fathers of that nobility. They would be known as **Khazars** who would fuse with the **Jewry** that we know today.

This has been a particularly difficult area to clarify since biases towards the Jews appear at every turn, both pro and con. An issue raised can lead to a plethora of "facts" which do not pass the test of **skepticism**. What appears fairly clear is that there was a lot of intermarriage going on between the **Israelites** and the **Hittites,** so that the **Khazars** were a blended group and the Jews, as we know them today, are not pure descendants of Abraham. Many people express very intense and very contradictory viewpoints about all of this. Everyone's prejudiced except me, I'm lily white.

Now we enter the world of the "biblical scholar." To be able to leave any bias aside, you have to be a "faithless biblical scholar," and you have to keep that **secret** to yourself. You have to be a "true biblical scholar" to *understand something understandable* about Canaanites and the Jews. Remember that this is in the general area of Israel, Jordan and Lebanon, I think. The **Israelites** were a Semitic people who spoke Hebrew in the land of Canaan between the 6th and 15th

115

centuries B.C. Somewhat later they inhabited the territories of Judaica and Galilee. The Israelites were descendants of Jacob, whose name was changed to Israel. Just for the record – – – Abraham comes first, his son is named Isaac. Isaac's sons were Esau (also known as Edom) and Jacob (renamed Israel). I'm really not trying to mess with your mind; life should be simpler.

When you try to do some reliable research in this area you just get confused, confused, confused, etc. For instance I found someone who said that Jacob "begot" I thought Israel and that Esau "begot" Edom. Do you think that the dictionary definition of "begot" has changed over 1000 or more years so that they were referring to name changes? Then there is the one which stated that the *Torah* and the *New Testament* describe the Edomites as descendants of Esau without clarifying that Esau's other name was Edom. I'm going to have a nervous breakdown. But I can understand how a researcher can make mistakes, even a simple typo can change the whole picture. The reason of course is that a good researcher can only do his work if he has a glass of scotch or bourbon in his hand. It eases the pain, the taste is good and consequences are forgotten. Please excuse me while I open another bottle of *Glenlivet.*

Now we can get back to the **Black Nobility**. Many of their precursors were known as the **Khazars** who ruled over a vast territory which included some of Europe, Russia, Ukraine, Azerbaijan and parts of Turkey, Georgia, Kazakistan, and lots more. They were a semi-nomadic Turkic group who had a major influence in that part of the world from around 622 to 1050. Some date their influence into the thirteenth century. They controlled the Silk Road and the roads of commerce between Europe and southwestern Asia. They apparently were major slave traders at that time. Jews traded with them and many Jews fled to Khazaria to escape persecution.

The **Edomites** were a Semitic people who apparently lived in the present location of Israel. Another expert said that they lived south of Judaica and the Dead Sea. I'm too tired to look it up. The Edomites intermarried with the Turks. These Turco-Edomites were later to be known as **Khazars**. The **Edomites** were descendants of Abraham. The **Canaanites** were non-Israelites who included the Hittites, the Philistines, the Phoenicians, the Jebusites and the Aramaeans. These Canaanites were not descendants from Abraham. The **Edomites** intermarried with the **Canaanites.**

116

The Khazarian luck ran out after persistent Russian invasions. There was not much left to the Empire by the time that Genghis Khan came to visit. They got out of town and went into Poland and towards Jerusalem. This **Edomite/Canaanite/Khazarian** band migrated to Italy and adopted the name **Sepharvaim**, became Venetians, and later inherited the title of the **Black Nobility**, as they married into the European royal and aristocratic houses. They were the ancestors of the people who were to be called the **Ashkenazi Jews**, who were to wield such formidable political and financial influences in France, Germany and Eastern Europe. The **Khazars** preempted the name of **Ashkenazi** because there was a prophecy that Ashkenaz would conquer Babylon. He was the grandson of Japheth and the brother of Togarmah, all related to Noah.

The people who write about history interchange names and dates and locations so freely that one tends to get mixed up quite easily. But there is a second group of **Khazars** going back to biblical times. They too had Hebraic and Canaanite origins. Let's add a few more to the above as we go along. You've heard of the Pharisees, Zealots, Assassins, Scribes, Amorites, Hittites, Philistines, and Sepharvaims. These **Edomite/Canaanites/Khazars** also migrated to Carthage where they called themselves **Punics.** But then Cato the Elder, a Roman Senator, repeatedly said, "Carthage must be destroyed." The Romans were so frustrated with his repeated utterance of that statement that they went out and completely destroyed Carthage.

This second group of **Edomite/Canaanites/Khazars** would be renamed **Sephardic Jews** when they hurriedly left and went to Spain and stayed there for 6 or 700 years. Sephardic means Spanish. It is said that in the 10th century A.D., around 960, the Khazar King Joseph is recorded in manuscript form as having corresponded with a Spanish Israelite Rabbi named Hasdi ibn Sharprut. Ibn Hasdi was the chief Minister of the Caliph of Córdoba in Spain. The manuscripts are actually in the Library of Christ Church in Oxford, England and in the Leningrad Public Library.

Israelites and Muslims mixed freely in Cordoba. The Khazarian King told Hasdai that the Khazars converted to Judaism in the 8th century A.D. after listening to the representatives of the three major faiths, Islam, Judaism and Christianity. The Khazarian interpretation of the Hebraic faith and laws required some reinvention. They called it **Judaism.** It apparently had little to do with the Israelite mindset. The king informed Rabbi Hasdai that the **Khazars** were of

Jewish descent. He had mandated that his genealogy be studied and he found that the **Khazars** could be traced directly to Japheth, the son of Noah in the Abraham tradition. "Know That We Are Descended from Japheth, through his son Togarmah. I have found in the genealogical books of my ancestors that Togarmah had ten sons... The seventh Khazar... I am a descendent of Khazar, the seventh son." In Jewish literature Togarmah is the founder of the Turks.

There is always someone who is going to give you a hard time. Apparently the experts think that his genealogy was somewhat flawed. Apparently Japheth had a son named Gomer who had a son named Togarmah who had a son named Khazar. The king jumped two generation. He may have been one of those speed readers. You can miss things pretty easily that way. The other experts claim that the **Khazars** were actually descended from the family of Magog, who was another son of Japheth. They don't seem to disagree that he was a descendant of Noah's.

The **Sephardic Jews** were forced out in 1481 when the Spanish Inquisition was established. Many of them were rather wealthy and scholarly and found their way to Holland which had a large navy and was involved in international commerce. They formed a much smaller community than the Ashkenazi Jews. The **Sephardic** wealth played a significant role in the foundation of the **Bank of Amsterdam** in 1609. The bank was very solvent and the money deposited was backed by the government. Banking had taken a great step forward. It was a new era. The **florin** became the standard currency, much as the dollar is today. Dutch financiers, including the Sephardic people, opened the **Bank of England in** 1694. These banks had the backing of the aristocratic classes and were the foundation stones of modern Western banking. The **Ashkenazi Jews** also contributed to opening these landmark banks.

The **Khazar** entourage having moved into Italy and Europe, we can proceed with the play. I'm told that the Crusades would not have been possible without the banking and financing of the Italians. The first three Crusades from 1063 to 1123 facilitated the consolidation of a wealthy ruling class, a banking class. These families grew extremely wealthy. One of the families that you have heard about is the **Medicis.** These families became known as the **Black Nobility** because of their brutal use of assassination, murder, bankruptcy, kidnapping, rape and whatever other dastardly deed that you can think of. They grew very powerful and very wealthy.

They would be useful to England. In 1600 I to do Queen Elizabeth I chartered the **East India Company** which was later renamed **United Company of Merchants of England Trading to the East Indies** in 1708. It was disbanded in 1873. The English grew the poppyseed initially in England and then later grew a great deal of it in Asia and engaged in a very active opium trade. The oligarchs of Genoa and Venice had a monopoly on trading rights since the 12th century. The **East India Company** needed them. At least a few dozen members of the **Black Nobility** became shareholders of the East India company and would later become members of the **Committee of 300**.

We've seen that the **Guelph** family is in the genealogy of the British Royal family. The **Guelphs** and the **Black Nobility** are said to have been with the Normans who conquered England in the 11th century and who supported William of Orange in the seizure of the throne of England. This laid the groundwork for the formation of the Bank of England and the East India Company which brought vast wealth and power to England for the next 200 years.

The **Guelphs** grew from their local Italian control of banking and international trade. The largest investment fund was the endowment of the **Basilia of St. Mark** which was closely associated with the Venetian state treasury. The wealthy Italian families put their money in it. There was so much money in it that it apparently formed the nucleus for opening the Bank of Amsterdam in the seventeenth century, followed by the creation of the Bank of England which dominated European finances in the eighteenth century. I guess that these **Sephardic** Jews and the **Ashkenazi** Jews collaborated in this undertaking. The Guelphs extended their Venetian and Roman influences northerly to Florence in Lombardy. So important was their influence that they became known as the **Lombards.** The Lombards were the bankers of the entire medieval world. They later moved their operations to Hamburg, Amsterdam and finally to London.

.

Oligarchies may just simply evolve in the **natural order.** It may have nothing to do with being evil from the start. Once you are there, you have to start thinking about your future and what use can be made of all this wealth and power. **Conspiracy theorists (CTs)** follow the evolution of this process. They conclude that their *modus operandi* is to cause division between parties, create chaos and instability leading to unemployment, economic depression with resultant wars and famine. Or maybe the war comes first?

119

It should be noted that there are many powerful Italian banks. The Banca del la Sviazzeria Itatiana handles flight capital investments to and from the United States and is located in Lugano, Switzerland. That is a pretty safe harbor and above scrutiny. The Bianca d'Italia works very closely with the European Central Bank. Bianca Monte Dei Paschi Di Siena is one of the most important banks and the Banca Di Roma is a long-distance bank for enterprises and firms.

The **Black Nobility** has really controlled the destiny of the Western world. The **Rothschild** family has been very influential and I'm going to spend some time in viewing how they have influenced the Western world. But first I'm going to highlight the names of banking families that have had an enormous influence. Many of them are nearing the thousand year mark. That may be where Hitler got his idea.

The **Oppenheimers** of gold and diamond mining fame. The **Sassoons**, opium producers in India. The **Goldsmids** and **Mocattas**, bullion merchants. **Montefiores**, purveyors of financial services to the Genoese nobility. There is a long list of the prominent banking families: **Warburg, Schiff, Meyer, Loeb, Radziwill, deMenil, Spadafora, Schroeder, von Thurn und Taxis, Wittlesbach, Lambert, Hambro, Luzzatto, Orsini and Weill.** By marriages and by recruitment many of these families show their power through the **Astors, Cabots, Russells, Morgans, Harrimans, Rockefellers** and **Belmonts.**

The name of **Rothschild** first appears in 1577. Mayer Amschel Rothschild (1744-1812), founder of the **House of Rothschild,** reveals something of his understanding of the world, "let me issue and control a nation's money and I care not who writes the laws." Some say that the family name was changed from Bauer. I'm certainly not going to take the time to try to find that out. The Houses of Rothschild flourished in London, Paris, Naples and Frankfurt. They kept financial ventures in family hands, so they could be said to have formed their own **Secret Society (SS).** Their banking structure was diversified, establishing branches in various centers around the world.

The **Rothschild** financial dynasty originated in Frankfurt, Germany. Although known as **Ashkenazi Jews** we know that they are **Khazars.** Five lines of the Austrian branch of the family were elevated to Austrian nobility, being given the hereditary titles of **Barons of the Habsburg Empire** in 1816. **Queen Victoria** elevated the Rothschilds to British nobility by giving them two hereditary titles of **Baronet** in

1847 and **Baron** in **1885.** The wealth has been spread out amongst hundreds of descendants who are heavily involved in the financial world and the necessary raw materials of the world that allow people to survive.

The Rothschilds were preeminent in the gold bullion trade prior to the Napoleonic Wars (1803-1815) and used their network to finance the British. They contributed an enormous sum, then upon hearing about the victory at Waterloo, Nathan Mayer Rothschild bought up the British and/or French government bonds and sold them two years later at a 40% profit. This was an enormous sum.

      Nathan Mayer Rothschild established N.M. Rothschild & Sons in London in 1811. He also financed the Prussian government in 1818. Nathan Mayer Rothschild is now the man who is quoted as saying, "I care not what puppet is placed upon the throne of England to rule the Empire on which the sun never sets. The man who controls Britain's money supply controls the British Empire, and I control the British money supply." The 19th century also saw the Rothschilds funding the **De Beers** enterprise, the **Rio Tinto** mining company, the creation of **Rhodesia** and the **Russo-Japanese War.**

The Rothschild family developed close relations with the **Vatican Bank** in the early 19th century. The Rothschild family is quite diversified and is omnipresent in the financial and industrial empires of the world. They have earned it with good management and a good work ethic. Of course they still belong to the human race and we will probably find that they have been involved in both good and bad. We'll see if Lord Acton's saying applies, "Power corrupts absolutely, and absolute power corrupts absolutely." I've already forgotten the exact quote, but you get the general idea.   There are many descendants who have distinguished themselves in many fields. I'm wondering why they don't have a large fan base. After all cricket, soccer and tennis champions are given rave accolades?

The **Rothschilds** have evolved into a dynasty which includes the families of **Astor, duPont, Kennedy, Morgan, Oppenheimer, Rockefeller, Sassoon, Schiff, Taft and Bundy.** Of course there are many conspiratorial stories involving all of these people. Mayer Amschel Rothschild is said to have been the power behind **Adam Weishaupt** who is given the credit for the creation of the **Illuminati.** The *Illuminati* was founded by a Jesuit student, **Adam Weishaupt,** in 1776. He apparently was critical of the church and governmental abuses and was an advocate of greater liberty and equality. His supporter was Ernest II, Duke of Saxe-Gotha-Altenburg of the house **Wettin**. Many researchers feel that the *Bavarian Illuminati* was controlled by the Jesuits. The **Illuminati** is said to play a very important role in the network of **Secret Societies.**

The **conspiracy theorists** keep mentioning the power of the **Illuminati**, but it must really be a very **secret society** since it is mentioned everywhere and by everyone but it's like an ether, you can't touch it, and if you even see it, it's immediately gone. It's really given me a headache.

The **CTs** believe that the **Illuminati's** mission was to divide the **goyim** (non-Jews) by using their political, economic, social and religious institutions in such a way as to destroy them. Is that pure **meshugana** (crap, bull, craziness)? I'm going to have to use that Yiddish term more frequently, since we are surrounded by it. The conspiracy theory is that Mayer Amschel Rothschild told Weishaupt to infiltrate the Continental Order of **Freemasons**, explain the Illuminati philosophy, and establish other Masonic lodges. **Weishaupt** is said to have recruited over 2000 people in educational, scientific, financial, industrial, artistic and intellectual people who were introduced to the methodology of subversion. You start by bribing or blackmailing people or converting people if you're lucky. Focus on colleges and universities and control the propaganda possibilities of the press. Recruit people into government positions and placed the faithful into that government.

The Bavarian authorities discovered one of **Weishaupt's** communications in written form and outlawed the *Bavarian Illuminati*. Apparently Weishaupt and his disciple Xavier Zwack were involved in a conspiracy with Robespierre. The existence of this conspiratorial material seems to be backed up by the publication of the Bavarian government in 1786 of the *"The Original Writings of The Order and Sect of The Illuminati."* This apparently was sent to the heads of church and state throughout Europe. So it does appear that the **Illuminati** did exist. The **Bavarian Illuminati was banned.** An influential group of people apparently were given umbrage by the **Freemasons at that time.** Professor John Robison of the University of Edinburg published a book in 1798, *"Proofs of a Conspiracy Against All the Religions and Governments of Europe Carried on in the Secret Meetings of Freemasons, Illuminati and Reading Societies."* Robison stated that he learned about this when, as a high degree Mason in the Scottish Right of Freemasonry, Weishaupt had given him a copy of his conspiracy manual.

The **Rothschilds** opened the **First Bank of the United States** in 1791 with a 20 year charter. In 1811 the charter was not renewed. The war of 1812 ensued with the Rothschilds' backing. But in 1816 the Rothschilds are given control of the **Second Bank of the United States** with a 20 year charter, but President Andrew Jackson put an end to that. The **Rothschild/Schiff** financial group would have to await the formation of the **Federal Reserve**. It's a private banking system. It's not federal at all, and although they require that all of the banks have reserves, they have none. The public has never been allowed to see their books and it is estimated that they make over $100 billion per year in profit.

In 1875 **Jacob Schiff** took control of **Kuhn, Loeb & Company** and financed the **Goulds, John D. Rockefeller's** Standard Oil, Edward **Harriman's** Railroad Empire, including the Union Pacific Railroad and the Southern Pacific Railroad, and the **Drexels** and the **Biddles**.

Jacob Schiff apparently was instrumental in founding the **NAACP**, allegedly to create discord. He also helped to set up the **Anti-Defamation League (ADL)** allegedly to protect any attack on the Rothschilds. Or you could just interpret that as a good guy who wanted everybody to be treated fairly. There are a lot of scary stories involving this particular fellow.

The **CTs** feel that the Rothschilds encouraged the division of the North and the South that led to the **American Civil War** for their own financial benefits. They also wanted to lend money to **Lincoln** at a 40% rate. They must not have been very happy when Lincoln *printed his own money*. **Lord John Maynard Keynes**, here I come! **Lord Keynes** would later say, "there is no subtler, no surer means of overturning the existing basis of society than to debauch the currency. The process engages all the hidden forces of economic law on the side of destruction, and does it in a manner which not one man in a million is able to diagnose."

You have to learn to move in and out of all these different conspiracy theories which are *almost always* germinating from seeds of truth. Congressman **Charles A. Lindbergh** revealed the content of the **Bankers Manifesto of 1892**, "We must proceed with caution and guard every move made, for the lower order of people are already showing signs of restless commotion. Prudence will therefore show a policy of apparently yielding to the popular will until our plans are so far consummated that we can declare her designs without fear of any organized resistance. The Farmers Alliance and Knights of Labor organizations in the United States should be carefully watched by our trusted men, and we must take immediate steps to control these organizations in our interests or disrupt them. At the coming Omaha Convention to be held on July 4th (1892), our men must attend and direct its movement, or else it will be set on foot such antagonism to our designs as may require force to overcome. This at the present time would be premature. We are not yet ready for such a crisis. *Capital must protect itself in every possible manner through combination (conspiracy) and legislation.* The courts must be called to our aid, debts must be collected, bonds and mortgages foreclosed as rapidly as possible. Went through the process is the law, the *common people* have lost their homes, they will be more tractable and *easily governed through the influence of the strong arm of the government* applied to a central power of *Imperial wealth under the control of the leading financiers.* People without homes will not quarrel with their leaders. History repeats itself in regular cycles. This truth is well-known among our principal men who are engaged in forming an *imperialism of the world.* While they are doing this, the people must be kept in a state of political antagonism. The question of *tariff reform* must be urged through the organization known as the Democratic Party, and the question of protection with the reciprocity must be forced to view through the Republican Party. By thus *dividing voters*, we can get them to expand their energies in fighting over questions of no importance to us, except as teachers to the common herd. Thus, *by discrete action*, we can secure all that has been so generously planned and successfully accomplished." Well, that seems pretty clear.

The **Rothschilds** purchased the **Reuters** news agency towards the end of the 19th century, recognizing that there was increasing need for control of the news media. They also have influence over **Wolff** in Germany and **Havas** in France. **US Congressman Oscar Callaway** accused **J.P. Morgan** of being just a front for the **Rothschilds** and his having taken over the media industry, "In March, 1915, the J.P. Morgan interests, the steel, shipbuilding, and powder interest, and their subsidiary organizations, got together twelve men been high up in the newspaper world and employ them to select the most influential newspapers in the United States and sufficient number of them to control generally the policy of the daily press – – – – They found it was

124

only necessary to purchase the control of twenty-five of the greatest papers – – – An agreement was reached. The policy of the papers was bought, to be paid for by the month, an editor was furnished for each paper to properly supervise and edit the information regarding the questions of preparedness, militarism, financial policies, and other things of national and international nature considered vital to the interests of the purchasers."

I believe that it was in the 1930s that a Rockefeller did the same thing. I'll let you know later on.

The *Sphere of Influence* of the **Rothschild** family has been enormous. I'll just list a few examples. The Rothschilds were influential in the **Zionist** movement to create Israel. They were also active during the days of Hitler. The Rothschilds controlled **I. G. Farben** which was a leading producer of chemicals in the world and the largest producer of steel. That company used slave labor in the concentration camps and created the lethal Zyklon B gas that was used to exterminate the Jews.

Prescott Bush, father of future American presidents, had his company seized in 1942 under the, *"Trading With The Enemy" Act.* In 1987 Edmund de Rothschild created the *World Conservation Bank* which was designed to transfer debts from Third World countries, and in return the countries would give their land to the bank. **Kofi Annan**, Secretary-General to the United Nations is married to a Rothschild. Into the 21st century most of the national central banks appeared to be under the influence of the Rothschild family. The exceptions appear to be Iran, North Korea, Sudan, Cuba and Libya.

So we are again faced with that dichotomy, that contradiction, that millions of Jews have been sacrificed and continue to be viewed as victims, while their elite controls the world's international monetary systems with tremendous political clout. Who would've thunk it?

I'll try to finish up with the **Guelphs** shortly. In the 12th-century there were two very powerful families in Germany. The **Welfs** controlled Bavaria in Southeast Germany. The capital was Munich. Their Italianized name was **Guelphs.** Their rivals were the **Hohenstaufens** who were located in the southwest corner of Germany, in Swabia. Their family castle was named **Weibling**, which Latinized became **Ghibellines.** The **Guelphs** were in the main the republican, commercial, burgher party. The Guelphs came from wealthy mercantile families. The **Ghibelline's** wealth was based on agricultural estates. They represented the old feudal aristocracy of Italy.

The King of Italy, **Frederick I Barbarossa**, attempted to conquer and rule Italy in the 12th century. He was crowned Holy Roman Emperor in 1155. This was a time when the Pope had great temporal power, but the papacy was about to lose it. The Royals were taking the power away from the pope. They even had two popes at one time. **Frederick** was hampered in his four or five invasions of Italy by stubborn resistance and the fact that he had to constantly put out fires in Germany. **Frederick** had the **Ghibellines** as part of his army.

The Lombard league and its allies, defending the liberties of the urban communes against the Emperor's encroachment, were known as **Guelphs**. Apparently the Italian and the German fusion of families became known as *the Guelphs.* **The Guelphs** supported the Pope. Genoa and Florence were Guelph cities. Milan, Florence and Lucca were under the Guelph protection. Naples and Sicily were under the influence of the Holy See. Venice stood apart. Siena, Pavia, Pisa were under the influence of the **Ghibellines** who were enemies of the papacy.

Frederick had great deal of trouble with the popes as well as with the Italian cities. The German Imperial power failed after many battles. The struggle ended with the triumph of the Guelphs and Florence. The Guelphs finally defeated the Ghibellines in 1289 at Campaldino and Caprano. The Ghibellines later came to power. Went back and forth, but it was mostly at a political level. Both families were involved in all the intrigue and wars in Europe until western Europe, excluding the German Empire, was united in 1815. The German Empire was conquered in 1918 along with the Russian Empire and the Ottoman Empire during World War I. The thousand year war between the Guelphs and Ghibellines finally concluded with the Axis defeat in World War II and the introduction of nuclear weapons.

I've chosen the house of **Guelph** as a model for how powerful one family could be. I have a list of twenty-two **families** associated with the **Black Nobility**. They still have enormous power. I'll just name a few which you have probably heard of: **Guelph, Hanover, Grosvenor, Habsburg, Orsini, Farnese, Wettin, Liechtenstein, Hohenzollern, Bourbon, Orange, Grimaldi, Nassau** and **Savoy.**

The most powerful of the **Black Nobility** families are located in Italy, Germany, Switzerland, Britain, Holland and Greece in that order. Their roots may be traced back to the Venetian oligarchs, who are of **Khazar** extraction, and married into those Royal houses in the early part of the 12th century. The house of **Guelph** or **Windsor** in England is the most important, followed by the house of **Hanover** in Germany. Then there is the house of Grimaldi in Monaco, the house of Habsburg in Germany, the house of Savoy in Italy, the house of Orange in the Netherlands, the house of Lichtenstein in Lichtenstein. Apparently all the powerful people and institutions are linked to the House of Hanover with an underpinning of the House Guelph or Windsor. Small world isn't it? Like I always say, "powerful people only talk to powerful people, why should they do otherwise?"

Ultimately the real power is the control of raw materials. The **Black Nobility** has concentrated much of its wealth in the ownership and distribution of tangible property such as land, raw materials, oil, precious metals and minerals. They certainly control the commodity markets. We know that the **City of London Corporation** oversees the principal commodity exchanges which are located in London. The price of precious metals comes under their regulation. We'll speak about them a bit later.

The descendants of the **Black Nobility** reads like the *Who's Who* in the social register: the **Rothschilds, Kuhns, Loebs, Lehmans, Rockefellers, Sachs, Warburgs, Lazards, Leafs, Goldmans, Schiffs, Morgans, Schroeders, Bushs, Harrimans, Giustinianas, Hambros, Luzzatos, Ortolanies.** And let's not forget some of their influence on the Popes. The Medici Popes, Pius XII (Eugenio Pacelli) and Pope John Paul II were **Khazars**.

The powerful **Black Nobility** families have spawned powerful families essentially controlling the international banking and financing of the world, including the *United States Federal Reserve* banking system. The usual names come to mind: **Rockefellers, Rothschilds, Warburgs, St. Clairs, Astors, Oppenheimers, duPonts.** Let's not forget their involvement in the distribution of information. Reuters is still owned by the Rothschilds.

It's time to look at the "power player organizations" of the world. No matter how you try you'll find all these organization veiled in secrecy. So they naturally have to come under the category of **Secret Societies (SS)**. When you think of it "every organization" is a secret

127

society since it's working operation is always kept very secretive. Perhaps we should refer to **secret societies** as just plain old **private clubs**? Meanwhile we still can have some fun calling them **No Good Organizations (NGOs)**.

Let's have a little fun as we go along. First of all I would ask the question of why it is so difficult to illuminate a group that is called the **Illuminati**? We know that the Jesuits were given the *coup de grace* at that time, and that Weishaupt had been trained by the Jesuits. Ergo, the Jesuits are the force behind the **Illuminati**, and so, if the **Illuminati** is the force behind all the **secret societies,** then the **Jesuits** control the **secret societies** and hence the world. How do you like that for a great example of a **post hoc,** cause-and-effect, fallacy. In this investigation there are times where you do find a good deal of facts to support, at least somewhat, our wish **to jump to conclusions.** Since there are often few facts available, it is easy to conclude that **conspiracy theorists** are all *paranoid.*   Since we've gone this far together I'm just going to share some of the material that I've found which is either very questionable or very funny. But at least it will give you a good idea how wealth and ideologies impact the cultures that we know today. *Illusion, fun* or *fact?*

Some people think that the **Illuminati** was an 18th-century item which lasted only a few years and then vanished. Others think that it's composed of the **Masons,** the **Vatican** and the **Black Nobility.** Some think that it is the brains behind all the other organizations. Others think that the **Committee of 300** is the top dog. Others think that the **Round Table** is the prime mover. David Icke the says that it was formed in the late nineteenth century in London by **Cecil Rhodes** and is *"the Illuminati's operational center."*

Let's get right into the **Conspiracy Theorists'** version of the **Illuminati.** The **Knights Templar** are said to be the driving influence at the highest level of all the secret societies involved in the **Illuminati.** During my investigation I stumbled upon the writings of William Cooper in his article written in 1997 about **MAJESTYTWELVE** and his effort to cast some illumination on the philosophy of **Illuminism.** He states that the **Illuminati** refers to the combination of fraternal orders and secret societies, whose religion is based upon the *worship of Lucifer and the Sun.* The Coordinating Powers are found with the **Rockefeller** family and their Wall Street sidekicks in the United States, and with the **Rothschilds'** circle of friends both on Wall Street and in Europe. Cooper says that these two circles of influence use the secret societies by keeping them busy with reasonable projects without ever revealing the real purpose of the organization. People are really groupies so that is pretty understandable, and it's a real honor to be invited into any of those organizations. I can understand that.

Cooper is definitely against the goal of the **New World Order** as he states that the secret societies have goals of eliminating religion, nation states and private property, with the aim of themselves owning and controlling everyone and everything. That is a real mouthful. I certainly would like to be invited to join either the *Golden Order of Rockefeller* or the *Golden Order of Rothschild*. But, alas, that will never happen. But to have been born at another time and at another place!

The Round Table, the Royal Institute of International Affairs, the Church of Saint John the Divine, the Council on Foreign Relations, the Jason Society, the Skull and Bones Society, the Scroll and Key Fraternity, the highest Degrees of the New York and Scottish Rights of Freemasonry, the Ancient Order of Rosicrucians, and many other organizations make up the **Illuminati (Brotherhood),** with the **Knights Templar** behind the throne.

Cults and symbols go back thousands of years. This is all built into the secret societies. And it is impossible for a neophyte to try to understand any of it. And the fool, like myself, certainly can't begin to deal with it. So it is nice to see Cooper simplifying all of this, "Adam and Eve were held prisoners in the bonds of ignorance by an unjust and vindictive God in that Garden of Eden. They were set free from the chains by Lucifer (Prometheus chose through his agent Satan in the guise of a servant (ancient symbol of Wisdom) with the gift of Intellect (Fire)." Hence the origin of **Illuminati** – – Intellect, Light, Illumination – – the Enlightened One. I am now the enlightened one, and very appreciative of Cooper's efforts to give a concise understanding of all of this. But I'm not sure that anyone who is a current member of the *Golden Order of Rockefeller* or the *Golden Order of Rothschild* knows of the origin of all of this stuff. Most of them are probably tough powerbrokers without degrees in ethics and philosophy. The *Golden Ethereal Order of Jesuits* is said to be the third powerful order. I wonder if they believe in *Lucifer?*

Cooper makes a big point that the people at the top surround themselves with a bunch of fools and feast on their *naïveté*. He makes a point that the **Illuminati** has used **Karl Marx** as a beacon of light. If you have some time to look up this article on the Internet, you will find that he is very entertaining as he weaves mystical interpretations into the movies *Star Wars* and *The Lion King*. He goes on to state that the, "Apollo Space mission was carefully rehearsed and then filmed in large sound stages at the Atomic Energy Commission's Top Secret test site in the Nevada Desert and in a secured and guarded sound stage at the Walt Disney Studios within which was a huge scale mock-up of the moon." "All names, missions, landing sites, and events in the Apollo Space Program are the so-called metaphors, rituals, and symbolism of the **Illuminati's** secret religion." Cooper feels that the entire **NASA** space program defies any realistic understanding of physics and certainly of astrophysics. He goes on to give many examples of distorted reportings and interpretations of events which are all manifestations of the facilitation of tyranny.

Cooper does give a concise narration and interpretation of events that particularly concern the conspiracy theorists who feel that the secret societies are indeed conspiratorial. It really is worth the time. He certainly has a lot of facts which force you to go into your closet and dust off your **critical thinking** hat.

I read one of John Coleman's books about secret societies and conspiratorial theories. He apparently is a graduate of MI6 and spent years in his research in libraries and museums around the world, years in the British Museum and the library in Alexandria. He does have a lot of good solid stuff. But dotting the I's and crossing the T's is next to impossible with such an intertwined group of organizations and power people. I'm going to do my best to give you some highlights and some good solid information which you can use to see if your government, your political organizations and their espoused ethical philosophies are leading you down the so-called primrose path. I especially enjoy using terms like the *primrose path*. It actually means "a course of action that seems easy and appropriate but can actually end in calamity," which might be accompanied by a good deal of music in reference to the musical comedy *Primrose* or the violinist *William Primrose.* I have to have some fun while doing this. It can get quite depressing.

So here is a list of the ***power player organizations*** that I will be covering: **Committee of 300, Illuminati, Jesuits, Knights of Malta, Tavistock Institute, Club of Rome, Trilateral Commission, Round Table, Royal Institute of International Affairs, Council of Foreign Relations, Bilderberg Group, Masons,** and the **Knights Templar.** If I get exhausted I'll drop one or two of these **NGOs** from the list. I still find it difficult to understand why the **Round Table** network is an expression of the **Illuminati**. It may become clearer, so let's go on.

We'll move on to the **Committee of 300**. They are called the **Olympians**, but that name appears to be a bit inappropriate since everybody knows that they were only **12 Gods** in Greek mythology who were all related in some way to the supreme God, **Zeus**. I'm jumping ahead but apparently a lot of people involved in the study of **Secret Societies (SS)** say that the **Zeus** in the **Committee of 300** is **Queen Elizabeth II**. John Coleman says that the **Committee of 300** is modeled after the **British East India Company's Council of 300** which was founded by the British aristocracy in 1727. The **Black Nobility's** shares in this company were not insignificant.. The British and **Black Nobility** families fell into the addiction to *untold* and unbelievable wealth as their customers fell into the addiction of opium. It is said that the committee was established early in the 19th century, although it did not take on its present form until 1897, when the China opium trade was legalized. It is rather strange that I haven't found references to any of the locations where they meet. I did find one... on **Queen Elizabeth II's** boat. They must have employed **Royal carrier pigeons**, diplomats and later the telegraph to chitchat about world affairs. It may be extraordinary for them to have any meetings at all, what with **Skype** and teleconferencing.

There appears to be a reliance on a "few written words" that such an organization actually exists. **Walther Rathenau,** who was the financial advisor to the **Rothschilds,** wrote in the *Neue freie Presse* in 1909, "only 300 men, each of whom knows all the others, govern the fate of Europe. They select their own successors from their own entourage. These men have the means in their hands of putting an end to the form of state which they find unreasonable." Six months later he was assassinated.

We have been told that "**new money**" is gone by the third-generation. This is absolutely not true of "**old money**." The **old** families truly understand how to hold onto power and wealth. The **Committee of 300** and the **Black Nobility** have infiltrated every aspect of human life, and control the financial institutions and governments with calculated intermarriages and "*agreements.*" They have survived way past three generations.

Warren Buffett really turns out to be a fool if you think in these terms, as well as **Bill Gates,** if they're going to spend all their money and not leave it to their progeny to challenge the **Black Nobility.** Of course both Warren Buffett and Bill Gates are already named in these **SS.** You can understand how difficult it is to make sense of all of this when you keep stumbling into contradictions.

One thing is certain. Powerful people do not spend any time with the riff-raff. They are in the business of growth and development and don't want to stumble into failure. So many of the same influential and powerful people, together with businesses and organizations, belong to several of these elitist clubs. The inner core of several of them amounts to 100 to 150 people. It's obvious that they are doing business. It would be sheer *fool*ishness for them to become *fools* like myself, the ultimate *fool.*

Who are these people who belong to this real or mythical committee? You can find their names on the Internet. Recent members of the **Committee of 300** are **Queen Elizabeth II, William Waldorf Astor-4th Viscount Astor,** Silvio Berlusconi, Ben Bernake, Warren Buffett, George H. W. Bush, Milibands, David Cameron, Prince Charles of Wales, **4 De Rothschilds,** Jacob Rothschild-4th Baron Rothschild, **Alan Greenspan,** John Kerry, Colin Powell, **3 Rockefellers,** Paul Volcker, **George Soros** and right below him in the alphabetized list I find Arlen Specter. Surely James Bond will save us from the evils of George Soros, one of the villains associated with *SPECTRE (Special Executive for Counter-intelligence, Terrorism, Revenge and Extortion).* **George Soros** is truly a villain in the **globalization** scheme involved in his hoped for **New World Order.** He is is said to be involved in the financial world of the **Rothschilds.**

The name of **Henry Kissinger** comes up as a member of all the **NGOs.** Since he is on center stage most of the time I am forced to conclude that he is the front man, the so-called hired gun, and not the *deus ex machina.* I was surprised to find **John Kerry**'s name on the list. His full name is listed as John **Forbes** Kerry. I had no idea that he would be considered to be so powerful. Massachusetts born people thought that he was Irish. But I find that his paternal grandparents were **Jews...Kohn and Lowe.** He married the **Heinz** money, Teresa Simoes-Ferreira Heinz who is said to be worth in the billion dollar range. His mother was a **Forbes.** There was a rumor that he married into money, but I'm not so sure now. Anyway it's irrelevant. I can just hear you saying, "there's a lot of that in this book."

Madeleine Albright is an Ashkenazi Jew who is a member of the **Committee of 300**. She was interviewed on 60 Minutes by correspondent Lesley Stahl, in reference to the years of United States economic sanctions against Iraq, "We have heard that half a million children have died. I mean, that is more children than died in Hiroshima. And, you know, is the price worth it?" To which Ambassador Albright replied, "I think that is a very hard choice, but the price, we think, the price is worth it." You can always read something sinister into anybody's remarks. Population control is one of the goals of the organizations working towards a **New World Order.** But that question is a beautiful example of a **fallacy** in which you juxtapose two unrelated items and have the *victim* connect them for you. She fell for it. People who don't hold her into high regard have always referred to her level of *brightness.*

We tend to think of **royalty** as figureheads now. That's totally off the mark. A lot of the names of Royal Houses appear on the list of the **Committee of 300**, and their names are there because of wealth, not because of the title. The **Royal Houses** of Britain, Yugoslavia, Belgium, France, Austria, Germany, Denmark, Netherlands, Spain, Italy, Lichtenstein, Luxembourg, Saudi Arabia, Russia and of course the Pope. I do recognize many of these names, but many are unknown to me. But why would a fool be familiar with any of these names?

But I have never heard of **Nicky Oppenheimer** who is the chairman of the **De Beers** diamond mining company. He apparently sold his 40% interest in **De Beers** to **Anglo American**, a diversified mining company. Surprise! He already owns a good deal of **Anglo American.** When you want to follow the money, that is one that is fairly easy to track. But it gives you an idea of what these people have in their pockets when they get included in a list like this. But he's a relatively poor man, his net worth is somewhere in the vicinity of $6 billion. The opium money was moved into the **gold, oil and diamond businesses.**

Some say that **Queen Elizabeth II,** or the **Round Table,** or the **Committee of 300 is** at the top of the pyramid controlling the government and financial institutions of the world. Others say that it is the **Illuminati** which controls the world through **Freemasonry,** the **Vatican,** and the **Black Nobility.** As we go along you will see that they are all interrelated, and no organization or individual person has established a proper right to performing the ritual of a *proskynesis* to the Queen.

Some feel that **Queen Elizabeth II** controls the <u>City of</u> <u>London Corporation</u>. "**The City**" is the puppeteer of international financial and business services. It's said that the City of London pays its people about $100,000 per year with unlimited expenses, but they are on a very short leash. They are cut loose if they make any mistakes. It is indeed the center of *global finance. The London Stock Exchange, Lloyd's of London* and the **Bank of England** are all in "*the city.*" 500 or more banks are also located there. It is also the largest foreign exchange market and a world leader in the insurance industry. It might be said that whoever controls "*the city*" controls the world. "**The City**" is said to be *Madame, la Directrice,* pointing to tax havens, and as polite as she is, directing the ill-gotten gains of the drug barons. Of course that's when you get into *hyperbole* in dealing with all of these **SSs**.

"**The City**" is a very small territorial part of London City, just a square mile of space, but it is very influential and the English Parliament has no authority over it. It actually imposes its will on the House of Commons. It's lobbyist, called "*remembrancer*" sits behind the speaker's chair. I like it, this is fun. "**The City**" has twenty-five electoral wards, twenty-one of them are controlled by a banking corporations. There are actually 108 livery companies that vote. The forces *that be* facilitate the voting decisions of the delegates. So "**The City**" is the umbrella over the the **Bank of International Settlements**, the **Federal Reserve,** the **European Central Bank,** the **IMF** and the **World Bank**. This **megacolossus** of bankers furnish the financial regulators who meet regularly as the **Group of Seven (G-7)**, the **Group of Twenty (G-20)** and the **Group of Thirty (G-30)**.

The **G-7** came into being in 1975 when the finance ministers of the US, the UK, France, Germany, Italy, Canada and Japan met. It meets several times a year and and represents 50% of the global GDP. The **G-20** was formed in 1999 and meets once a year. It is composed of the finance ministers and the central bank governors of the US, the UK, France, Germany, Italy, Canada, Japan, Australia, Saudi Arabia, Turkey, Russia, Indonesia, India, South Korea, China, Argentina, Brazil, Mexico, Canada, South Africa and the EU. They represent 84% of the global GDP. The **Rockefeller Foundation** initiated the formation of the **G-30** in 1978. It's supposed to be a private international body. The heads of central banks and major private banks and some academicians discuss issues relevant to foreign exchange, currency, international capital markets, international financial institutions, supervision of central banks and the supervision of financial centers.

It's obviously *very influential* in both the governmental and financial worlds. So you can see that the **Bank of America, Wells Fargo, Lloyd's, Credit Suisse, Société Générale, Deutsche Bank** and the **Imperial banks** of the world all have friends in high places.

We've been following the trail of wealth in the Western world. I hate to figure out what is going on with the rest of the world. These fellows in the West are certainly on the move. But we have not discussed their ethical or philosophical underpinnings, other than materialism. We certainly can't blame them for that, after all we all indulge in that. But there are scores of statements made by members of these groups that cause one to shudder. We'll find some of these quotes as we go along. Meanwhile it is either Icke or Coleman who has put together a list of issues and objectives that the **NGOs.** seem to have in common.

The ultimate goal appears to put together a unified monetary and church system under the aegis of the **New World Order.** The undermining and ultimate destruction of national identities and the powerful religions would have to be facilitated. You can break the back of any manufacturing industry by eliminating tariffs and implementing free trade. In so doing you can increase unemployment and eliminate the middle class. By using drugs and mass propaganda over the media you can convince people that the welfare state is in their best interests.

Limited wars and famine can eliminate the population problem. Keeping the youth focused on movies, music, videos and cellular apps allows you to use all sorts of mind control techniques. The Russian technique of creating crises and manipulating the intensity of these crises keeps people on the defensive. The aim is to penetrate all governments and destroy their sovereign integrity. Giving power to world government institutions such as the *UN, IMF, World Bank, World Courts* will dismantle national sovereignty. **Globalization** and free trade can be used to collapse the economies of the world and create political chaos. Limited global wars and worldwide terrorism is a wonderful way of collapsing nations and the cultures. Finally the penetration and corruption of American education is to be a high priority.

I'm not a member of the **conspiracy theorists**, but I'm seeing this happening. Do you think it's the **natural order** or is a natural order being strong-armed? Do you think that the **Tavistock Institute**, which the **CTs** accuse of being in charge of mind control, is using *Twitter* to

135

undermine world governments?

We'll move on to the **Round Table** which was founded in 1909. **Cecil Rhodes** acquired diamond concessions in South Africa in the latter part of the 19th century. He created an enormous personal fortune which led to the creation of the **De Beers Consolidated Mines Company** in 1888 and of **Consolidated Goldfields.** We know of him because he left the educational endowment which allowed the Brits, the Germans and the Americans to apply for *Rhodes Scholarships* for the express purpose of enabling those countries' future leaders to mingle in an attempt to create an *Anglo-Saxon Empire* across the world. The son of **Baron Lionel Rothschild, Nathaniel Mayer,** funded **Cecil Rhodes** development of the **British South Africa Company** and the **De Beers** diamond conglomerate. He apparently administered Rhodes' estate after his death in 1902.

Cecil Rhodes was to be the impetus behind the formation of the **Round Table** which was to be devoted to "the extension of British rule throughout the world." His goal included the "ultimate recovery of the United States as an integral part of the British Empire" and would culminate in "consolidation of the whole Empire, the inauguration of a system of Colonial Representation in the Imperial Parliament which may tend to weld together the disjointed members of the Empire, and finally the foundation of so great a power as to hereafter render wars impossible and promote the best interests of humanity." That's certainly *a grand design.*

Rhodes was initiated into *Freemasonry* at the Apollo University Lodge No. 357. On April 17, 1877, he was raised to Master Mason in the same lodge. Rhodes also joined a *Scottish Rite Lodge* at Oxford called Prince Rose Croix Lodge No. 30. Later in life he came to view English Freemasonry and its conspiracy as impotent and defunct.

During this period of time **Lionel George Curtis** advocated for British Imperial federalism and a *world state.* His vision influenced the development of the Commonwealth of Nations. He became secretary to **Sir Alfred Milner,** British High Commissioner in South Africa, who founded the quarterly *Round Table.* Lionel Curtis was the empire's leading ideologist around the time of WWI. In 1919 Curtis led a delegation of British and American experts to organize the **Royal Institute of International Affairs**.

In his third will **Rhodes** left his entire estate to **Freemason Lord Nathan Rothschild** as trustee. Rhodes stipulated that his gigantic fortune be used by his disciples to carry out the program he envisioned. **Rothschild** appointed **Freemason Alfred Milner** to head up the Secret Society for which Rhodes' first will made provision. Lord Milner once remarked of himself, "My patriotism knows no geographical but only racial limits. I am a British Race patriot."

Upon his appointment by Rothschild to chair Rhodes's secret society, Milner recruited a group of young men from Oxford and Tonybee Hall to assist him in organizing his administration of the new society. All were respected English Freemasons. Among them were Rudyard Kipling, Arthur Balfour, Lord Rothschild, and some Oxford College graduates known as "Milner's Kindergarten." In 1909, Milner's Kindergarten, with some other English Masons, founded the **Round Table**. The grandfather of all modern British Masonic "think tanks" was born. Ironically, when the society Rhodes had envisioned was finally organized after his death, its membership consisted only of **English Freemasons. "The Round Table,"** as it was known, soon became the most powerful appendage of the British Brotherhood.

Three powerful think tank offshoots of the **Round Table** are (1) the **Royal Institute of International Affairs (RIIA)**, organized in 1919 in London; (2) the **Council on Foreign Relations (CFR)**, organized in 1921 in New York City; and (3) the **Institute of Pacific Relations (IPR),** organized in 1925 for the twelve countries holding territory in what today we call the Pacific Rim. The **Round Table** had a profound influence of these organizations.

We now have a timeline. The **Committee of 300** was organized before the 20th century. The **Round Table** was founded in 1909. The **Tavistock Institute** came into being in 1921 and the **Bilderberg Group** was formed in 1952. The **Council of Rome** stepped to the podium in 1968 and the **Trilateral Commission** was on stage by 1973. But they would be considered Johnny-come-latelys if you consider that the **Society of Jesus** was founded in 1534, and was funded by Francis Borgia, apparently the great-grandson of both Pope Alexander's VI and King Ferdinand II of Aragon. But that is only of importance if you believe that the Jesuits are part of that whole **Illuminati** picture. From a historical point of view it is interesting to note that **Pope Paul III** of the **Black Nobility** Farnese family saved **St. Ignatius of Loyola** from persecution by the Inquisition in 1527.

It's time to look at the **Tavistock Institute of Human Relations**. **Wellington House** first opened its doors in 1913 in London. **Lord Northcliffe was** the director. The future director of studies at the **Royal Institute of International Affairs, Arnold Toynbee,** was assisted by **Walter Lippmann** and **Edward Benays,** who was the nephew of **Sigmund Freud. Lord Northcliffe** was related to the **Rothschilds** by marriage. The British Royal family, the **Rockefellers** and the **Rothschilds** appear to have funded the organization. The goal was to create a proper public opinion during a time of trouble. They seem to be involved in finding a way to treat "shell shock" during the war. This appears to be a rather **secretive** organization and people trying to study it indicate that it is all very confusing.

It's said that that the **Tavistock Clinic** opened in 1920 and embraced a wide range of psychological approaches. The Duke of Bedford, **Marquis of Tavistock,** donated the building to the Institute in 1921 to study the effect of shell shock on British soldiers, hence the name. In 1946 or 1947 some of the members were studying military issues and founded the **Tavistock Institute of Human Relations.** The Institute was to study issues having to do with society and organizations. Some people feel that it's been very influential in developing propaganda strategies and some of their brainwashing techniques were used by Korea during the war. It continues to be active in behavioral science research.

It may be that their research is done in conjunction with universities, foundations, even with the CIA and perhaps some of those secret societies. The **conspiracy theorists** feels that they have been working on ways of breaking down family units and societal cultures. We know that many countries are involved in these types of research. One of them may be this Institute. We often find, rather belatedly, that much research has been done which we would never approve of, *had we known*.

VII

20th CENTURY WEALTH & POWER

We have covered about 2000 years in our attempt to understand how our financial institutions have grown so powerful and where the wealth has been secured. The ideas and organizations which came into being around the time of the **League of Nations** would lead us on a new cultural path with a further concentration of wealth and power in the hands of the **Black Nobility. Woodrow Wilson** was the President of the United States from 1913 to 1921. He pushed through the *Federal Reserve Act, Federal Trade Commission Act,* the *Clayton Antitrust Act,* the *Federal Farm Loan Act* and then the *income tax.* He also became an advocate of women's suffrage. He was the epitome of the modern liberal. Following the armistice of World War 1 he went to Paris in 1919 to try to create the *League of Nations* and shape the *Treaty of Versailles.* He became famous for his *Fourteen Points* which **Walter Lippmann** helped him draft. The Senate rejected the Treaty of Versailles.

President Woodrow Wilson asked Walter Lippmann to put together a group of scholars who would work on drafting the League of Nations Constitution. **Walter Lippmann** was one of the founding editors of "*The New Republic.*" His view of the voters was that they were "largely ignorant about issues and policies and lacked the confidence to participate in public life." He was awarded two Pulitzer prizes although he referred to the masses as the "the welded herd," who must be governed by "a specialized class whose interests reach beyond the locality." He favored the *Fabian Society* that was being promoted by socialists like **Beatrice Webb, Sidney Webb, H. G. Wells** and **George Bernard Shaw.** In 1908 he and eight other Harvard students organized the *Intercollegiate Socialist Society (I SS),* a coordinating body founded by such people as Jack London, Upton Sinclair, Norman Thomas and Clarence Darrow. Quite famous people. In 1910 he came under the influence of **Graham Wallas.**

In 1917 **Lippmann** started working for Woodrow Wilson. **Edward M. House** and he helped to draft the *Fourteen Points Peace Programme.* Walter Lippmann, a 28 year old Harvard graduate, recruited scholars who were to assemble the data that they thought necessary to make the world safe for democracy. **Edward M. House** was Wilson's national security advisor. Walter Lippmann said, "We are skimming the cream of the younger and more imaginative scholars." These scholars were referred to as *"The Inquiry."* Only 23 of them made it to Paris because of space limitations on the presidential cruiser. They met with the British and continued their relationship once they returned home.

A former Secretary of State under Theodore Roosevelt, Elihu Root, introduced the young group of scholars to an influential club of New York financiers and international lawyers. This select group called itself the **Council on Foreign Relations**. It began with 108 members of high-ranking officers of banking, manufacturing, and trading, together with lawyers and representatives of finance companies. There were two conflicting and perhaps parallel objectives, world peace and greater profits. Motivation was lacking and it went dormant for a while.

The scholars of *"The Inquiry"* had envisioned the implementation of **The American Institute of International Affairs** when they were first in Paris. Scholars on both side of the Atlantic wanted this organization to be implemented. They came to recognize that the Atlantic really divided them in more than one way and that they should go their separate ways. So they went their separate ways.**The Royal Institute of International Affairs (RIIA)** is the most influential *think tank* in Europe. Its aim is to promote debate in the international affair arena. The **Rothschilds/Lambert** families of Brussels were influential at its inception. The Lambert family is part of the Rothschilds family. The founder of the Rothschild family stipulated that the power would be with the males, but the females married into many other influential families which allowed a network of financial and political power to extend beyond what the "inconceivable could conceive."

The Institute was initially founded in 1920 and named the British Institute of International Affairs. The Council on Foreign Relations was incorporated a year later in 1921 in the United States. The British Institute changed its name to the Royal Institute of International Affairs in 1926. It is now known by its residential location, the Chatham House. It is linked to the *Brookings Institute* and the *American Enterprise Institute.*

Research is always difficult. I found a quote from the RIIA's Annual Report for 1942-1943, "When the Institute was founded through the inspiration of Mister Lionel Curtis during the Peace

140

Conference of Paris in 1919, those associated with him in laying the foundation from a group of comparatively young men and women." Of course this is the fellow from the Round Table. His boss was Sir Alfred Milner who was playing a hand here; he also had a working relationship with J.P. Morgan & Co. There has always been a close relationship with the Council on Foreign Relations (FRC) in the United States which was controlled by J.P. Morgan & Co. from the very beginning. The Carnegie Foundation was funding the young Americans.

The so-called Milner Group dominated the RIIA during the early years and obviously imbued it with the goals of the Round Table. As we go along we find linkage here, linkage there, linkage everywhere. 23 companies contributed to the RIIA in 1929. Most had a member of the Milner Group on their boards of directors. Some of the names are Rothschilds, Lloyds Bank, Lazard Brothers, Hambros' Bank, Bearing Brothers, Bank of England. Chatham House is heavily funded by companies like AIG, Chevron, Royal Dutch Shell and the money people such as Bloomberg, Morgan Stanley and Goldman Sachs. Memberships and contributions come from many large corporations, institutions and foreign governments.

Chatham House moved to establish branches in the British dominions including India, Canada and Australia. The new organizations always relied on Round Table members to put them together. Chatham House also influenced the *Institutes of Pacific Relations* as well as the *United Nations*. The Milner Group thus has had an enormous amount of power throughout the world. So much power in the hands of such a small group. They are the power behind the RIIA.

We've been talking about the concept of **shadow governments (cryptocracy)** for some time. It's pretty clear that *heavy money* has a great deal of influence on governments, which of course comes from organizations, corporations and individuals. New members of the US Congress never get selected without the money of the *shadow government*. The power is not with the politician but with the *shadow government.*

You should be familiar with the **Chatham House Rule** which allows any guest to discuss the results of the seminar, but never to reveal who attended the seminar or what any individual said. The **RIIA** invites many prominent speakers to speak about their specialty in

141

international affairs so that there is a lot of good information that emanates from the Institute. It's what happens behind closed doors and what their **New World Order** agenda includes that really counts.

So we move on to the Americans side to discuss the **Council on Foreign Relations.** The new **Council on Foreign Relations** was assured of financial support. The money came from **J. P. Morgan, Bernard Baruch, Otto Kahn, Jacob Schiff, Paul Warburg** and **John D. Rockefeller.** The initial membership numbered about 400. Elihu Root, Herbert Lehman, Averill Harriman and John Foster Dulles were there from the beginning. Membership was limited to "high-ranking officers of banking, manufacturing, trading and finance companies, together with many lawyers." Jews were early members, but there were no women. It began as a **Secret Society** since it was very private and confidential. The certificate of incorporation was drawn in 1921. They now have over 4000 members and membership covers people in government, scholars, businessmen, journalists and lawyers. They are said to be interested in government action leading to greater equality around the world.

You'll remember the name of **Jacob Schiff.** He helped to found the *ACLU* and the *Anti-Defamation League.* Prior to his death in 1920 Jacob Schiff helped Bernard Baruch and Colonel Edward Mandel House to found the **Council on Foreign Relations**. Jacob Schiff was a pretty savvy guy who obviously wanted to protect the **Rothschilds'** influence with both the financial and political institutions. The membership was huge and included virtually every powerful American industrialist and banker, as well as their foundations. There would be money available to influence the politicians.

The credit for founding the **CFR** appears to be given to **Edward Mandell House,** He wrote the book *"Philip Dru: administrator."* House was a Marxist whose goal was to socialize the United States,*"Socialism is dreamed of by Karl Marx".* House is given credit for quite a number of accomplishments. He helped to establish the *American Central Back*, known as the *Federal Reserve,* in 1913. **Karl Marx** recommended a graduated income tax; **Edward Mandel House** had it ratified.

CFR attracted men of power. In the 1920s money from the **Rockefeller Foundation** and the **Carnegie Foundation** poured in. In 1940 **President Roosevelt** empowered the **CFR** to work with the State

Department. That gave the Council its enormous power and should have been renamed the **Council on American Governmental Affairs**. With 4000 members in the organization, they regularly provide members, by the dozens or hundreds, to support *standing* and *ad hoc committees* of the US federal government. The **CFR** has seen a *one world socialist system* as superior to the chaos evident in the world. **FDR** has been supportive of this goal. **FDR** had his own agenda, "no country, however rich, can't afford the waste of its human resources. Demoralization caused by vast unemployment is our greatest extravagance. Morally, it is the greatest menace to our social order."

Members of the Council have included Eisenhower, Nixon, Dewey, Stevenson, Kennedy, Hubert Humphrey and McGovern. You've heard of *NBC* and *CBS*, the *New York Times*, the *Washington Post, Time, Newsweek, Fortune* and *Business Week*. Many of their leaders are **members**. *Wall Street* banking interests and the *CIA* directors are regular members of the **CFR**.

Of importance is the **CFR's** dominance over the *Free Press*. John D. Rockefeller set up magazines such as *Life* and *Time*. He financed *Samuel Newhouse* who has a chain of newspapers across the country and bought up the *Washington Post, Newsweek* and *The Weekly Magazine*. The control of radio, television and the motion picture industries were left to the international bankers from **Globe, Goldman Sachs**, the **Warburgs** and the **Lehmans. Governor Nelson Rockefeller** in his 1962 lectures at Harvard University urged the United States to submerge its national identity and its sovereignty to a **new political order. David Rockefeller** is quoted as saying, "The world is now much more sophisticated and prepared to march towards a world government. The supernational sovereignty of an intellectual elite and world bankers is surely preferable to the national auto-determination practiced in the past centuries." We all instinctively realize that the concentration of power in the hands of a few hundred people, in a world populated by a 7 billion people, is going to give anybody the creeps. So let's see what the still small voices crying in the wilderness have to say about this.

Professor Carroll Quigley characterized the **CFR** as "a front group for **J. P. Morgan & Co.** in association with a very small **American Round Table Group**." The **Rockefellers** came to be more influential. Almost all 20th century US Secretaries of State have been members of the **CFR. David Rockefeller's** family donated the land on which the United Nations stands. He has been a **chairman** of the **CFR**.

James Warburg, son of **CFR** founder Paul Warburg, and a member of FDR's brain trust, testified before the Senate Foreign Relations Committee in 1950, "we shall have **world government** whether or not you like it – – by conquest or consent."

I'll include some of the current **CFR** membership names. John Abiz-**US Central Command,** Madeleine Albright-former **Secretary of State, Gates Foundation,** J. Tomilson Hill-the **Blackstone Group,** Shirley Jackson-**Rensselaer Polytechnic Institute,** James Owens-**Caterpillar, Bank of America, Chevron Corporation, Goldman Sachs, J.P. Morgan Chase & Co, Alcoa, Barclays, BP, Citigroup, Credit Suisse, Deutsche Bank, Lazard, Shell, Soros Fund, Anglo-American, Boeing, Duke Energy, Credit Agricole Corporate and Investment Bank, Google, Microsoft, Hitachi, News Corporation, Pepsi, Rothschilds, T. Rowe Price group, Zürich Insurance Group, Banca d'Italia, Michael Bloomberg, Mayor of New York City.** There are also lists of present and past politicians and influential people from around the world. There is also **Karenna Gore Schiff,** daughter of Al Gore. We've already seen that the **Schiff** name appears prominently in the **Rothschild** family. You certainly would be impressed at the number of ex- and current politicians as well as *so-called **thinking*** intellectuals who have joined the ranks. I wonder if **Al Gore** is new to the **Rothschild** bloodline?

We know that **Colonel House** helped to ratify the *Federal Reserve System.* It is easy to see how the *private* American Central Bank can easily be fused with the existing supranational banking cartels. You just need to walk one step into the room to see that the **CFR** has a wonderful view of the oligarchs controlling the manufacturing, petroleum and industrial-military complexes.

Talk about establishing real power. The first **Rothschild World Bank,** "*Bank for International Settlements (BIS)*" was established in Basle, Switzerland in 1930. This *BIS* is not accountable to any government and provides banking services only to central banks. This is a system which is modeled after the *Venetian/Genoese style banking,* called *fondi,* which controls national currency and credit without government interference. *Fondo* means family fortune in Italian, and that's how banking started in Italy. The central banks determine what interest rate will be charged to everyone, including the government. They wield incredible power, and as you know, absolute power corrupts absolutely.

There is always a pecking order. *Dominant investment bankers* really dominate the chief *central bankers* in the world of finance. These "*merchant bankers*" operate out of private banks. The **Rothschilds** built their influence by keeping their banks closed to outsiders. They control the flow of credit and investments on both a national and international scale. You know about the **Libor** scandal. They have the capacity to influence the discount rate and they choose their borrowers carefully, whether they be governments, corporations or private individuals.

Abraham Lincoln was prescient as we view some of his statements, "I see in the near future a crisis approaching that unnerves me and causes me to trouble for the safety of my country. Corporations have been enthroned, an era of corruption in high places will follow, and the money-power of the country will endeavor to prolong its reign by working upon the prejudices of the people until the wealth is aggregated in a few hands and the Republic is destroyed."

And we have seen that **Jacob Schiff's** *ACLU*, mostly comprised of Ashkenazi Jews, has done a number on the Constitution and the moral culture of the United States. We know that the *ACLU* had socialists and communists as its founding members, so that shouldn't surprise us. If you understand that the proponents of a **New World Order** see the disintegration of the American culture and its government as prerequisites to its emergence, then it makes sense. It is probably another example of using naïve, goodhearted people, for a perfidious purpose. Most of the lawyers, about 5000 of them, who work for the *ACLU* are probably well motivated folks. We all know that the leadership of any organization is privy to its own agenda, but uses our own built-in naivety to reach its unstated goal. I like to use redundancies. It makes you feel better.

Under the banners of "*Free Speech* and *Equality* and *Liberty*," you can reduce everything to the absurd so that privacy, free speech and individual achievement can be voluntarily sacrificed to an oppressive regime. Once you frame things in terms of helping and saving people, you can do anything you want. **Michael Bloomberg**, the Mayor of New York City, says that you **can't** sell a soft drink if it's any larger than a few ounces, **can't** eat any calorie filled meal without feeling guilty, **can't** live in an apartment which is larger than 500 ft.^{2}, **can't** cross a bridge without paying at least four dollars, **can't** have you car windows tinted too much ($50 per window), **can't** buy a pack of cigarettes for less than $10, **can't** smoke in any public building, **can't,** can't, can't, etc.... it all gets pretty crazy. Even the august body of the **American Medical Association** has decided that *obesity* is a *disease*. On second thought that does make sense, the **AMA** can manufacture a variety of charges for treating people who have no intention of being treated for the *illusion of a disease*.

In 1988 **Jacob Schiff's** *Anti-Defamation League* initiated a nationwide competition for law students to draft anti-hate legislation for minority groups. The winner of the competition, Joseph Ribacoff, proposed that any words which stimulated suspicion, friction, hate and possible violence must be *criminalized*. That's real **meshugana**. "Be chary of your words, even in jest; beware the *hate police!*"

Felix Frankfurter said, "The real rulers in Washington are invisible and exercise power from behind the scenes." **President Franklin Roosevelt** wrote, "The real truth of the matter is, as you and I know, that a financial element in the large centers has owned the government ever since the days of Andrew Jackson." People have repeatedly said that he simply needed a central bank with a monopoly over the supply of money and credit. They have that in England with the Bank of England and in the United States with the Federal Reserve System. The wealthy have Foundations which are often started with tax-deductible money and are never taxed. They can use that money for good and evil purposes. A lot of it is used for propaganda. An organization such as the **Council on Foreign Relations (CFR)** can use such money to have academicians and experts write articles for whatever purpose and can disseminate those articles through their control of the mass media.

Some say that the most powerful secret organization in the world is the **Bilderberg Group,** organized in 1952. It held its first meeting in 1954. A Polish politician named Jozef Retinger was promoting the better understanding between the cultures of the United States and Western Europe. He was an advocate of the unification of Europe. It is said that he approached Prince Bernhard of the Netherlands who managed to link the Belgium Prime Minister, the head of Unilever, Walter Smith (CIA) and Charles Jackson (advisor to Eisenhower) in a coordinated effort to form the Bilderberg Group. Denis Healey, a member of the Royal Institute of International Affairs, assisted him in putting the organization together. Denis Healey was also a member of the socialist *Fabian Society.* The Bilderberg Group started with 50 delegates from 11 countries in Western Europe along with 11 Americans. They were to meet on an annual basis. Prince

Bernhard has invited Henry Kissinger and David Rockefeller to join meetings. Everyone is sworn to secrecy. No one gets invited back if they talk about the contents of the meetings. In that sense it's a Super Secret Society.

During World War II **Prince Bernhard** was a fighter and bomber pilot for the Dutch. He demonstrated courage. It is said that he also helped to found the Rotary International. In 1976 he apparently stepped down as Chairman of the Bilderberg Group after it was noted that he had taken a **million-dollar bribe** from Lockheed for influencing the Royal Dutch Air Force to buy their fighter jets.

This is pretty factual material. Now we can add some of this conspiratorial stuff, "Prince Bernhard of Netherlands and the CIA brought the hidden ruling body of the **Illuminati** into the public knowledge... as the **Bilderberg Group** this is the official alliance that makes up the world governing body. The core of the Bilderberg group consists of three committees with thirteen members each. Thus the heart of the Bilderberg group consists of 39 total members of the **Illuminati**. The three committees are made up exclusively of members of all the different secret groups that make up the **Illuminati,** the **Freemasons,** the **Vatican** and the **Black Nobility**. The committee works out of offices in Switzerland."

At the *Bilderberg Conference* in Baden-Baden, Germany, **David Rockefeller (Rothschild)** said, "We are grateful to the *Washington Post,* the *New York Times, Time Magazine,* and other great publications whose direct jurors have attended our meetings and respected their promises of discretion for almost 40 years. It would have been impossible for us to develop our plan for the world, if we had been subjected to the lights of publicity during those years. But the world is now more sophisticated and prepared to March towards a world government. The super-national sovereignty of an intellectual elite and world bankers is surely preferable to the national auto-determination practiced in past centuries." You don't need to be a member of the **Illuminati** to comprehend what he just said. *Intent... non-secretive.*

About 150 people attended the **Bilderberg Group** meeting in 2013. To be a member of the Bilderberg Group you usually have to be in charge of a multinational bank, a global corporation or a nation. It's best to fold a corner of this page. I'm going to list some of the attendees and you can compare this list with the other organizations. Let's get to

147

it. David Cameron, **Great Britain, Prime Minister**; Henri de Castries, chairman of AXA; Paul Achleitner, **Deutsche Bank AG**; Marcus Agius, chairman, **Barclays**. wife is Katherine **de Rothschild**. The father was a cofounder of Bilderberg; Roger Altman, Evercore Partners, formerly with **Lehman Brothers**; Ali Babacan, Turkey Deputy Prime Minister for Economic and Financial Affairs; Francisco Baqlsemao, Portugal, former Prime Minister; Jose Barroso, President, **European Commission**; Nicolas Baverez, France, into national law firm with offices in 17 nations specializing in privatization; Franco Bernabe, Italy, Chairman and CEO of **Telecom Italia**; Jeff Bezos, USA, Founder and CEO, **Amazon.com**; Anders Borg, Sweden, Minister for Finance; Svein Brandtzaeg, Norway, President and CEO; Norsk Hydro ASA, fourth-largest integrated electrical generation and aluminum producer in the world; Peter Carrington, Great Britain, Foreign Minister and **NATO** Secretary General. He is a leading figure in the *Pilgrims Society.* He was a director of several banks including **Rothschild NM**; Edmund Clark, Canada, CEO TD Bank Group in Toronto; Sherard Cowper-Coles, Great Britain; **BAE** systems which is connected to a *British arms scandal*; Enrico Cucchiani, Italy, CEO, Intesa Sampaolo SPA, banking with 7246 branches in Italy and overseas; Etienne Davignon, Belgium, Minister of State, involved in a *weapon scandal* in Africa, Ian Davis, Great Britain, senior partner Emeritus, McKenzie & company, 17,000 consultants who serve senior management and governments; Robert Dudley, Great Britain, Group Chief Executive, **British Petroleum**; John Elkann, Italy, Chairman **Fiat**, grandson in a hair of Gianni Agnelli, Fiat owns **Ferrari, Maserati** and **Chrysler**. Henry Kissinger and Carla Bruni attended his wedding; Borje Ekholm, Sweden, President and CEO, Investor AB which runs **NASDAQ** OMX; homas Enders, Germany, CEO, **Airbus**; Michael Evans, USA, **Goldman, Sachs & Co**; Mark Fishman, USA, president, Novartis institutes; Douglas Flint, Great Britain, **HSBC**; Timothy Geither, USA, Secretary of the Treasury. His first job was working for Kissinger Associates; Michael Gfoeller, USA, checkered career. Also works with Exxon-mobile for government affairs; Donald Graham, USA, Chairman and CEO, **The Washington Post**; Stuart Gulliver, Great Britain, HSBC; Simon Henry, Great Britain, CFO, **Royal Dutch Shell**; Paul Hermelin, France, Chairman and CEO Capgemini Group,IT consulting firm with 125,000 employees worldwide; Kenneth Jacobs, USA, Chairman and CEO of **Rothschild owned Lazard**; Thomas Jordan, Swiss, Chairman, **Swiss National Bank**; Vernon Jordan, Junior, USA, Senior Managing Director, Lazard; Alexander Karp, USA, CEO, company was created with seed money from the CIA; John Kerr, Great Britain, Deputy Chairman of Royal

Dutch Shell; Henry Kissinger, USA, Klaus Kleinfeld, USA, Chairman and CEO, **Alcoa**; Klaas Knot, Netherlands, president of the Dutch central bank,**De Hederlandsche Bank**; **Mustafa Koc,** Turkey, Chairman, Koc Holding A.S. only son of **Turkey's wealthiest man**; Henry Kravis, USA, firm bought out **R.J. Reynolds**; Stefan Lofven, Sweden, Party Leader, **Social Democratic Party**. He is a friend of the Wallenbergs, a very wealthy family; Peter Loscher, Germany, President and CEO, **Siemens AG**; Jessica Tuchman Mathews, USA, president, **Carnegie Endowment** for International Peace; John Micklethwait, Great Britain, Editor-in-Chief, **The Economist** which is owned by the **Rothschilds**; Mario Monti, international, four-month Prime Minister and a former **Goldman Sachs VP**; Craig Mundie, USA, **Microsoft** Corporation; Alberto Nagel, Italy, CEO, **Mediobanca**, an international investment bank; H.M. Beatrix, the recently retired Queen of the Netherlands. Her father founded Bilderberg. Her family owns a large part of Royal Dutch Shall along with the Queen of England and the Rothschilds; Jorma Ollila, Finland, Chairman, Royal Dutch Shell. Chairman of **Nokia**; David Petraeus, USA, general, former CIA Director Robert Rubin, USA, Co-Chair, **Council on Foreign Relations**. He was the head of Citibank's private bank which *laundered drug money*; Eric Schmidt, USA, Executive Chairman, **Google**. Their superior search engine was designed by the CIA-DARPA people probably in the condition that the CIA and the NSA could use it to spy; Jean-Dominique Senard, France, CEO, **Michelin Group**; Peter Sutherland, Ireland, Chairman, **Goldman Sachs International**; Peter Thiel, USA, President, Clarium Capital/Thiel Capital involved with the **CIA** and **NSA** doing Internet business. Partial owner of **Facebook** and **PayPal**; Jacob Wallenberg, Sweden, member of the famous **Wallenberg** family. Director of several banks and of **Coca-Cola**; Kevin Warsh, USA, Hoover Institution, **Federal Reserve Board of Governors**; James Wolfensohn, USA, former head of the **World Bank**; David Wright, Great Britain, **Barclays**; Robert Zoellick, USA, former President, **The World Bank Group**, was also a managing director of **Goldman Sachs**. I warned you that you should skip over this, but it is a lot different than simply saying, "a lot of important people and corporate members attended."

The Bilderberg Group is Europe's version of the Council on Foreign Relations. The Bilderberg Group is associated with the network of powerful banking families going back to Crusader times with the old *fondi central-bank concepts.* The Lazards appear to be doing better than the Rothschilds at the moment. The *British and Dutch East India Companies* and the Black Nobility were the first to put that together. These private merchant bankers are now part of an international group of industrialists and financiers. It's a small world, Paul Volcker, former *Federal Reserve Board Chairman*, became Chairman of the European banking firm, *J. Rothschild, Wolfensohn & Company.*

It's time for us to turn our attention to the **Club of Rome** which was organized in 1968 by members of the **Morgenthau** group on the basis of a telephone call made by the late **Aurelio Peccei.** The **Morgenthau** group is a member of the **National Association of Securities Dealers** and many other securities organizations. The **Club of Rome** was born in 1968 in **Rockefeller's** house in Bellagio, Italy and comprised seventy-five industrialists, economists and scientists from twenty-five nations.

Amelio Peccei wrote the book *Human Quality*. He was an Italian industrialist with close relations to the *Olivetti Corporation* and *Fiat*. He headed the Atlantic Institutes Economic Council for three decades while he was the CEO for Giovanni Agnelli's Fiat motor company. Agnelli was a member of the ancient Chadian Black Nobility family and one of the more important members of the Committee of 300.

The United States Association of the Club of Rome (USACOR) was formed in 1976.. It appears that Henry Kissinger is the big gun for this organization. The majority of the Club of Rome executives were drawn from *NATO*. The Committee of 300 and the Round Table rely a great deal on the Club of Rome and the Bilderberg Group for much of the muscle in the important foreign policy areas

In September 17, 1973 the **Club of Rome** published a report entitled the "*Regionalized and Adaptive Model of the Global World System.*" The report revealed the club's intention to divide the world into ten economic/political regions, called "*Kingdoms*", which would unite the entire world under a common leadership. This would serve to fuse the Anglo-American financiers with the old **Black Nobility** families of Europe. They also put that plan into a book by the title of Mankind at the Turning Point. Here's where it gets scary. During the 1980s the club of Rome contributed significantly to the development of the concept of sustainability which played an important role in highlighting the interdependence of environment and economics. In August, 1982 the "*Executive Intelligence Review*" released a document entitled "Global 2000: Blueprint for Genocide" which included a statement that, "Throughout the world, the **Club of Rome** has said that genocide should be used to eliminate people whom they referred to as "useless eaters." **Ted Turner** is a member of the **COR** and is quoted as saying "a total population of 250 to 300,000,000, a 95% decline from the present levels, would be ideal."

The **Club of Rome** now has *thirty* worldwide national associations with a membership of over 1500 people in five continents. Its original goal was to have the **New World Order** in place by 2000. We already know that the plan to gain control of the world includes the disruption of economies by facilitating recessions and depression. Economic crises lead to severe social disruption on either a national or international level. This inevitably leads to a decrease in private ownership, greater government involvement, rising unemployment which leads to national and/or global masses of people who are ripe for the picking. With every one *twittering* it is much easier to cripple governments, to turn prosperous nations into easy prey for the **New World Order** to devour. Some feel that they can best coordinate this by helping the **World Council of Churches** and the **Parliament of World Religions** to counter established religions by developing a pantheistic/humanist philosophy which the common people would turn to. Sort of like *religion for the masses* which then could change its name to the **New World Religion**. I just thought I would add a little color to this.

The **Club** believes in the establishment of a world court, a global tax and a global police force together with the control of currencies. Socialism and collectivism moving towards communism seems to be its way. **Henry Kissinger**'s name keeps coming up. They say that his theme, when he spoke in 1976 at the **United States Association of the Club of Rome,** was about shutting down the US economy ever so gradually. His lecture apparently was not put in print. I don't have a list of its current members.

The **Club of Rome** must be a member of *SLICK*, commonly known as **Socialists Longing for Idealistic Communist Kharma**. Kharma is used in the sense of working towards bettering oneself and being rewarded for.

Let's look at the **Trilateral Commission** which came into existence in 1973. **David Rockefeller,** Chairman of the **Chase Manhattan Bank**, asked **Zbigniew Brezinski** to put it together. This organization would foster better understanding between America,

Western Europe and the Pacific Asian area. The goals of the **Trilateral Commission** are: "Close Trilateral cooperation in keeping the peace, in managing the world economy, and fostering economic redevelopment, and in alleviating world poverty will improve the chances of a smooth, and peaceful evolution of the global system."
The **Brookings Institute** and foreign policy experts were among the early members. **Alan Greenspan** and **Paul Volcker** were included. Those two gentlemen would later chair the **Federal Reserve**. They now have a membership of about 400 people.

Noam Chomsky and **Senator Barry Goldwater** have both criticized the organization for attempting to spread ultraliberal doctrines into the classrooms of every day schools and universities, as well as in churches and other institutions. It has been accused of being one of the tools being used to establish the **New World Order** with its influence in financial, political and intellectual areas.

Brezinski wrote _Between Two Ages_ in which he said, "national sovereignty is no longer a viable concept." He followed that zinger with, "Marxism represents a further vital, and creative stage in the maturing of man's universal vision. Marxism is simultaneously a victory of the eternal, active man over the Internet, passive man, and a victory of reason over belief." Do you find a hint about his political and economic philosophies in that statement? Is there a reasonable alternate to Marxism after we have viewed the consequences of its use in the Communist world?

I guess we can see some of the motivation of the **Trilateral Commission** in helping the **Chase Manhattan Bank** to interact with the **IMF**. The bank had loaned a lot of money to the developing countries and repayment was very much in question. Encouraging a revision and loosening of the **IMF**'s philosophy towards their lending practices in the Third World would prove to be very helpful. Senator Barry Goldwater simply saw the commission as heavily motivated for the multinational consolidation of the commercial and banking interests.

The **Trilateral Commission** is made up of past American Presidents, Ambassadors, Wall Street investors, international bankers, wealthy industrialists, Senators, Congressmen, NATO and Pentagon military representatives. Let's look up a few names. Paul Arthur Allair-**Xerox**, Dwayne Andreas- **Archer Daniels Midland**, Michael, Armacost-**Brookings Institute**, Riley Becktel-**Becktel**, Susan

Berresford-**Ford foundation**, Geoffrey Boisi-**JP Morgan Chase,** Lord Brittan-**UBS Warburg, London,** Frank Carlucci-**The Carlyle Group,** Richard Conroy-**Conroy Diamonds & Gold,** E. Gerald Corrigan-**Goldman Sachs,** Lynn Davis-**Rand Corporation,** Richard Fisher-**Morgan Stanley Dean Witter,** Stanley Fischer-**IMF,** Paolo Fresco-**GE,** Leslie Geib-**Council on Foreign Relations,** General Lord Guthrie-**NM Rothschild & Sons,** Richard Holbrooke-**Credit's Suisse First Corporation,** Robert Hormats-**Goldman Sachs,** Samuel Johnson-**Mobil Corporation,** Sir Mark Boody-Stuart-**Royal Dutch/Shell group,** Alessandro Profumo-**Unicredito Italiaon, Milan,** John Rockefeller IV-**U**.**S. Senate,** Albert Shanker-**American Federation of Teachers** and many politicians. You can see that there are many powerful and influential people listed, and there are another 350.

VIII

AMERICAN PLUTOCRACY
OPIUM & SLAVE TRADING

It's probably time to discuss the ancestry of *American Plutocracy*. We really have to go back 1000 years and see what the **Knights Templar** were all about. The **Poorer Fellow-Soldiers of Christ and of the Temple of Solomon** came into being in 1120 after the First Crusade recaptured Jerusalem in 1099. The pilgrims were in great danger. King Baldwin II of Jerusalem created a monastic order for the protection of such pilgrims. The **Templars,** as they were known, were given a home on the Temple Mount which was believed to be above the ruins of the Temple of Solomon. Their leader was Hugh de Payns. The order was officially recognized by the Catholic Church in 1129 after Saint Bernard of Clairvaux intervened on their behalf. They would be known by their white mantles with the striking Red Cross. They received a great deal of charitable donations and in 1139 the Pope exempted them from obedience to local laws and from any taxation. They became quite powerful and may have had as many as 20,000 men during that period of time. Their original mission of protecting pilgrims expanded to that of a very powerful fighting force which helped to fight Saladin's army.

The Knights Templar became an elite fighting force which was paid handsomely for their military prowess by various governments. This was truly an elitist group, with wealth and good breeding as requirements for admission. Banking became the business of the Templars in 1150 when they began caring for the valuables of the pilgrims. You would consider this a deposit in current day language. The pilgrims would be given a letter describing the deposits, which then was presented to other Templar Houses, and funds could be withdrawn during their travels. The Templar "banks" charged "rents" for the money that they loaned since "interest," known as "usury," was prohibited by the church. Banking, as it is known today, was an institution founded by the Knights Templar. They actively competed with the Italian family bankers of Florence, Venice and Lombardy who also developed *deposit banking.* They had fortresses, and the Templar banks secured the possessions of merchants, Knights and royalty and allowed them to be moved internationally. There were charges for the transaction. A network of fortified houses throughout Europe and the Holy Lands served as the predecessor of the modern branch banking

154

system. Their banking system was extensive and it is said that they had as many as 15,000 Templar Banks as well as an entire Navy.

The Templars owned land in Germany, Hungary and France and elsewhere. They controlled 9000 estates that had been donated to the order by European landowners. They took business away from the bank of Venice, Genoa, Lucca and Florence. So it would appear that at one time the **Ashkenazi Jews** and the **Knights Templar** were competing for the same business.

In 1207 the **Templars** became shipowners and they did a lot of trading. They apparently did a lot of privateering. A *Privateer* had to have the permission of a king to plunder, otherwise he was known as a *pirate*. I just love the *Jesuits*, they are so good at *casuistry*. At some point the **Black Nobility** banking families worked in cooperation with the **Knights Templar**. They were needed to finance the Crusades and in the transport of the Crusaders.

King Philip IV of France, called *Philip the Fair,* was heavily indebted to the **Knights Templar**. He needed their money as he persecuted the Jews and the Lombards for their wealth. On October 13, 1307, in the name of *fairness,* King Philip raided the **Templar** headquarters, arrested 15,000 soldiers, tortured and killed everyone from the *Order* which he could get his hands on. He did fail to get their enormous treasury in France. Some say that they took it to Scotland. No one is really sure what really happened to most of the Templars. Some certainly went to Switzerland. The **Templar** bankers with a modern form of banking certainly could be well maintained in Switzerland. Protected by the Swiss cantons and the Alpine passes, the massive wealth of the European elite could be well protected by the Swiss guard. Switzerland remained neutral at times of war and could be counted on to maintained the secret banking procedures that have been in place in Switzerland for a long time.

Surprise! There was a lot of corruption in those days, both in the clergical and secular realms. **Pope Clement V** was **King Philip IV's** pawn. The King instructed the Pope to issue a *papal bull* in 1307 instructing all Christian monarchs in Europe to arrest all the **Knights Templar** and to seize all their assets. The **King of England** was delighted since he too was heavily indebted to the **Templars**. **Pope Clement V** dissolved the *Order* in 1312.

Philip failed to get hold of their huge fleet which numbered in the thousands. They sailed to northern Europe and into the northern ports of Africa. There must've been tens of thousands of **Knights Templars** who got away. Many feel that they sought refuge in Scotland in the *Masonic Lodges* and were granted umbrage. It's felt that the **Masons** and the **Knights Templar** are largely responsible for influencing the American commitments to liberty, freedom and democracy. The **Masonic** St. Clair family was instrumental in protecting a new *Templar Order*. They changed their name to **Sinclair**. I wonder if they are the people in the oil business? But **Secret Societies**, like any other person or organization, need to save themselves by any means. The **Knights Templar** simply went underground for several hundred years

The **Order** changed its name to the **Order of Christ** in Portugal. **Prince Henry the Navigator** led the Portuguese order for 20 years. **Prince Henry**, the **Grand Master of the Knights of Christ,** made advancements in the art of navigation prior to the voyages of discovery. Members of the Royal Society advanced astronomy and the medical arts. They contributed a good deal to modern sciences. Since the Inquisition lasted well into the 15th century and learning and experimentation were considered heretical, they had to have a lot of guts. The legacy of the *Inquisition* was that all later **Templar** organizations understood the value of *secrecy* to avoid religious persecution. Part of the Templar fleet probably operated out of Portugal. Some of it may have gone to Scotland. The rest of it remained in the Mediterranean

Once the **Knights Templar** were forced out of business, they still had to make a living. Many of them became pirates who plundered the ships of France and Spain. If you don't have any skills, piracy is a good alternate, and it was usually quite lucrative if you knew your business. The **Knights Templar** knew the seas well and were proficient at commerce and finances. The pirates organized themselves into fraternal brotherhoods and transformed themselves into the *Templar Pirate Fighting Fleet.* Their white flag emblazoned with the Red Cross was known as the *jolie rouge* by the French. *Rouge* is red in French. Hence the term *Jolly Roger* came to be associated with Pirates for a long time. The flag often had the adornment of the Skull & Bones symbol. I think that they still fly the Skull & Bones flag at Yale. That society was founded in 1832 by William Russell and Alfonso Taft.

The breakup of the **Templars** was directly responsible for the dramatic rise in piracy that plagued Europe, America and even the Indian Ocean. For the same reason that Masonic organizations grew into labor and artisan guilds that protected the livelihood of their members, individuals in the smuggling business needed to be considered trustworthy. Pirates were banded together by covenants and eventually pirate ships were subject to democratic rule. The *Pirates* needed some connections. As the remnants of the **Templars** became organizing lodges, old ties were restored. *Masonry,* more or less underground until the early 18th century, provided lodging, employment, food , and cover.

Piracy became a very big business and was highly profitable. Several of the pirate bases were in Scotland, Ireland and America. The **Pirates** were protected by **Masonic** cells that extended to the courthouses and capital buildings. Smuggling also grew from Salem and Newport to the Caribbean. Bermuda was a place of sanctuary and facilitated the trade of pirates.. About two thirds of the 18th century trade in Bermuda was illegal, hence trading partners had to maintain secrecy. It appears to have been a **bastion of Freemasonry**.

Masonic lodges became involved in the slave trade. The slave trading ports were controlled by a handful of families bound by Masonic and family ties. The *Knights of Christ* organized the import of human cargo to Europe and licensed the trade in the Americas. The *Knights of Christ* started the trans-Mediterranean trade of Africans to finance **Prince Henry the Navigator**'s explorations. They later brought the trade across the Atlantic. The Spanish and Portuguese crowns, acting through a host of military orders, licensed the right to explore, conquer and subjugate foreign peoples and lands to other governments. They in turn organized trading companies. The sea captains of Genoa bought the licenses. The banking and merchant families from France to Flanders lent the money that paid for the licenses and mounted the expeditions. The early slave trade had to do with buying slaves , not capturing them. Once an Empire was in place in a new region, it also issued licenses granting rights to buy and sell slaves. The licenses first went to the *elite families* who later financed expeditions to the Americans.

The **Royals Houses of Europe** were the ultimate beneficiaries of the business; for a share of the profits, they granted licenses to elite merchants and businessmen who were part of the court. The licenses to trade in slaves were sold by the merchants and businessmen to the highest bidder, allowing newcomers to join the merchant class, but you had to have connections.

The Dutch most likely introduced both tobacco and opium smoking to China. In 1729 the Chinese Emperor prohibited the sale and use of opium. But that didn't work and there was a twenty fold increase in the import of opium by 1799. There was again a tenfold increase by the year 1838. By that time the Chinese imports of opium made the drug the largest revenue producing commodity in the world. The drug merchants included Americans. The opium came from the **East India Company's** factories in India. Two Opium Wars, won by the British in 1860, allowed the trade to flourish. The Indian farmers were forced to sell the opium to the **British East India Company**, which was then transferred to English and American merchants.

The Forbes family brought drug smuggling to its highest level of profitability and left a legacy that extends into modern times. The roots go back to Scotland in the 13th century when Sir Alexander Forbes was granted lands in 1423 and was made a Lord of Parliament in 1445. The Forbes family was situated in Massachusetts well before 1745 and connected with the families that would become *America's "aristocracy."* The Forbes money made in the opium trade was invested in land and industry. John and Robert Forbes would lead the way to the family fortune. John Forbes (1813-1898) started his career at age 15 in the Boston County house of his uncles James and Thomas Perkins. He represented the Perkins syndicate in Canton. In 1837, at the age of 24, he returned from Canton so wealthy that he could finance the construction of several railroads, including the Michigan Central Railroad. He led a group of capitalists who would raise millions to complete acquisitions of companies. He built several other railroads. Forbes bought the island of Naushon, just south of Woods Hole around Cape Cod. It was a *protectorate for smugglers*. Forbes married into the Hathaway's. The Hathaway, Forbes, and Perkins families merged.

A handful of *elite American families* connected to counterparts in England and France took over the business of *slavery* importation. When the American Revolution broke out **Benjamin Franklin** turned to the **Masonic** elite of France who controlled the slave trade to get arms, supplies and military support. **Masonic** military lodges from Europe brought their fighting units from Europe to help the 13 colonies fight for independence on their own soil. The **Masonic St. Andrew's Lodge** in Boston would instigate the *Boston tea party.*

The **Masons** would become involved in the *Sons of Liberty*, the *Committees of Correspondence*, the *Continental Congress*, and finally with fighting militia units. Lodges were necessarily organized in secret. Oaths might be taken in Masonic fraternal lodges. The climax came when French forces, enlisted from Masonic channels, arrived under the command of high-ranking Masons and Knights of St. John and defeated the British at Yorktown under the command of **Comte de Rochambeau.**

Smuggling and privateering provided a foundation for many of America's political dynasties who remain in power to this day. **John Jacob Astor,** who once held 50% of the American personal wealth, joined the **Masonic Lodge.** *Passing the bar* is a term that originated in the **Templar** stronghold in London. Membership in a military Lodge was required for promotion in the military.

Profits from drug running, smuggling, slave trading and piracy are directly responsible for the founding of several of the country's most important banks and insurance companies. . A New England's Insurance business prospered through profits earned from insuring opium and slave ships. The railroad systems and the telephonic communication industry were funded from the profits of the illegal drug smuggling. The **Brahmins** and other **Royal American Families** would have to include the *new and improved* **Templars** for their competence in the maritime drug and slave trade. But more to the point, they should thank the **Masons.**

It's time to familiarize ourselves with some historical data regarding *Freemasonry.* It appears that the first documentation of the existence of **Masonic Lodges** dates back to 1771 with the opening of the **First Grand Lodge** in London. The earliest **Masonic** text contains some sort of history of the craft of masonry. The earliest official English document to refer to **Masons** was written in Latin or Norman French in London in 1212 and later in 1391. The **Lodge** and **Guild** were first mentioned in 1278. The oldest known work of this type, the *Halliwell manuscript, or Regius poem* dates from 1390 and states that the craft of masonry began with Euclid in Egypt and came to England in the reign of **King Athelstan.** Shortly afterwards, around 1425, the *Cooke manuscript* traced masonry to **Jabal** mentioned in *Genesis*, 4:20-22. It tells how this knowledge came to Euclid, from him to the Christians of Israel while they were in Egypt and so on through the elaborate path to **Athelstan.** (927-939AD). The **Templars** are linked to the timeline of *Freemasonry* through the imagery of the carvings in the

Rosslyn Chapel in Scotland, where the **Templars** are rumored to have sought refuge after the dissolution of the *Order.* Myths apparently are interwoven here. The *Crusader Masons* were said to have revived the craft from secrets that they recovered in the Holy Land. The **Knights Templar** also became involved in this myth. Myths and reality survive side-by-side.

Somewhere around 1539 the lodges of **Masons** were brought under the control of two crown appointed officials. The *craft skills* were abolished in England in 1547. In 1548 "the bill of conspiracies of the victuallers and craftsmen" was passed, revoking their monopolies. The formation of the **First Grand Lodge** in London came to be in 1717. The Constitution of the *Freemasons*, *For the Use of the Lodges* in London and Westminster was published in 1723.

The *Order of the Quest* was set up in America before the middle of the 17th century. Most of the *founders* of the United States government were **Masons**. The oldest Masonic text called the *Regius manuscript* was exported to the British colonies in North America by the 1730s. The *founding fathers* rose to great wealth and passed their wealth and power on for generations to come. It was protected by the institutions they put in place. The family wealth of the **Roosevelts** was built on drug running. It appears that the Delano side of Franklin Delano Roosevelt had a prominent merchant who was an opium smuggler. He made a fortune, lost it and returned to drug running.

Smuggling and privateering provided a foundation for many of America's political dynasties which remain in power to this day. Illegal drug trafficking provided riches for the elite when slave trading no longer did. The core of *American aristocracy* worked alongside the British during the first half of the 19th century. The powerful families were mostly connected through **Masonic Lodges** on both sides of the Atlantic. Entrance into the **Masonic Lodges** was by invitation only. Wealth was a prerequisite. The *first families* received invitations. The **Masons** (with their network of lodges, governors, mayors and judges) licensed and protected pirate captains, and themselves invested in the pirate voyages.

The **Masons** have been a part of American culture for a long time. The *Rotary Club* was founded by **Paul P. Harris** in 1905. The *Rotary* lapel badge, the *Rotary Wheel*, carries the symbol of *Freemasonry*. The membership was dominated by *Freemasons* for many years. I've been a *Rotarian* myself and I didn't think that it was

160

any part of a *Masonic Lodge*. The **Pope** once said that membership in the *Freemasonry* was a *mortal sin* and members could not receive *Holy Communion*. I wonder if that fits into the *Infallibility Clause* of the *Roman Catholic Church?* The **Protestant** objections were based more on an uncomfortable association with *mysticism, occultism* and *Satanism.*

We already know that **John Jacob Astor was** a Mason. Our oldest colleges and universities were named after slave traders and opium dealers. The families of New York and New England donated the money earned in the illegal drug trade, which provided funds for the establishment of Harvard, Yale, Columbia, Brown and Princeton Universities. The same people invested in the development of the railroad and in textile mills, founding banks and insurance companies, which kept the family wealth intact for generations to come. We honor politicians and families whose fortunes can be traced to the initiatives of the **Knights Templar** and the **Masons** through their competencies in drug smuggling and slave trading..

The *founding fathers*, in the formation of the **Constitution of the United States**, put into place legal instruments which would protect future institutions. The **Newport Insurance Company,** the **Bristol Insurance Company,** the **Mount Hope Insurance Company** and **Aetna** contributed a great deal to the New England economy. They were maritime insurers who became wealthy by insuring the pirate and slave trade. **Aetna** later issued an apology for its role in insuring the lives of slaves, who were considered as property at the time.

John Hancock was a wealthy **Mason** whose ship *Liberty* provided work for one third of Bostonians. Some believe that Britain's insistence on enforcing its laws against smuggling was a major reason for the revolution. The colonies relied on smugglers to provide food, arms and supplies during the revolution.

Philip Livingston signed the *Declaration of Independence*. The Livingston descendants include the **Bushes, Eleanor Roosevelt** and the **Astors**. The **Livingston** family of New York was one of the foremost colonial families in America with ownership of a vast land tract secured by Royal charter. **John Livingston** was a pioneer fur trader who married a **van Rensselaer. Johnston Livingston** made a lot of money with his interest in **American Express** and **Crawford Livingston** made his fortune in the railroad industry. **Edward R. Livingston** was the celebrated lawyer who acquitted **Jean Lafitte**

when he was tried in **Louisiana**. **Lafitte** engaged in smuggling in illicit trade. He said that he was simply a *privateer.* He was tried because he shot one of his men because he boldly said that he was *"a pirate and was proud of."*

    Thomas Perkins was a preeminent opium dealer in America. **Perkins** also made a lot of money in the slave business. His name is synonymous with *Wealth*. He was the power broker behind the **Boston Brahmin** class. The *first families* of Boston were from Salem and they amassed their fortune from shipping and made their *old money* in the opium trade. The **Lowell's, Phillips and Saltonstalls** made their money in opium The **Sturgis** family headed the **Barings Bank** which financed the opium trade. The women in the **Sturgis** clan married into the **J.P. Morgan** family, **John Pierpont Morgan.**

    The **Colts**, of revolver fame, also married into the slave trading money. **Samuel Colt** founded a bank which later was known as the **Fleet Boston Financial**. Another **Colt** founded the **US Rubber Company.**

    The *Skull and Bones* at **Yale** was founded in 1832 with money from the China trade..The *Skull and Bones* membership names include family members of the **Harrimans, Bushes, Tafts, Whitneys, Bundys, Weyerhaeusers, Goodyears, Sloans, Stimsons, Phelps, Kellogg's, Vanderbilts,** and **Lovetts.**

    But let's not forget the **Jews. Masonry** welcomed the Jews in America. **Moses Hay**, a Portuguese Sephardic Jew, founded the *Bank of Boston*. The **Jews** were located in Rhode Island, from where they trafficked in the slave trade. Slave trading was regulated by the **Masonic Lodges**, which was composed of elite shipowners. Membership meant that you could navigate the treacherous waters of both New England and the Atlantic Ocean in a much safer fashion, since the *pirates* had to be licensed. The Newport Lodge's membership consisted mostly of Jews.

    The current day worth of **John D. Rockefeller** would be about $700 billion. That wealth did not come from the opium and slave trading businesses. He was born in 1839 to a profligate father and a mother who taught Johnny to be thrifty. He was a resourceful and well behaved boy who studied bookkeeping. He and **Maurice B. Clark** went into the business of wholesale foodstuffs. They built an oil refinery in 1863. The growth of the railroads was on and an oil fueled economy was born. In 1866, his brother **William Rockefeller** built another refinery. They borrowed money and reinvested the profits. In 1870 **Standard Oil** was born. By 1880 it refined over 90% of the oil in the United States. They did use monopolistic philosophies but they did build an empire out of nothing. **John D. Rockefeller** spent his last 40 years in the philanthropy business, mostly for good causes. He did *not* make his money from **opium** or **slave trading.**

Theodore Roosevelt, Jr. was born in 1858 into a wealthy family which was in the hardware business and in the plate-glass importing business. His uncle **James Dunwoody Billoch** was a secret agent in Great Britain during the **Civil War.** He apparently had a lot to do with the destruction of the United States merchant fleet and was instrumental in procuring the ships that brought the supplies through the Union blockade.

Where did the **Bush** family wealth come from? Were they in the opium and slave trading businesses? Their lineage is rather interesting. I'm going to show you what I found on the Internet, and it will include a lot of extra stuff. "George Herbert Walker Bush's lineage goes back to King Edward I of England. He also is descended from King Henry I and King Henry II, both of England, and William I and Robert II, both of Scotland. Bush has common ancestors with 15 American presidents: Washington, Fillmore, Pierce, Lincoln, Grant, Hayes, Garfield, Cleveland, both Roosevelts, Taft, Coolidge, Hoover, Nixon and Ford.

Other presidents who have connections to British royalty are George Washington, the two Adamses, Millard Fillmore, Rutherford Hayes, Grover Cleveland, Theodore Roosevelt, William Taft, Woodrow Wilson, Calvin Coolidge, Franklin Roosevelt, Harry Truman, Richard Nixon and Ronald Reagan. Mrs. Ronald Wilson Reagan was descended from Henry I, king of France, and Henry I, king of England. Mrs. George Herbert Walker Bush is descended from Henry II, king of England, and other notables. There are other royal descents of first ladies but these will serve as examples...George Herbert Walker Bush has kinship with Presidents Nixon, Taft, Hayes, Pierce, Coolidge, Hoover, Franklin Roosevelt, Grant, Ford, Cleveland, Garfield, Washington, Fillmore, Theodore Roosevelt, Lincoln, John Quincy Adams, and John Adams Jr.

Talk about intermarriages! So that's how it's done. The genealogist really have to have a great deal of time, and a great deal of patience and certainly a passing facility with languages and the scripts of the early languages. Have you ever tried to read *Boewulf* in the original script? The single surviving manuscript is known as the *Nowell Codex.* It's a much harder task to read that manuscript than **Boewulf** had in trying to subdue the monster, **Grendel.**

Let's get back to the origin of the wealth of the **Bushes.** It's a little difficult to keep straight since the names of the progeny seem repetitive. The first known progenitor was from Bristol, Plimouth colony. His name was **Richard Bush (1676 - 1732). Samuel Bush (1863 – 1948)** was the great-grandfather of **George Walker Bush (1946 -).** He took over the presidency of the **Buckeye Steel Castings Company** when **Frank Rockefeller**, brother of **John D. Rockefeller**, retired. They did business with the railroad baron, **Edward Henry Harriman. George Herbert Walker (1875 – 1953)** enters the picture. He was a wealthy American banker and businessman. **George** helped to organize the St. Louis World's Fair in 1904. The **Walker Cup** carries his name. He became President of **W. A. Harriman & Co.** His son-in-law was **Prescott Bush (1895 – 1972).** This is **George Walker Bush's** grandfather. **Prescott Bush** became a senator from Connecticut and a partner of **Harriman & Company**, before it was merged with **Brown Brothers & Company** (a merchant bank founded in Philadelphia in 1818) to form the largest private bank in America, **Brown Brothers Harriman & Co.** in 1931. The **George Herbert Walker Bush (1924 -)** and **George Walker Bush (1946 -)** oil businesses have prospered and both have been Presidents of the United States. So it appears that they did not inherit any opium seeds.

Franklin Delano Roosevelt's wealth was secured by the family's foresight to purchase cheap land on Manhattan Island during the great depression of 1837. They became *wealthy land barons.* **FDR's** maternal grandfather, **Warren Delano**, made his money in the China trade which included trafficking in opium. It took a bit of scouting, but I finally found a **Roosevelt** whose family made some money from **opium.**

Beginning with the **Black Nobility**, we have been able to trace the continuum of wealth through the *banking* and *aristocratic Italian, Germanic, British* and *American plutocratic families.* That is a real *mouthful....* the history of *wealth's travels* and *travails* for a *thousand years.*

These *plutocratic families* now control the trade in, and the tangible things themselves in **land, oil, minerals, precious metals and raw materials.** Many of these families grow even wealthier by simply renting the land. And we have discovered that you do not have to be *conspiratorially intentioned* to see that powerful, moneyed people and many influential organizations have openly stated that a **New World Order** is the way to go.

IX

BIRTH OF AMERICAN SOCIALISM

Why does a philosophy of *Socialism* dominate the *intelligentsia* of the great universities and colleges of the United States? Nobody seems to have an answer, it's like finding oneself in *Alice in Wonderland.* How did we get here? Well, I've been looking into this and it's starting to make sense. *Intelligence* is not synonymous with *common sense.*

Researching is terribly hard, but it's a lot easier if you're looking at what has transpired for just 100 years. We give the faculty members a lot more credit than they deserve. They are representative of the human condition; they may be pretty good in their specialized fields, but unreliable outside of their area of expertise. We give them credit for being inquisitive and surmised that they might be looking for alternatives to the capitalist system after having participated in the *Great Depression.* There were not a lot of alternate systems on the table at the time, just socialism and communism. But that was the *wrong* guess. They *"didn't have a lick of common sense."* Other intellectuals managed to brainwash them. They had forgotten that their **critical thinking** caps were in the closet. The systematic propaganda from other intellectuals made them easy prey. There is an elitist pride in being a member of one of those great universities

This is *not* a scholarly work. I'm not even going to try to be very precise about the origins of what I've found. I've been finding a lot of dates, and names, and statements that are very conflicting. There is a lot of guesswork. Many people use the creative genius of **it logically follows** to fill in the gaps. It's often necessary to do that, but you should be clear to the reader that it is just that, a guess. I have done my best to verify things. John Coleman is a graduate of *MI6 intelligence* who has spent some years studying the archives in Egyptian and British institutions. He's added to and clarified a lot of what I have been able to find.

This chapter is about **Socialism** The earliest thinkers to be called "socialists" were the Frenchmen **Henri de Saint-Simon** (1760-1825) and **François-Marie-Charles Fourier** (1772-1837) and the Welshman **Robert Owen** ((1771-1858). All three of them were visionaries with little political sense. The democratic revolutions of the

first half of the 19th century had no relationship with the ideas of the
Communist Manifesto. It remained for the *International Working
Men's Association* to spread the delightful Marxist philosophy upon
the European continent.

The word **socialism** had been around since 1835. It's attributed
to **Robert Owen**. **Fabian** refers to the manner in which the Roman
General **Quintus Fabius Maximus** fought against **Hannibal**. He
sought victory by delay and harassment rather than by decisive battles.
The founding idea of the *Fabian Society* is attributed to **Thomas
Davidson**, a Scottish philosopher. He believed that restrictive social
relations hindered the development of man's potential to be a god. He
believed that people would become increasingly moral as they became
aware of their own self-divinity. The growth of one's own spiritual
potential would lead both to a lessened emphasis on materialism and to
a reform of the human society. This fellow was a first graduate at
Aberdeen University and spoke eight languages including Arabic. I
guess that he qualifies for inclusion in the *intellectual elitist* class.

Fabian Socialism began as a debating society in 1883. Some
say that the *Fabian Society* was founded in 1884 by **Beatrice** and
Sidney Webb, George Bernard Shaw and H.G. Wells. Another version
is that it was **Edward Pease**, a successful stockbroker and Quaker,
together with Frank Podmor, Edith Nesbit and Hubert Bland, who
founded the *Fabian Society*. Sidney and Beatrice Webb apparently ran
the society from its inception. Early members included **Annie Besant**
and **Graham Wallas**. The group hoped to establish a socialist state in
Great Britain by a gradual series of reforms. Their aim was to use
education as a vehicle for socialist propaganda. This little seedling had
a profound effect on education and politics both in the US and in
Britain.

Edward Pease and the two **Webbs** were trustees of the fund
used to establish the *London School of Economics* in 1895. **Professor
Graham Wallas** was also a co-founder of the *London School of
Economics* which proved to be very influential in the United
States. You might guess that it would have a socialist bent. **Pease** also
served on the *Labour Representation Committee*, the forerunner of the
Labour Party, for 14 years. Some people just seem to get around. **Sir
Victor Gollancz**, a respected British book publisher, and many
intellectuals helped to influence the Labour Party and the *London
School of Economics*. **Beatrice Webb** was a guiding force in securing
control of the *Labour Party*. She concentrated on the sons of the

famous at **Oxford University.**

Sidney Webb, 1ˢᵗ Baron Passfield, was a cofounder of the *London School of Economics.* He served as both *Secretary of State for the Colonies* and *Secretary of State for Dominion Affairs* in 1929 when he was raised to the peerage as **Baron Passfield.** He and his wife wrote *Soviet Communism and The Truth About Soviet Russia* documenting their support of the Soviet Union and their pro-Stalinist ideology. From *socialism* to *communism* in one easy step.

Annie Besant was a prominent British socialist and was quite active in the *women's rights* movement .She became president of *Theosophical Society* in India. She established the first overseas *Lodge of the International Order of Co-Freemasonry* in England. Most of the women involved in the *Fabian Society* women's civil rights movement were very wealthy. Considering the influence that they have had on our culture, it lends some validity to the *Islamic* suppression of education and individual rights.

Miss Jane Addams was no exception to this world of wealth. She and her female companion, **Ellen G.Starr,** founded the *Hull House* in Chicago in 1889 from whence she had a lot of political clout. It would prove to be a powerful socialists *think tank.* **Jane Addams** and **Josephine Lowell** charted the *National Consumers League (NCL)* in 1899, which under its first general secretary, **Florence Kelley,** promoted fairness in the marketplace for both workers and consumers. She also helped to develop the *NAACP* and she founded the *Women's International League* and was awarded the Nobel Prize in 1935. **Jane Addams** was to influence **Robert Morss Lovett** who was an associate editor of *The New Republic* for 20 years and who wrote the *Humanist Manifesto I* in 1933.

The names **Webb, Perkins, Mary Harriman Rumsey, Mary Williamson Averell Harriman, Addams** and **Besant** appear prominently in the women's movement. There have been many prominent women's rights socialist organizations. To name a few... *National Council of Jewish Women, League of Women's Voters, National Consumers League,* and the *Women's International League.*

But let's look at what preceded English socialism. **Robert Owen** was a wealthy Welsh industrialist who turned to social reform and socialism. In 1825 he founded a colony called **New Harmony** in Indiana. It only lasted from 1825 to 1829. Robert Owen was a principal backer of John Quincy Adams' presidential campaign. His name comes up in the context of several ideas and movements. He coined the word **socialism.** He also was a business partner of a cotton manufacturer by the name of Engels, whose son, **Friedrich Engels,** later became **Owen's** political disciple, and still later, together with **Karl Marx,** gave the the world the intellectual spark for the *Communist* movement. So perhaps **Robert Owen** is a *villainous creature.* In an altruistic venture into socialism, he fueled the spark of oppression and serfdom. Oh well! We shall see that theme over and over again where *good people* are either used by or as *conduits* to *villainous goals.*

On a more inspirational note let's turn to the *Transcendental Movement* which appeared just after the collapse of *New Harmony.* It appears to have originated with **Ralph Waldo Emerson.** The movement started around 1830 and lasted for about 40 years. Professor Ashton Nichols defined it as "the search for truth that might be true at all times in all places, the belief that evidence for such a spiritual truth might be found in and through the physical world, and the idea that each individual had the capacity to experience this truth in a personal way."

We've referred to the two 18th-century groups of great thinkers, one in America and one in Great Britain. We called one group the *Founding Fathers* and the second the *Adam-Mill-Bentham-Ricardo-Malthus group.* The 19th century group of American thinkers all lived around Beacon Hill in Boston. Their names were **Emerson, Thoreau, Margaret Fuller, the Alcotts, the Parkers,** and the **Peabody sisters.** They moved away from the restrictions of the Calvinistic ideas of the time, and saw man, nature and an open view of what constituted God as all intertwined. They stressed individual responsibility, and found insights in the forces that were revealed through nature. They believed very strongly in the *need for education* and in *liberty* in a controlled, responsible form. They would break out from the oppression of religion and put the responsibility on the individual to form his own relationship with his God. Oriental literature was being made available at that time.

Thoreau certainly was an eccentric, a hermit for two years, who wrote the rather famous book *Walden.* I think he was the first guy to use the expression, "keep it simple, stupid!" Thoreau famously refused to pay his taxes on principle. This concept of "civil disobedience" led to its use by **Gandhi** and **Martin Luther King, Jr.** The movement also believed in the equality of all men and all women.

The *Transcendentalist's* abolitionist and feminist ideas were influential well into the 20th century. This doesn't sound like terrible stuff, does it?

Transcendentalist utopians founded the ***Brook Farm Institute of Agriculture and Education*** in 1841. A Unitarian minister by the name of George Ripley was responsible for opening it. **Nathaniel Hawthorne** and **Ralph Waldo Emerson** were members of that community. The philosophy was one of balancing work and leisure for the common benefit. It was felt that the leisure time could be spent in reading and meditation to better oneself and the community. They founded a school which apparently was very well respected and brought in most of the income. But a fellow by the name of **Charles Fourier** entered the picture with his own concept of socialism which created some turmoil. He built a large structure for the development of his principles. The building burned down. That was the *coup de grace* and the farm had to close in 1847.

Josiah Warren was the first American anarchist. He founded *Utopia* in Ohio. Land was privately owned. The coin of the realm was not used as a means of exchange, labor was. You were paid in certificates indicating how many hours of work you had done. He opened a store which was called the "***Labor for Labor Store***"which was successful and operated for three years. These certificates could be exchanged at a local "time" store for products that took the same amount of time to produce.

The Socialist Labor Party (SLP) was founded in 1876. Its original name was the *Workingmen's Party of America.* The party was made up of German immigrants who brought Marxist ideals with them. The *SLP* was re-organized as a Marxist party in 1890. By the start of the 20th century it was the foremost American socialist party. American socialism was based on the ideology known today as "democratic socialism" which would transfer ownership of major industries to the employees, "capital to those who create it." They advocated universal suffrage so that the working class could vote. The *Socialist Labor Party* broke into two parties. The word socialist gets used over and over again; you'll have to reread a couple of sentences to make it clear for yourself. Morris Hillquit left the party in 1901, and fusing with the *Social Democratic Party,* he formed the *Socialist Party of America.* Eugene Victor "Gene" Debs of the *Social Democratic Party* (the original party) gained national recognition in the socialist movement and was one of the founding members of the *Industrial*

Workers of the World. "Gene" Debs had converted to socialism in 1897.The socialist movement became organized, energized and adept at using *collective bargaining.* They formed unions and refused to work. These strikes led to the crippling of plant and mine production.

The *American Federation of Labor* was formed in 1886 and came under the direction of Samuel Gompers. The *AFL* organized only skilled workers and tried to minimize its *striking* power. It became the most powerful and largest union. It's lack of unskilled union membership and its refusal to use the power of the strike later led to significant loss of membership. 1886 saw demonstrations and strikes in Chicago and Milwaukee. There was a lot of labor unrest in the late 19th century and early 20th century. The most prominent unions of the time were the *American Federation of Labor, the Knights of Labor,* and the *Industrial Workers of the World.*

Morris Hillquit founded the *Socialist Party of America* in 1901 or 1902 and was also in attendance at the meeting of the *ISS* in 1905, and was elected to the executive committee. The *ISS (Intercollegiate Socialists Society)* was the brainchild of Upton Sinclair. The birth of the *American Fabian Society* began on that date in 1905. William Forster was at that meeting. He went on to play a leading role in the *Communist Party* in the US. About 100 supporters of the new organization met in a Manhattan restaurant and elected Jack London president, Upton Sinclair first vice president and millionaire philanthropists J. Graham Phelps Stokes as second vice president. Other founding members were Norman Thomas and Florence Kelly.

The *ISS* opened the doors to universities, spreading socialist programs among impressionable students. It changed the face of education in the United States. Upton Sinclair and Jack London were prime movers who went around the country preaching the *Fabian Socialist Gospel* to both students and professors at many universities and socialist clubs.

The *ISS,* the *Intercollegiate Socialist Society,* was active from 1905 to 1921. In 1921 it changed its name to the *League for Industrial Democracy (LID).* It became the base for left-wing intellectuals. During the great depression it organized radio stations and broadcast propaganda for the New Deal. It's goal was to provide "education for increasing democracy in our economic, political and cultural life." It was supported by **Eleanor Roosevelt, Florence Kelly,** and **Frances Perkins.**

171

The year 1909 saw the foundation of the *NAACP*, the *National Association for the Advancement of Colored People*. Some of the founding members were W. E. B. Du Bois, Henry Moskowitz, Mary White Ovington, Charles Edward Russell, William English Walling and Florence Kelley. Mary White Ovington was a well-educated social worker who worked within the *NAACP* for 38 years. Ovington wrote for radical journals and newspapers such as *The Masses* and the *New York Evening Post*. She may have assisted Florence Kelly in writing the briefs for Louis Brandeis.

In 1907 Florence Kelly and Josephine Goldmark, Brandeis's sister-in-law, hired Brandeis to represent the state of Oregon in *Muller vs. Oregon* involving the constitutionality of limiting the working hours of female laundry workers. They relied on statistics from medical and sociological journals. It was the first case in which extra-legal data was used rather than legal arguments. This precedent would be known as the *Brandeis brief*. Kelly and her associates employed more than 200 socialist researchers worldwide to gather information favorable to socialism which made up the bulk of the material that comprised the *Brandeis brief* court documents.

Florence Kelley was an American social and political reformer who worked to establish minimum wages and children's rights in the sweatshops. She began her career as a social worker and later became an attorney. Her married name was Weschenewtsky. She was born in 1859 in an affluent home to a father who had turned from business to abolitionistic causes. She had a strong desire to change things, "by the legislative route" if they cannot be done by constitutional means. She and the *Social Security* lady, Frances Perkins, both saw that it would be best to avoid the limitations of the Constitution. She studied at the University of Europe in Zürich and became a follower of Karl Marx and Friedrich Engels. She translated Engles' *The Conditions of the Working Class in England in 1844* which was published in 1887. Kelly joined the *Intercollegiate Socialist Society* in 1905. One of her students was Frances Perkins, who is given credit for implementing *Social Security*. Florence Kelly became a resident at *Hull House* from 1891 through 1899, joining Jane Addams in her endeavors.

Florence Kelley was the founder of the *National Women's Trade Union League*. She was the national secretary of the socialist *National Consumers League (NCL)* for 34 years. She persuaded Eleanor Roosevelt to join the organization. The goal was to encourage the federal government to preempt the powers of the state in the areas of health, education and police powers. It appears that Frances Perkins, Eleanor Roosevelt and Kelly all worked together as a united front towards ever-increasing socialism. All of these women understood the concept of networking very well. Unlike the men, they did not require large secret societies to implement their agendas. They, of course, were pretty wealthy women. It's hard to get anything done if you're poor. Eleanor Roosevelt was strongly involved with the feminist movement. Her lesbian relationship with Lorena Hicock has been documented.

Talk about wealth, I'll introduce you to Dorothy Payne Whitney. She was born 1887 and died in 1968. Her father was William C. Whitney who, at the time of his death, was one of the largest landowners in the eastern United States. Dorothy, at age 17, inherited $45 million. She married Willard Dickerman Straight and became known as Dorothy Whitney Straight. She came right out of top-drawer American society. Her brother was a partner in J.P. Morgan and she had carte blanche entrance into the *Fabian Socialist* circles in London, New York and Washington. The Whitney Straits financed the American Fabian socialist publication, *The New Republic* in 1914.

A similar magazine called the *New Statesman* was founded in London in 1913 and was connected with the members of the *Fabian Socialist Society*. It was founded by Sidney and Beatrice Webb with the support of George Bernard Shaw. John Maynard Keynes, chairman of the *Nation's* board, which changed its name to the *New Statesman,* was influential in both magazines. It had a history of supporting communism because it feared that any criticism of communism would be taken as propaganda against socialism. Kingsley Martin supported that position when he took over as editor in 1930. In 2006, the editor of the *New Statesman* said that it had remained "true to its heritage of radical politics."

Dorothy Payne Whitney's son was **Michael Whitney Straight**, a confessed *KGB* spy. A document from the Soviet archives concerning a report from recruiter Anthony Blunt made in 1943 to the *KGB* states, "as you already know the actual recruits worldwide took were Michael Straight." He was part of the Soviet spying network which included Donald McLean, Guy Burgess and Kim Philby. He became a *Communists Party* member and part of an intellectual's secret society while at Cambridge University in the mid-1930s. He served in the United States Army Air Force beginning in 1942 as a B-17 Flying Fortress pilot. He later became the publisher of his family owned *The New Republic* magazine. Subject to government scrutiny, it is said that he informed a family friend, **Arthur Schlesinger, Jr,** that he had been a *KGB* spy. He apparently escaped prosecution for being such a good boy and for being so honest. He was a speechwriter for **Franklin Delano Roosevelt.** It's a small world, isn't it? It certainly is good to have friends in high places.

Alexandra Kollontai was a Russian Communist revolutionary who had many troubles with human relationships. She wrote *Communism and the Family* which is a savage attack on marriage and family. Her followers call themselves members of the "*International League of Peace and Freedom.*" Kollontay visited the United States in 1916 in 1917 and influenced the socialist movement. She was an exponent of free love and nationalization of children.

Let's take a quick look at how President Wilson got into office. Enter *"the man"*, Colonel Edward Mandel House. Colonel was an honorary title. House apparently was really a Huis, of Dutch descent. His father, Thomas William House, was the agent for the London Rothschilds. He came out of the Civil War with a huge fortune. Eddie inherited the vast fortune and learned socialism while at school in England. House, with his wealth and connections, took over the Democratic Party in the United States. He became a key player with the *Fabian* socialite elite and with Sir William Wiseman who was with *British Intelligence MI6,* functioning as its North American station chief.

We've mentioned that he was known for his novel, "*Philip Dru: Administrator,*" in which his character Dru leads the democrats of the West against the aristocrats of the East and becomes the dictator of America. Dru says "I agree with you that this much to be desired state of society cannot be altogether reached by laws, however drastic. Socialism as dreamed of by Karl Marx cannot be entirely brought about by a comprehensive system of state ownership and by the leveling of wealth. If that were done without a spiritual leavening, the results would be largely as you suggest." House explained that Dru was speaking for House, "For a long time it had seemed to me that our Government was too complicated in its machinery and that we had outgrown our Constitution. It has been my constant wonder that our people were willing to go along without protests with such an inefficient machine." Some socialist underpinnings, don't you think?

Colonel House was president Wilson's personal foreign policy advisor throughout World War I. He also managed the 1916 presidential campaign very skillfully. House was the man who asked Walter Lippmann to organize the scholars who would formulate a Constitution for the League of Nations, the so-called *"Inquiry."*

Walter Lippmann also had a relationship with *British intelligence* and *MI6*. He visited with Colonel House on a regular basis, discussing how to get Wilson reelected and how to push him away from neutrality. Strongly socialist in his views, he was very influential in the business, legal and banking circles of the United States. He had tremendous power through his syndicated press columns. He was a natural born *convincer.* **Lippmann** had learned at the **Tavistock Institute of Human Relations** to be a good salesman, to slowly encourage people in the United States to accept socialistic concepts in education, economics, religion and politics. We know that if you keep people busy, as we do with the **quick** generation, that you can flood them with propaganda and nonsense and they won't even notice it.

Wilson was not happy with House's negotiated settlements with the British and had little to do with him after that. The Colonel then turned his attention towards Franklin Delano Roosevelt. He was not to be influential in that relationship. He probably will be remembered as the man who introduced a new style of government in which presidents were to surround themselves with many advisers who could avoid the scrutiny of the electorate. Wilson's circle did include Louis Brandeis, Felix Frankfurter, Walter Lippmann, Bernard Burr Oak, Sidney Hillman, and Florence Kelly. FDR surrounded himself with *CFR* advisors.

The *ACLU*, the *American Civil Liberties Union*, was founded in 1920, allegedly to defend and preserve the individual rights and liberties of Americans. If you look at the *Columbia Encyclopedia* you'll find that many of the founding members were *Communists* and *Socialists*. Jacob Schiff took some credit for having helped to found the organization. Understanding that one of the goals of the secret societies is to create discord and hence disruption, this organization has been doing a lot of that. The lawyers are Ashkenazi Jews. They have significantly changed the American culture by undermining religious and social values, under the banner of *we care*. It may not be a coincidence that the *League of Women Voters* was also founded in 1920. Although it alleges neutrality, it has been a powerful force in the movement toward Socialism.

175

The Socialists were against entry into World War I. President Woodrow Wilson signed the **Espionage Act** in 1917. Scores of Socialists were convicted and jailed. **Debs** was sentenced to 10 years in prison. He did serve six months.

In 1918 Woodrow Wilson required collective bargaining, effectively making unions legal. He also created a new division called the **General Intelligence Division** inside the Justice Department led by **J. Edgar Hoover.** The Socialist Party reached its peak in 1912 and declined after World War I. Strikes were beaten down by force American socialism failed to make a widespread impact in the union movement, not so in the political arena in Washington.

Let's go back to British socialism. **Sidney Webb, 1ˢᵗ Baron of Passfield**, was a prominent member of the Labour Party. He apparently had a major part in drafting the *"Four Pillars"* after World War I. Those **Pillars** would give government a great deal of authority to curb unemployment through public works and institute government housing and social programs. The railroads and utilities would be immediately nationalized. Education would also be nationalized with the government providing all the training. Graduated income taxes would be instituted. Buried in the fine print was a warrant for capitalism and its system of production and competition, leading to an unlimited welfare state with nationalization of major industries, and the bolstering of the *League of Nations,* giving it international economic control.

The aims of the *Fabian Society* include the reorganization of society by the emancipation of land and industrial capital from individual ownership to the community for the general benefit. The *Fabian socialism* also speaks to creating such financial collapses that nations would face overwhelming unemployment problems, and collapse into a welfare state.

A carpetbagger, by the name of **Mark Starr,** brought British **socialism** to the United States. He became an educational director of the *International Ladies Garment Workers Union.* **Starr** was also the vice president of the *American Federation of Teachers.* He was pretty influential and was appointed to the *United States Advisory Commission* by President Truman.

What do we know about **Professor Graham Wallas,** co-founder of the *London School of Economics*? He was a socialist educator, a member of the *Fabian Society*, who apparently was quite influential in the United States. Beatrice Webb said of him, "To his disciples he appears a brilliant man, first-rate lecturer, a very genius for teaching...... a skillful propagandist and an admirable and most popular University Extension lecturer."

The "*New Republic*" founded a socialist think tank called the *New School for Social Research* in New York City. He lectured there. He was teaching socialism at Philadelphia University in 1902. He taught **Walter Lippmann** and delivered the *Lowell Lectures at Harvard.* **Walter Lippmann** was the fellow who enlisted the scholars who worked on Wilson's "*Fourteen Points*" and who later became members of the **Council on Foreign Relations.**

Graham Wallas wrote _The Great Society_ which formed the core ideas of the *New Deal*, the *New Frontier* and the *Great Society.* He believed that the Industrial Revolution had created a lot of problems for mankind. The people needed a "kinder and gentler state" with more nurturance and welfare. He seemed to think that there was a need for a stronger international government. **Wallas** made it plain, when he was teaching at the *London School of Economics*, that people should be led one step at a time on the road to socialism.

His view of the average man failed to have kindly overtones. He had his own ideas of how people think. Contrary to the popular view that people think rationally, he thought that they were creatures that acted irrationally. People did not behave intelligently. He believed that the government would be better able to understand itself if psychology was introduced into the political sciences. They gave two economists Nobel prizes for thinking that people in the market acted irrationally. The Nobel people appear to have bypassed him. He was a friend of **Felix Frankfurter**.

Harold Laski, a British economist and socialist, also became a very influential spokesman for socialism. He is a real *Frankenstein* in this tale of a virus infiltrating the American educational system. His mother was named **Sarah Frankenstein**. He was a professor at the *London School of Economics* from 1926 to 1950, and an executive member of the socialist *Fabian Society* during 1922 to 1936. His Labor Party's Constitution, adopted in 1918 had made the "common ownership of the means of production, distribution and exchange" the basis upon which was to be secured "for the workers by hand or by bringing the full fruits of their industry and the most equitable distribution thereof that may be possible." He believed in a planned economy based on public ownership of the means of production. Initially he stated, "But," he said, "men will still be able to make fortunes,"... "although they will be subject to heavy taxation upon income, and still heavier duties upon their estates at death." The revenue thus produced would then be used for extensive social services. "The achievement of greater economic equality would involve slow and painful experiment." This was included in his *Grammar of Politics.*

By age 30 he was an avowed **Marxist.** He firmed up his view that the state should take over the operation of private enterprise. He believed that a worker's revolution would be necessary and it might be violent. He actually served as **chairman** of the *British Labor Party* in 1945. He believed that nations would eventually be internationally controlled and based on social welfare, which opponents call the *welfare state.* He believed that the *plutocrats* would have to be violently overthrown. He felt that nation states would have to yield to an international **New World Order.**

Laski felt that the ideology of the *middle classes* was used as a justification to take away the wealth and power of the aristocrats. "The preaching of individualism and freedom...if not obtained, what is needed, by general consent, we shall have to use violence even if it means revolution." He stressed the need for equality. It was all good stuff and it was extremely well received on the campuses of the *intelligentsia of America!* I think that I've made it fairly clear that he was preaching revolution since I've mentioned it at least three times.

Laski and **Wallas** were quite civilized and engaging, and very influential. They influenced the "great academicians" of American universities and colleges. They went on lecture tours. **Harold Laski** was one of the favorite contributors to the *New Republic.* **Laski**'s circle included **Felix Frankfurter, Supreme Court Justice Oliver Wendell Holmes, Walter Lippmann, Edmund Wilson, Victor Gollancz** and **Franz Neumann. Laski** lectured at **McGill University, Yale, Harvard.** He was one of the most popular guest lecturers in New York City. **Laski** was the close companion of **Felix Frankfurter,** who himself was constantly attacking the United States Constitution. **Laski** was a regular house guest at **Frankfurter's** homes in Boston and Washington. **Graham Wallas** also had a lot of influence over **Frankfurter.**

Walter Reuther was a son of a trade union and socialist activist from Wheeling, West Virginia. Unemployed during the Great Depression he went to the **Soviet Union** and found employment in an auto factory. He later went to work for General Motors and became an active member of the **United Auto Workers.** In 1929 he enrolled at Detroit City College to study law and became president of a social service club (socialist party). He arranged for leading socialists such as Norman Thomas to speak at meetings. He was elected president of the *UAW* in 1946. After World War II he supported civil rights and social welfare legislation. Walter Reuther served on the committee of the *LID* when he became a member in the 1940s. He was *honored guest at a Fabian socialist dinner party* in London in 1949.

At this point we need to move into the **FDR** era of the 30s. We are looking for some insights into what appears to be creeping socialism. I think we've already covered some of the widely publicized Roosevelt programs known as the **New Deal. Stuart Chase** wrote an article for the *New Republic* entitled "A New Deal for America" in 1932. This would appear to be the origin of the term. **Chase** was an engineer and an economist who was influenced by *Fabian Socialism* and strongly supported their causes.

We all know about the highlights associated with **FDR's** administration, so let's look for some low lights. As we know the **Delano** portion of his name made a fortune out of the opium trade and his friend, Bernard Baruch, had a monopoly on the copper industry which allowed him to make millions out of World War I. Roosevelt's *National Recovery Act* actually reduced tariffs at a time when 12 million people were out of work. It is to be noted that **Lord Beaverbrook**, the *British Fabian socialist*, encouraged the White House to transfer billions of dollars into Germany during the 30s.

Henry Wallace was **Secretary of Agriculture** from 1933 to 1940 and Secretary of Commerce from 1945 to 1946. The American agricultural industry was coming out of its infancy and was becoming very efficient and productive, but Henry Wallace encouraged the policy of plowing the products of the earth into the ground, the slaughtering of animals, and paying for fertile land to lie fallow. This program, originating from the mind of **Professor Rexford Tugwell**, was advocated by the *Fabian Socialists*, thus placing agricultural land under government control. **Baron Israel Moses Seiff**, a member of several socialist organizations, a prominent British businessman and president of the *Political and Economic Planning think tank*, lobbied for this. He was involved in the retail business and later became chairman of Marks & Spencer, worldwide retailers of clothing and foodstuffs.

Harry Hopkins was the Edward Mandel House to Franklin Delano Roosevelt. He was the architect of the *WPA* and gave strong support to the $50 billion Lend-Lease program at the inception of World War II. He entered the field of social work as an administrator in New York City and was referred to Roosevelt by Macy's president. He built the government business into the largest employer in the nation, probably in the world. He was the go between to Churchill during World War II. He had tremendous influence in the diplomatic field.

President Roosevelt was surrounded by *Fabian Socialists* in his administration. Reagan's administration was also filled by bureaucrats with socialist ideologies, although he apparently was not aware of it. Many of the appointments were members of the *Heritage Foundation* which is a conservative *think tank*. But you've heard the saying, "things rarely are what they seem." John Coleman says that the power behind the foundation at the time was **Sir Peter Vickers Hall**, who was a leading member of the *Fabian Society.*

Harold L. Ickes (Secretary of the Interior), Wallace, Hopkins and **Frankfurter** were the powers behind the throne. A strong contender for such a position would be **John Maynard Keynes** who was a strong advocate of deficit spending and increased taxation. I think that he was an advocate of the *multiplier theory.* But was this the classic *wolf within a sheep's clothing?* He expressed a rather infamous opinion,"there is no subtler, no surer means of overturning the existing basis of society than to debauch the currency. The process engages all the hidden forces of economic law on the side of destruction, and does it in a manner which not one man in a million is able to diagnose." I think that I already mentioned that quotation. **Lord Keynes** had many people in his clique; **Felix Frankfurter, Walter Lippmann, Colonel House, Walt Whitman Rostow, Dean Acheson** and **Bernard Baruch** should be included

In 1941 the *Union for Democratic Action (UDA)* was formed by former members of the *Socialist Party of America* and the *Committee to Defend America by Aiding the Allies*, as well as by labor unions, liberal politicians and theologians. The *UDA* was co-founded by liberal theologian Reinhold Niebuhr, a member of the *Socialist Party of America*, and by James Isaac Loeb, the *International Ladies*

Garment Workers Union, and others. The organization and its members held influential positions in the presidential administration of FDR. The *UDA* supported a strongly interventionist, internationalist foreign policy and a pro-union, liberal domestic policy. It was strongly anti-Communist.

James Isaac Loeb advocated disbanding the *UDA.* It reappeared when the *Americans for Democratic Action (ADA)* was formed on January 4, 1947 which considered Communists wrong and a threat to the United States. Founding members of the *ADA* were Hubert Humphrey, John Kenneth Galbraith, Walter Reuther, Eleanor Roosevelt and Arthur Schlesinger. Jr. The *ADA* has had allegiances to the socialist cause and influence within the Democratic Party. The *ADA's* philosophy was freely expressed in the *New Statesma*n, a socialist publication. Members of the <u>Royal Institute of</u> <u>International Affairs</u> and the <u>CFR</u> lent them some of their ideas.

Frances Perkins was the **US Secretary of Labor** from 1933 to 1945. She was a graduate of Mount Holyoke College and was trained as a teacher. She did graduate work at the University of Pennsylvania and Columbia University. **Frances** was a reformer at heart and did push for changes in the New York State legislature. Her mentor was **Florence Kelley.** She and her friends would write booklets and pamphlets and circulate them through schools and universities and encourage the readers to write reviews and articles in the news media. It took a good deal of energy. She was involved in the women's movement, legislation involving unemployment compensation, child labor laws and the 40 hour work week. She helped put the labor movement into the New Deal coalition. *Social Security* was her idea. In 1962 she recounted how she managed to get around the Constitution to be able to accomplish this. Supreme Court Justice **Harlan Stone** told her, privately, that she could do this by using the taxing power of the US. She quoted him later as saying, "The taxing power of the Federal Government, my dear, the taxing power is sufficient for everything you want and need." A new law was enacted based on the power to levy payroll taxes.

The Supreme Court ruled 7-2 in favor of the *Social Security* program in 1937. Justices Brandeis and Stone were prescient here. So the *taxing power* of the US allowed *Social Security* and *Medicare* to become part of our history. Unfortunately someone should've explained to her that it was nothing but a *Ponzi* scheme since it was the current worker who had to pay the retirement or disability pension and there is

181

no guarantee that the economy will be always in an expansionary mode. It was not an annuity, but it gave Roosevelt a lot of extra money when the program started.

But let's give her the benefit of the doubt, or should we? We all know that it was a **Ponzi** *scheme*. It's a fairly simple scheme which was around for a long time. After all **Carlo Pietro Giovanni Guglielmo Tebaldo Ponzi** had been first sentenced in 1920 and I believe was finally deported in 1934. She had to know that she was involved in a **Ponzi** *scheme*. And she was well-educated and must have read **Charles Dickens'** *Martin Chuzzlewit* and *Little Dorrit* published in the mid-19th century. William F Miller had used the same scheme in 1899. And this from a nice socialist lady!

I suppose the Supreme Court was not asked to rule if a **Ponzi** *scheme* was legal. After all, they are very bright men, so are they all, come I to say that they are all very bright men.

The Constitution has been slowly eroded as it has been freely interpreted, its metal weakened, by the Supreme Court. **Roosevelt** appointed *eight new members to the Supreme Court.* The names of these members, inclined to be favorable to socialistic ideologies, were **Justices Hugo Black, Stanley F. Reed, Felix Frankfurter, William O. Douglas, Frank Murphy, James F. Byrnes, Robert H. Jackson, and Wiley Blount Rutledge.** The names of **Earl Warren, Warren Burger, Abe Fortas, Louis Brandeis,** and **Harlan Stone** demonstrated similar leanings.

Dean Gooderham Acheson was **Secretary of State** under President Truman from 1949 to 1953. He played a key role in the Cold War politics. He was involved in the Marshall Plan and the North Atlantic Treaty Organization (1949). He persuaded Truman to become involved in the Korean War in 1950. He also was instrumental in sending advisers to help the French in Indochina. While at Harvard Law School from 1914 to 1918 he came under the influence of **Felix Frankfurter** who was very influential in enhancing the cause of socialism. **Acheson** was also a law clerk to **Brandeis**, also an influential socialist. **Dean Acheson** became a partner in the law firm of **Covington, Burling and Rublee, Atcheson & Shorb.** Some of their clients would represent the companies or family members of rather important stature such as **Price Waterhouse, J. P. Morgan, Andrew Mellon, Kuhn, Loeb,** and **Felix Frankfurter.** Of interest is the fact that he promoted **Alger Hiss, Stuart Service, John Carter Vincent,**

Lauchlin Currie, all <u>**communist spies,**</u> to high positions in the State Department. The Republicans in the House of Representatives wanted him removed. Joseph McCarthy identified Acheson as one of the problems in the administration.

But we are now double-**Dean-ed,** I hope that doesn't mean double-down.   **Dean Rusk** was the **Secretary of State** from 1961 to 1969 under **JFK** and **Lyndon Johnson.** The definition of **"rusk"** is a *hard, dry biscuit or a twice-baked bread.* I guess you have to do something to distinguish yourself from a dry biscuit. Oh, oh! he was a *Rhodes Scholar* and received the *Cecil Peace Prize* in 1933. The ghost of **Cecil Rhodes** must have been very happy. He worked for the United Nations and at the time suggested that Korea should be split at the 38th parallel North into two spheres of influence between the US and the Soviet Union.   His advice apparently led to the decision to forbid **General Douglas MacArthur** to attack the Red Chinese army, as it was poised to cross the Yalu. He later became president of the **Rockefeller Foundation. Plutocratic** names keep coming up. I guess that is to be expected if you're really governed by the **plutocracy.** Well, I guess I did witness a double down. I meant the term as used in the casino, not in the sexual arena.

Walt Whitman Rostow was an economist who had a great deal to do with shaping US foreign policy in Southeast Asia during the 1960s. His parents were active socialists and named their three sons in memory of three prominent socialist: **Eugene V. Debs, Ralph Waldo Emerson** and **Walt Whitman.** A much more popular appellation in the past was George Washington Jefferson. I wonder what the socialist gene is called? Anyway, you always stumble upon something that's different and interesting. The virus of socialism must have infected the poor lad. He graduated from Yale University and was a *Rhodes Scholar* from 1936 to 1938. He also received his PhD from Yale. During World War II he was a major in the *(OSS)* which was responsible for espionage and helping the resistance movement in Europe. Of course we know that the *Rhodes Scholarship* is an **invitation** to joining the **New World Order** movement. **Clinton** was also a *Rhodes Scholar.* That may be the reason that **Walt Whitman Rostow** had been declared *a great security risk* by the State Department intelligence agency and the Air Force intelligence agency. He wrote in <u>*The United States in the World Arena,*</u> "It is a legitimate American National objective to see an end of nationhood as it has been historically *defined."*

He remained in a powerful position as an unelected representative of the American Socialists with an open door to Eisenhower, Kennedy and Johnson. Rostow appears to have had a good deal to do with diminishing the American defense capacity. He met Vasily Kuznetsov, a Kremlin foreign minister, to discuss America's first strike capability. Following his return, **Robert McNamara** cut back drastically on the missile-defense system, and the nuclear bomb production was curtailed. As a reward **Rostow** was appointed to Presidents Johnson's *National Security Council* in 1964. He played a prominent role in shaping the US foreign policy in Southeast Asia during the 1960s; he strongly supported US involvement in the Vietnam War. **Rustow** arranged for the ground forces to be sent to Vietnam against the advice of the Joint Chiefs of Staff. He served as a major security advisor in both the Kennedy and Johnson administrations.

There was plenty of blame to go around concerning the Vietnam War. McNamara is given the credit for being the architect of the Vietnam War. He wrote *In Retrospect* in which he enumerated about 11 lessons that he had learned. He apparently had ignored some advice. Here is sort of a *mea culpa*:

1. We misjudged the geopolitical intentions of the Viet Cong, the DRV, China and the USSR, and exaggerated the dangers to the United States of its actions.
2. We viewed the people and leaders of South Vietnam in our own experience.
3. We underestimated the power of nationalism to motivate a people to fight and die for their beliefs and values.
4. We were profoundly ignorant of the history, culture, and politics of the people in the area.
5. We failed to recognize the limitations of modern, high-tech military equipment, forces, and doctrine.
6. We failed to draw Congress and the American people into a full and frank discussion and debate of the pros and cons of becoming involved in large-scale military engagement in Southeast Asia.
7. We did not explain fully what was happening and why we were doing what we did. We failed to maintain national unity.
8. We failed to recognize that neither our people nor our leaders are omniscient. We do not have the God-given right to shape every nation in our own image or as we choose.
9. We erred in taking unilateral military action not supported by multinational forces and the international community.

10. We failed to recognize that in international affairs there may be problems for which there are no immediate solutions.

11. We failed to organize the top echelons of the executive branch to deal effectively with the extraordinarily complex range of issues at hand.

There is a quote from a former West Pointer and a former CIA Vietnam Chief of Station, by the name of DeSilva, "McNamara simply had no comprehension of how the war should be handled – – – fundamentally we lost because we were arrogant, prideful, and dumb."

Sounds like some stuff relating to America's military interventions in the Middle East. So it goes... the best and the brightest can be wrong, and very wrong indeed. Remember that it is your obligation to use your own **critical thinking.**

Arthur Schlesinger, Jr. it is also a well-publicized name. **Schlesinger, Eleanor Roosevelt, Hubert Humphrey** and **John Kenneth Galbraith** where the inspirational figures in the founding of the *ADA.* **Schlesinger's** biographical material reads like a *Who's Who* of influential, socialistically inclined Democrat Party members in the political, acting, writing and artistic fields. As we go along I'll be including many of the intellectual and political names that I find on the list. I'll omit the actors and writers since I'm really out of touch with those people.

He's quoted a lot. "We're not going to achieve a *new world order* without paying for it in blood as well as in words and money." He wrote in the *Partisan Review* in 1947, "there seems no inherent obstacle to the gradual implementing of socialism in the United States through a series of new deals which is a process of backing into socialism."

You really don't have to believe in **secret societies** or conspiracies to recognize that mankind records many political, financial, intellectual and philosophical movements which may or may not have effected any significant change. *Specialty Groups* have always separated themselves from the common herd. That applies to trade groups or any other group, be it financial, political, religious or whatever. *Powerful people* do not associate with the *common man.* Is that *prejudice?* **Henry Kissinger** is said not to discuss very much with *his barber.* And we all know that we would just love to jump into the *powerful people group* if we had the chance.

Let's review what we have learned about the goals of socialism. Socialism was an abstract concept before I started doing some of this research. Its mold from the abstract to the concrete now, and its foundations in America a peer to be made out of pretty solid concrete. We need to overstate a bit here so that it's very clear. The implementation of socialism was to be achieved slowly and without obvious violence, although socialism would benefit from national and international instability and wars. The aim was to slowly **penetrate** *established institutions* with a philosophy which overtly was filled with hope and kindness, such as equality for all and the protection of the innocent. The "well-intentioned innocents" could easily be converted, and the wealthy and intellectual elite would also be easy prey to convert. Of course the plutocrats would be excepted although their names would be attached to the movement. Of importance was to penetrate the educational system with *ideas of fairness* and social service, putting a stop to vocational schools and information about the world (eliminating geography) and the basic scientific studies. Reading is an essential part of *getting educated*, but socialism, with its strong propaganda mechanism enhanced by current technologies, has been able to bypass this. The **Rockefeller** *media* and associated publications easily disseminate socialistic propaganda. Under the guise of women's rights, they have put women to work and eliminated them as mothers and as custodians of the education of their children. The children have no homework. The goal of undermining marriage and putting the *education in the hands of the government*, rather than of the family, has been achieved. With a strong push in favor of minority rights, racial preferences and the *cultural acceptance of the least favored* members of society through the use of sexual and violent propaganda on the television, the cultural values have been seriously eroded. The *ACLU* has played a prominent part. *Religious values* are steadily attacked and *eroded*. Meanwhile the financial, cultural and governmental institutions find themselves to be minions of socialism. Under the guise of a paternalistic government which cares, we find that tariffs have been eliminated with the result that **manufacturing industries have disappeared** and good paying private *jobs no longer exist.* There is also a movement to tax property rights out of existence and to totally abolish any inheritance. The Internet has facilitated *total government control* with current documentation that the government records every private interaction. There has been a successful *erosion of the separation of powers in our government,* so that the Supreme Court changes the Constitution and takes the rights away from Congress; the presidency has usurped all sorts of powers given to the federal Congress, and also many of those given to the states, explicitly protected by the Constitution. As part of this agenda of destabilizing the nation state, the utopian solution can be found by following *the yellow brick road* which leads to the *New World Order*. *Socialism*, while espousing new hope for the individual, *actually takes away the liberty* of the individual. Much of this thinking is actually based upon the concept that the *average man is* really part of an inferior race, *homo dyssapiens*.

What have I missed? I don't think that I've made it clear enough that the focus is on massive state welfare, nationalization of industries, confiscation of wealth via taxation, except for the plutocracy. Abbreviated, the *goals of socialism* are rather simple, *the abolition of everything* – – *government, property rights, family, religion, nation states and human dignity.*

I still have difficulty understanding why a wealthy and powerful people are not afraid that all this power war be eventually turned against them? Perhaps I should consult with Lord Acton and ask him if *wealth* and *power* really makes you a *God*?

Let's review a little bit of the philosophy. The *Fabian Society* "therefore aims at the reorganization of society by the emancipation of land and industrial capital from individual ownership and turning them into the community for the general benefit. In this way only can natural and acquired advantages of the country be shared by the whole people." Many of the people involved in this process have been high-minded people. *Intellectuals* can be *unidimensional*, meaning that they are focused on only one issue, and they, figuratively, cannot tell the forests from the trees. Intellectuals can be used without having any understanding that they are but puppets, and very hard working and very well motivated puppets.

Goals and philosophies have changed over the years. The Macedonians and Romans ruled the world by the sword, and the sword was mightier than the word. Being corrupt and powerful was acceptable for a long period of time and the **Medicis** and the **Popes** did not seem to be bothered by this *positive* social philosophy. The Western world has now stumbled its way into a philosophical preference for *why can't we all get along?* I can think of *several hundred reasons*. You can too. This is now *Utopia on a grand scale!* Won't we be surprised if it doesn't work! Times have certainly changed. We now have our weapons of mass destruction which we can activate without getting out of our chairs. And with this technological revolution it may no longer be necessary to use the sword to conquer people. Technology can conquer *the spiritual and physical nature of homo dyssapiens.*

A *Liberal education* is a medieval concept which espouses the development of knowledge and skills and ethical values. In the 20th century more emphasis was placed on sciences and technical skills. But that has changed considerably with the evolution of *religious socialistic values* which is quite apart from developing any type of skill set and certainly places **critical thinking** in the shadows. It actually discourages it. The **Greeks** of ancient times were mostly concerned about the rights and obligations of citizens. A broad based education was offered which produced a well-rounded citizen aware of his place and responsibility in the society. **Socrates** played an important part in this, emphasizing that it was the duty of the student to form his own opinion through reason rather than indoctrination. It's obvious that education is fostered in the home. The school room adds another dimension. The late 19th and early 20th century American schools really required children to learned a great deal about many many subjects. College graduates now are unable to pass eighth-grade tests that the children easily passed back around 1910. The American educational system doesn't support the development of individualism since this would undermine the state mandated education which produces non-critical conformists. I don't think that most educators realize that they are doing this to the kids.

There are always competing choices within an educational system, but that is eliminated when the government issues educational policies and practices. The socialist preoccupation with cultural, ethnic and religious issues within the context of so many different cultural backgrounds has led to a robotized philosophy of overly respecting aberrant lifestyles and quite moronic points of view. This has led to the hiring of "word reviewers" to delete any word in any sentence, in any paragraph, in any book which could even be faintly interpreted as offensive to an ignorant or paranoid few. Religion has even been expunged from history books, and certainly there is no need for any geography anymore, certainly if we believe that we are all creatures of the world. This is true **Aristotelian logic** and I'm sure that **Aristotle** would be very proud of me. It's interesting that some say that state and local governments have too much influence in the education of their local students. That's a laugh when they always do what the federal government tells them to do for fear of losing their funding.

I guess it's time to study the effects of **socialism** on American education. We know that **Harold Laski** lectured at the *London School of Economics* and that he and **Wallas** toured the American institutions as salesmen for socialism and they were quite successful. **Laski** was known as a brilliant lecturer who humiliated people who raised any questions. Ralph Miliband, one of **Laski**'s students, was really enthralled by him and said, "His lectures taught... A faith that ideas mattered, the knowledge was important and its pursuit exciting... His seminars taught tolerance, the willingness to listen although one disagreed, the values of ideas being confronted..... It was also a sieve of ideas, a gymnastics of the mind carried on with vigor and directed unobtrusively with superb craftsmanship... That by helping young people he was helping the future and bringing nearer that brave world in which he so passionately believed."

The 10th Amendment of the Constitution reserves the right to educate for the states. The federal government is prohibited from meddling in education. There has been a horrible decline in education with landmark cases being decided by socialist judges. Let's look at **Everson v. Board of Education** brought before the New Jersey Supreme Court in 1943. Mr. Everson objected to the funding of transportation for children attending religious schools. New Jersey allowed the town to continue funding transportation to all schools. The *ACLU* took the case to the Supreme Court where **Justice Black** was holding court. The Supreme Court was actually packed with socialists, several of whom were *Masons*. The court applied the *Establishment Clause in the Bill of Rights to State Law.* The original interpretation was that "Congress shall make no law respecting an establishment of religion," without imposing any restrictions on the states. The Establishment Clause had been interpreted as prohibiting the establishment of a national religion by Congress, together with treating all religions equally.

The **Black** court, and I mean *black*, stated that the religious power of the States would now be subject to the *Due Process Clause* of the 14th Amendment. The courts have outlawed prayers in school, they have banned oral Bible readings and attendance at prayer services on school property. Longtime traditions and customs such as singing Christmas carols are prohibited. Religious instruction by teachers has been prohibited

The *National Education Association (NEA)* is philosophically based in socialism. It has advocated the deletion of history, geography

189

and civics. There certainly is a lack of teaching and emphasis about the American Revolution, the ideas of the **Founding Fathers**, and any study of the American Constitution. *Minority rights* and *feel good studies* have replaced the archaic philosophies of education. We certainly do not want to overtax those poor students with things that do not apply at all anymore, and interfere with the educational impact of concentrating on video games for six hours a day.

If you believe that that there has been a malicious and concerted effort to undermine American education, then you need to turn to the writings of the people who point to the **Tavistock Institute.** I found very little.

The **Everson v. Board of Education** set things in motion. In 1945 the *National Education Association (NEA)* sponsored legislation that would not allow federal funding of private schools.. The *Supreme* Justices barred the Christian education curriculum from public schools. Another example of *the slippery slope.* Remember that **Justice Black (ominous)** was a *Mason.* John Coleman quotes from some *Masonic* tenents regarding education, "Next to this, the form of learned literary society is best suited for our purposes and had not *Masonry* existed, this cover would have been employed and it may be much more than a cover, it may be a powerful, engine in our hands. By establishing reading societies and subscription libraries and taking these under our direction and supplying them through our labors, we may turn the public mind which way we will... We must win the common people in every corner. This will be obtained chiefly by means of schools, and by open, party behavior, popularity and tolerance of their prejudices which at leisure ruled out and dispel... We must acquire the direction of education, of church management-- of the professional chair and of the pulpit."

Then there is the case of **Brown v. Board of Education** which is another landmark decision making separate but equal unconstitutional. I'm thinking of how crazy this can all be. This really appears to be a very good thing by helping the blacks to overcome oppression. *Affirmative action* has been helpful to the **blacks** who have shown the motivation and capacity to use that advantage. It has now outgrown its purpose. A good example of that is the fact that there are many slots open for blacks at the college level, but the reservoir has run dry. We move on into that **Neverland** of the elimination of all discrimination and prejudice where everyone must forcibly be taught to think and act in prescribed ways. But taken to its logical extreme, and

190

extreme we have seen it to be, then this is the new *Law of Meshugana*, yes, the *Law of Craziness*. *It logically follows*... that all sexes, all mixtures of them, must have *no* boundaries; that there can be *no* Women's club, *no* Men's club; *no* ethnic club, such as the Italian Club; *no* private golf courses; *no* exclusion of child molesters; and certainly *no* exclusion from the *Bilderberg Group*.

We've covered the fact that every one is born with comparisons and prejudices and choices right from birth. That is part of the **natural order**, and here we are trying to force an *unnatural order* into every American human being. Let's put a clear definition to the noun *prejudice*. *Prejudice* is *the innate capacity to recognize differences between both animate and inanimate objects without moral judgment*.

The court which heard the **Brown v. Board of Education** relied rather heavily on the report of **Karl Gunnar Myrdal** which concluded that American education was giving the blacks a raw deal. His report had quite an impact on the Supreme Court. **Karl Gunnar Myrdal** was paid $250,000 by a **Carnegie Foundation** to study race relations in the United States.. I wonder who authorized did you authorize this war was a clone you authorize this part well I'm wondering whether Chloe authorize that since you already had one well yeah you both get one for both one for each now don't let that you go out and close the door I don't what the dogs to have a chance to get this close the door please that?

Myrdal and his wife toured the United States and described the American people as "narrow minded whites, written by evangelical mystic religion." He described the southern white as "poor, uneducated, coarse and dirty." He certainly sounds like a fellow without prejudice. **Myrdal** had a history of working for **Walt Whitman Rostow.** He also had made statements showing contempt for the Constitution. He published his impartial findings in his book, "*An American Dilemma: The Negro Problem and Modern Democracy.*" His meritorious work was rewarded when he received the Nobel prize in economics in 1974. There always seems to be a story behind every story. We often feel a lot better not knowing what the real story is.

The founding ideas imbued in our Constitution are not taught in our schools. The Supreme Court attack on its principles is never discussed. The *secret* stories behind its **reevaluation** by the *Supremest Court* is not known to most of us. The students would just have too much information. With the creeping indoctrination of students, the resultant adult does not have enough information to make any informed judgment. The very roots of his own existence are unknown.

Key educational positions, particularly at the level of professors and college presidents, are occupied by socialists. Socialists are in the diplomatic service, in the United States State Department, in the House and Senate, in key banking positions which control the money of the nation. They also occupy important positions in the military and communication businesses. They make public opinion and they are entrenched.

That the American citizenry has accepted the *disintegration of the American family*, as they say in the Supreme Court parlance, can be viewed as a "*landmark decision.*" The *ghost of a family* simply allows the children, and the resultant adults, to sit in front of the television and watch movies and listen to *shaken rap*. And the girls are now free to engage in the new culture of *sexual liberalism* (devoid of significant emotional relationships), enhanced by a *drug additive.*

Has **Socialism** made inroads into the religious area? But what is religion? The **Biblical God** was an all powerful man who was very vengeful. **Jesus** came along and taught tolerance and forgiveness, but the **Inquisition** grilled people and put them to death. The Church told people that the Bible was not subject to revision, and any questioners should be referred to the death chambers. Now the Church merely *Excommunicates* people with the promise of eternal damnation.

I need to look up the definition of what religion is. One definition includes "*the worship of a super human controlling power, God of God's.*" A second definition is "*a cause, principle, or system of beliefs held to with ardor and faith.*" The theologian **Paul Tillich** said that faith is "the state of being alternatively concerned is itself a religion." Paul Tillich is also quoted as saying, "Religion is the state of being grasped by an ultimate concern, a concern which qualifies all other concerns as preliminary and which itself contains the answer to the question of the meaning of life." John Dewey defines it thus, "the religious is any activity pursued on behalf of an ideal and against obstacles and in spite of threats of personal loss because of his general and enduring value." Another simply says "**details of belief as taught or discussed.**" That sounds a lot like any basic belief, *Socialism*. Ergo, *Socialism has become a Religion.* The bureaucracy and the government ideology has become a religion.

But socialists say religion is a problem. *Religious people* are characterized as compassionate, caring people who are interested in the rights of people and the poor. These are important issues. But the ecumenical movement is one which appears to dilute religion, rather than strengthening it. It's sort of a, "Can't we all get along? approach. The Roman church appears to be helping the cause of socialism. It's become prominent in the *Fellowship of Child Molestation.* The Church has lost a lot of its faithful by not changing with the times. You go to hell if you practice birth control, let alone abortions. Their priests have to be celibate, and forgo all their natural social and sexual urges.

Years ago I was talking to a former *Mafia* bag man, turned lawyer and administrator, about why the *Church* was closing all of its schools and many of its churches in the United States. My memory is not that good, so I'll just paraphrase him, "Follow the money, they have so much money that they don't need any paltry contributions from the members." We know that if you conquer land and you don't keep any boots on the ground, you lose the land. So the *Church is aiding the cause of Socialism*, whether through naïveté or a malicious method to its madness.

Many prominent **theologians** seem to have been converted to the *Socialist Church*. It's like having **Laski** and **Wallas** spreading the gospel from the pulpit. A prominent member of the *Socialist Church* was **Harry F. Ward** who taught ethics at the *Union Theological Seminary* from 1918 to 1941. He came under the influence of **Jane Addams**, founder of *Hull House.* He grew rather radical and saw the church as the instrument to rectify the structural failings of society. He resigned from the *ACLU* when the organization was forced to bar Communists from holding office. He did a great deal of lecturing and was involved in many socialist movements.

The *Union Theological Seminary in the City of New York* was established in 1836 under the aegis of the Presbyterian Church. It was known as a center of *liberal Christianity* and was the birthplace of the *Black Liberation Theology* and the *Womanist Theology.* The Seminary is known to have had an outstanding faculty and has taught students from around the world. You can only imagine the significant impact that they have had on budding theologians. It is now known by its alternate name, the *Union Theological Socialist Seminary (UTSS).*

Another *contributing* theologian was named **Karl Paul Reinhold Niebuhr**. He was a professor at the **Union Theological**

Seminary for over 30 years. He is characterized as being a very good speaker and very influential in public affairs. Oozing of *humility* he viewed most theologians as having lesser minds. In 1938 **Niebuhr** joined the socialist *American Association of University Professors.* He's one of the founders of the *ADA* and a member of the *LID.* He was a fan of **Graham Wallas.** He espoused a **Marxist** philosophy and was appointed by **Rockefeller** to the "*Commission* on *Freedom of the Press*" and later to the **Council on Foreign Relations**. He wanted the idealists to become more like himself, a realist. **Arthur Schlesinger Jr.** said that he was, "the most influential American theologian of the 20th century."

The *Federal Council of Churches (FCC),* which was founded in 1908, later known as the *World Council of Churches (WCC),* had a socialist focus on the fields of education and labor relations from its inception. **Mark Starr,** the British socialist appointed by **Roosevelt** to a number of government posts, apparently used the church to distribute *Fabian Society* literature. It apparently has been funded by the **Carnegie** and **Rockefeller** foundations. It is now known by the name of the *National Council of the Churches of Christ in the USA (NCC),* and is composed of 37 Christian faith groups in the United States, with 45 million adherents.

It would appear that the *main Socialist religious activity* in the United States is centered in the *Riverside Church* which is funded by the *New York City Rockefeller Foundation. "The New York Times"* in 2008 described it as "a stronghold of activism and political debate throughout its 75 year history." The Dulles family dominated the *Federal Council of Churches of Christ in America (FCCA).* In 1935 the *United States Navy intelligence service* said of the *FCCA* – – – "this is a large radical pacifist organization – – – it's leadership consists of a small radical group that is always very active in an matter against national defense." The Dies committee took sworn testimony from an expert who said "apparently, in.lieu of promoting Christianity among its several members it (the *FCCA*) more represents a huge political machine and appears to meddle in radical politics. It's directorate indicates that it into locks with many of the most radical organizations.".

The *Fellowship of Faiths* has also been influential in diluting the influence of the major religions by promoting the ecumenical movement and forcing all the religions to espouse to that wonderful doctrine of *Why Can't We All Get Along?* It has been around since

1921.

Our culture now believes that **God** needs to be a tolerant person, at least on paper. But our **God** is really **Socialism** which seeks to curtail personal freedom and embraces a new **pantheistic** religion of the **New World Order** and the **United Nations,** which of course themselves bow in **proskinesis** at the altar of the wealthy descendants of the **Black Nobility** who espouse socialism for everybody else but their **plutocratic** family circle. I guess that's as succinct as I can get. I'm sure you'll say it's just a whole lot of **meshugana.**

I had no idea that this would be such an adventure when I went off the beaten path. I certainly have learned a lot.

X

SYNESTHESIA IN THE AMERICAN EDUCATIONAL
REVOLUTION

.   My friend read the chapter on education, "The only good thing
in that chapter was the one about the doctors, where they waste 20
years in the educational system to get a *political* diploma, an M.D.
They then spend another 4 years in *residency training* learning how to
treat patients. I don't know when the educational system changed from
teaching people practical things to one of abstract thinking. Murderers
were hired as professors. They kill creative thinking and the art of
survival. You really specialize in chaff. You really should put some
thinking into this so-called *thinking book.*"

     A political diploma? I remember him saying, "an engineer
doesn't know how to do anything until he's worked with a practicing
engineer for at least a year." That's really the same with lawyers, they
have no idea what the practice of law is all about until they've been
with the firm for at least a year. My friend is really fixated on the idea
that wisdom only comes down to experience.

     I know that we don't use 95% of what we've learned in school.
We forget a lot of the stuff that we should remember and a lot gets
rusty. Steve Jobs and Bill Gates didn't see much potential in academe.
We know that the great thinkers, observers and inventors of the past
were motivated by individual effort and often had to resist the
established thinking of the time. Eventually the great universities
became museums with tenured people, holders of the keys to the doors
locked to creativity.

     My friend has been a part of academia and industry. He's
found that scientific progress bypasses the educational system and is
now found in industry and its labs. Intel created the semiconductor.
Diversity comes into the picture here. Put people into a room with a
problem, and let them give one another different ideas. A point of
departure for further inquiry will be found. Intuition and common
sense play key roles in the process. My friend says, "the whole
educational process is a waste of time." I agree with him. I can see the
end of the educational system as we know it. It's so expensive that we
can no longer afford it. The parents don't put the effort into it. The kids
are part of the *me generation*. The quality of the teachers is going

down as each generation reflects the lowered standards.

I have been saying, somewhat in jest, that we should close the schools since anyone can use a hand held computer and instantly get an answer to any question. Of course it may not be the right one, but it usually will give you something in the neighborhood of what you're looking for. Who needs to learn all that information? You don't even have to learn to multiply.

We now have access to an incredible amount of information on the Internet. And there is a human compulsion to put data about oneself or one's field of interest. It's probably a recognizable psychiatric disorder. People are out there putting all sorts of information on *Facebook* and *Twitter* and whatever else is available. A ton of software gives you easy access to scientific and mathematical computer programs that already know what your wish list is. You don't have to pull a genie out of the bottle anymore, and if you do pull a genie out of a bottle, he simply refers you to the computer program, or if necessary, to a computer programmer.

So my computer friend has come to the conclusion that knowledge should be abandoned in the educational process. It's available if you need it. There are computer models for virtually anything. The mathematician or the scientific expert can always get with the computer guy and put together a program that you need.

You know as well as I that geometry, trigonometry and calculus are almost never used. The basic useful concepts can be taught in a few hours. So let's not focus on knowledge or "data collection." The study of the arts might actually be more useful. Does rote memory encourage people to think?

We know that kids are naturally inquisitive. A good parent can be an incredibly good teacher before the kids go to school. Kids are always asking questions. They just naturally pick up all the information that parents are willing to talk about. The more the parents know, the more the kids can learn. Parents can teach children how to be observant and help explain why things are as they are and why things work. Before children go to school they know how to answer phones, use computers, tablets and all sorts of state-of-the-art tools. They learn how to dress themselves, how to eat, how to tie shoelaces, how to take batteries out of flashlights, how to pull toys apart, and how to get under your skin. There are a lot of timeouts if they are to develop a conscience, social skills and a sense of priorities. Parenting is not an easy job.

Our society tries to avoid intrusiveness into the family structure. I think there is some sort of story in the Bible about putting seed into a bad soil and that the seed is not going to grow. That applies to parenting. Many children enter the school system with little chance of succeeding. The parents don't know how to be parents, many of them use drugs and alcohol to excess, many are very unstable, many lack moral values and don't care what happens to the kids. Once the children enter school, the harm to the kids rapidly surfaces and the teachers have a lot of work to do.

Children are inquisitive as they enter school. They haven't learned how to hate school yet. They can learn that fairly easily. That choo-choo train of learning is just chugging along until it is derailed by the **Grand Educator**. Educators are adults who forget what children are all about. Although they will deny it, they structure the educational process as if the child were an adult. It's really counterintuitive. It damages the whole way that kids naturally learn, enjoy the learning process, put efforts into it and enhance their creative potential. And that's a whole lot of presumptive verbiage on my part.

That's how a bureaucracy functions. It has grown up in the bureaucracy, it is rewarded by following the dictates of bureaucracy, it doesn't get promoted if it asks questions of the bureaucracy. You have to be a robot to succeed, otherwise your choo-choo train is going to be derailed. Why is my thinking at a choo-choo train level? You know what indoctrination is all about. It feels good to be part of a system. I believe that most of the people in the system think that they are doing something good. That seems to be changing, most of the teachers now feel that they are victims. The principals know that they can't withstand many parental complaints without getting fired by the superintendent or his designated bouncer. It is part of that **natural order** of things.

So what should we be doing. We recognize that the primary and secondary schools are rather sickened and in failing health. It is natural to point at a problem. Looking at the reasons is another issue, especially if the root cause is the parent. The American parent has abandoned his or her responsibility. It apparently is all part of a cultural shock. People used to strive to better themselves. People were pretty poor in the 19th century. But the average person was looking to identify with people who had achieved something. If you look at those

198

old photographs, many with sepia tones, they all had *going to church and meeting clothes*. And they used to go to church. Now people go to fancy restaurants and to church in jeans and don't even have *going to church and meeting clothes*. The culture has done a 180 and tries to emulate the poorer standards of the society. It's another one of these issues, like terrorism, which is so multifaceted in causation that it defies explanation. Everyone has a different explanation. Maybe we should have another chapter on, "how many explanations can you think of?"

American citizens and educators have been aware of the problem for a long time. Education is truly on a **slippery slope** and no one has thrown it a life-saving rope, let alone a winch to help it come back up. Throwing money at the problem has done nothing to help it. And with the declining economy, there is less of that available. Are we facing the problem of the Gordian knot? That's an interesting Greek legend. Gordius was a peasant who was made king. In gratitude he tied his oxcart with a very complex knot and dedicated it to Zeus. The legend goes that whoever could untie the knot would rule Asia. Alexander the Great apparently was not a great puzzle solver and simply cut the knot with his sword. It really has to do with an old Aristotelian logical puzzle which really can't be solved. But that would make this paragraph a bit longer, and I know that you are tiring of my side comments by now.

But what about higher education? We've seen that highly educated graduates leave school heavily indebted, with little prospect of ever repaying the debt, only to find the absence of something. The something is akin to the Gordian knot, a mythical job. Has he been sold a bill of goods by the culture and educators? We already know, short of technical schools, that graduates don't know how to work in the fields that the education purported to teach them. They now start the process of on-the-job training, be that as a medical doctor, a lawyer or engineer. Why not bypass the educational system and start them in the on-the-job training process, a *new and improved educational process*.

This book started as an inquiry into the nature of **thinking**. But we've learned that **critical thinking** is unnatural and has to be taught. It should be intuitive, but it ain't. So the prime focus of **education** needs to be on how to **teach critical thinking**.

There is some humor built into this. Recent presidents of Harvard University seem to highlight some of the flaws in our thinking processes. President Nathan Pusey urged the 321st graduating classes of Harvard University to go forth and do great things as highly educated men, and women since Radcliffe was included. This pinnacle of education was simply parroting a self-serving, self deception of academe. After all, he was just part of a few thousand years of the evolution of university education.

Let's go over that again. You'll remember that **Dr. Siaramsed** summed it up pretty well in his book, *The Sense of Nonsense*. He put it this way:

1- The 3R's go back 2500 years
2- Molding good conduct and character also goes back 2500 years
3- Socratic wisdom warred against political skills back 2500 years
4- Aristotle wanted state-controlled education
5- Athletics was important 2500 years ago; few people were educated
6- 900 years ago schools to educate the clergy were licensed
7- 900 years ago teachers were licensed by examination
8- 600 years ago the first liberal treatise was written
9- 500 years ago Luther pushed for peasant education
10- 500 years ago the grading system was born
11- 500 years ago the need for better pay for teachers was recognized
12- 500 years ago the need for more student freedom was noted
13- 500 years ago tutoring and individual attention were promoted
14- 500 years ago Puritans establish a fundamentalist theocracy
15- 400 years ago American schools stressed ancient language and literature
16- 300 years ago Franklin urged useful teaching in the schools
17- 200 years ago discipline and rote memory prevailed
18- 200 years ago the individual needs of the child were noted
19- 200 years ago the kindergarden was founded
20- 200 years ago Massachusetts set up a board of education
21- 150 years ago Vassar, a female college was founded
22- 150 years ago schools for teachers were founded
23- 150 years ago experimental schools allowed students to

self-teach

But let's get back to some issues having to do with recent Harvard presidents. **Lawrence Summers** was forced to resign when he tried to change the tenured bureaucracy of the University. But I think the *coup de grace* came as a result of his statement that women really did not have a high-end aptitude for science and engineering. He was the Secretary of Treasury for 2 years during the Clinton Administration. He has financially advised Obama. I don't know if he had much to do with the Obama contribution going to the banks rather than into an investment in the infrastructure of the nation. I wonder if Lawrence Summers is another budding Robert McNamara.

He was replaced by *Dr. Faustus*. That's right, the fellow who makes deals with **Lucifer**. I think that's rather droll. His name is **Drew Faust**. He seems to have a few problems to solve. 90% of the Harvard College students have A's, the rest fall off the precipice. It's an interesting variant of the bell shaped curve. And what to do about the fact that a very high percentage of students about to graduate have been caught cheating? It's not just a cultural change, it's a geometric shift.

The government has set the academic curriculum in stone, and despite their differences, the teachers unions are not about to allow much turf-changing. But let's proceed. In looking at that short evolution of the educational teaching system, we note that it reflects the **natural order.** It started with the clerics and the wealthy being educated, and 500 years ago Luther was pushing for some peasant education. So the peasants get educated minimally, and only the elite managed to go to college and to the University. It seems that you really can't drag the peasants into the elitist group. We've seen it fail.

So my friend is going to engineer a new educational system from the top down, or perhaps you could say that it's from the bottom up. Upon entering school the student will be exposed to the secrets of higher education and receive a better education than what is offered in our colleges today. "That's nonsense," you'll say. It does sound like nonsense but it does work. I'll prove it to you as I go along. It's like deductive reasoning, you put together a lot of information, become a generalist and then you choose to be a tradesman in some specialty. Can you find anything that's *illogical* in that analogy?

But before you read about this *new and improved version of education* I would refer you to a D.C. Phillips publication of 2008

201

entitled *Philosophy of Education*. It is an excellent summary of all the opinions and philosophies since the days of the Greeks. It is absolutely overwhelming in terms of its breath and depth of knowledge and perspectives. His bibliography will keep you in good reading for a few years. I cringe as I implore you to continue reading this humble and simplistic educational offering. Phillips refers to a Blackwell anthology, with 60 papers considered to be important in the field, and which also are representative of the range of work that is being done (Curren, 2007).

Just to give you a preview of what will happen after the first 8 years of education, the second phase of this *new and improved educational process* would start at age 13. Having finished his academic prerequisites, he would enter the workforce in an area which interests him. He would be an apprentice and learn from hands-on experience. He would have the satisfaction of enjoying what he was doing and learning and improving as he went along. A lot of people have been incredibly successful starting at the bottom. Anything that you need to know is just a scroll away on some sort of computer. I discussed this idea with a high school teacher. I found him to be a funny fellow. He said, "your friend's an idiot, he's as bad as that lady on BBC who wants to include pornography in the school curriculum." I personally think that my friend is a lot like a kamikaze pilot. His torpedo may not hit the target, but if he doesn't go out like a bomb, he'll certainly get a lot of attention.

So much for trying to get some humor into this. Let's get on with it. The world has significantly changed since the last major innovation occurred in education 150 years ago. Our culture has changed and our educational system is falling apart. Changes are occurring at lightning speed and it is the age of high-tech. Kids are pretty good at high-tech before they enter school. The average teacher is already being taught by the student. The way kids learn has basically changed and the educational system has to adapt to the **New Technological Age**. The teacher has quite a challenge. She (most teachers are a she) must endeavor to make a good and thinking person out of this *thing* walking into a classroom for the first time. This *thing* has a transformation experience in store.

The *thing* comes with many characteristics and propensities. It is naturally inquisitive, competitive, selfish, emotional, impulsive and devoid of critical thinking. His biased, judgmental tendencies can be modified as he is taught social skills, exposed to world cultures and is exposed to **critical thinking**.

We've seen where change does not necessarily mean progress, unless you choose to define progress as regression. We'll go back and plagiarize some ideas that go back 3 or 400 years. I'll quote from **Sellig M.K. Siaramsed's** famous book *The Sense of Nonsense More Tails from the Red Fox*, "Johann Heinrich Pestalozzi is given credit for the foundations of modern elementary education. He was a Swiss educational reformer who influenced American education. Experience was the fundamental idea. A person develops his own knowledge by his own investigation." Who said that before? Was that Aristotle? A new idea? I wonder if Pestalozzi read Aristotle? Education was focused on the individual needs of the child. Of course he spoke to the issue of everyone being well-rounded. This was before all the kids were getting fattened, so to say, well-rounded, by the fast food chains, for the slaughter. Pestalozzisms abounded: "*The art of education must be significantly raised in all its facets to become a science that is to be built on and proceed from the deepest knowledge of human nature...*" This "learning by head, hand and heart" apparently was responsible for illiteracy being eliminated in Switzerland by 1830. *"A person develops his own knowledge by his own investigation,"* is pretty scary stuff. We'll proceed with this in mind.

Reading has to be emphasized. It can be done from a book or from a computer tablet, or whatever. A visual imprint is very important in the learning process. You can let the students read from simple texts in many fields. They can choose the books, but they should be exposed to several fields. It's okay if they just find one topic and stick to that. They've already chosen their area of interest. We know that people naturally gravitate to areas of interests. Sports is a very popular area of interest. Others are drawn to dancing, music, movies and some even like bird books. There's always a kook around. He might have some of that *synesthesia* that we've talked about.

The students have to know how to read so that they can extract information in the future. Students can be encouraged to stand up and give a brief synopsis of what they have read. That enhances the scope of everybody's experience exponentially. The kid hasn't had to waste his time reading his peers' books but he hopefully gets a concise cream of the information that was in that book. I'm against giving grades in this context. We are simply encouraging students to find their own way. Some reward for putting in the effort would certainly not be discouraged, maybe some ice cream or cookies for the whole class.

The student is **inquisitive**. That's a natural teaching tool. A question and answer period should be an everyday occurrence. Let the kid ask any question that he wants. Encourage the other students to answer the question. The teacher should feel free to comment and answer the question. If she doesn't know the answer, she should own up to it. She can find the answer later and can also make it a class project. This can be done in two ways. The children can ask the parents and get them involved in what is happening in school. You can make a game out of looking things up in books and on the Internet. It can be great fun. You can also make the teacher cringe and the children can have fun teasing the teacher. School should be fun.

The student is **competitive**. That can be so useful. The teacher can put small groups into competitive teams to investigate anything, create anything, come up with their own games and choose things that they would like to do. They could then vote on the various proposals. The teacher could then raise the pros and cons, sneak up with **critical thinking**, and then have the kids vote on the proposals again.

The student is **emotional & impulsive**. Poor behaviors and poor decisions can be discussed by the students. It's a wonderful way of building social skills and **critical thinking**.

The study of *world cultures* and the *geographical locations of these world cultures* are just filled with avenues of investigation into **inquisitiveness, prejudice,** and **biases. Ignorance** is the dread disease to be feared in any educational process. The more you know about things in a general way, the better you are equipped to make decisions later on. And if the teachers have been skilled enough to teach you enough about the need to use **critical thinking**, you are prepared to face the work. Is this a sneaky way of teaching kids? You bet it is. Bring on the kamikaze pilot!

Critical thinking must lurk behind whatever facts are offered to the student, and certainly quite openly whenever an issue is being discussed. The students are simply asked what they think about the subject being discussed. Opinions are to be encouraged. They can have fun doing this. Hopefully the teacher will have some sense of humor and will encourage the students to disagree. School can really be a lot of fun especially if you're not being graded.

Without being accused of teaching religion in the schools by the *ACLU*, morality can be embedded in all discussions about cultures and their habits. Repetition is certainly a good way of doing this. It's good to be kind to people, to be fair to people, to respect other individuals and races, to be polite and to show some pleasure and enthusiasm when someone wins or achieves something. You should expect the same in return.

You could even show a video having to do with **good manners.** Somebody could put together a very funny video which would show some differences in what is considered good manners in different cultures. The **Three Stooges** could make some appearances. Good manners could certainly be a standard in the classroom. Maybe you can sneak some oriental philosophy in here, something having to do with being in harmony with one another. You could even use the names of **Confucius** and **Buddha** with a brief history of their lives and teachings. There is really nothing in there to offend the *ACLU*, so you don't have to be worried about being sued.

We know that people are trying to be creative and innovative in many areas... outside of the educational field. Maybe the Shanghai *city enclosed within a skyscraper* concept will work out and become a new standard. Perhaps the *kamikaze attack on education* will also catch on. It would be innovative to introduce the kids to the manual arts, how things work, and and to the basics that anyone needs to be able to function on a daily basis. This would include having some idea of how to use tools, such as a drill or a wrench, seeing a Phillips head screwdriver and an Allen wrench. It's good to know what is under the sink, how to turn the water off, where the electric breaker box is and what to do in case of an emergency. You should also know something about banks, stocks, bonds, mortgages, checks, credit cards and the antiquated cash system. There is a lot of simple, practical stuff that needs to be covered.

When reporters ask most adults simple questions about countries, continents and current events, they are stunned by the level of <u>uncovered ignorance</u>. The children should be exposed to earth sciences so that they understand why rain, cyclones and tides occur, what ecosystems are involved, where rocks, stones, gold and diamonds come from. That is a lot of interesting stuff which the kids run into every day. You might even *pique* the interest of the potential chef by introducing the students to various food groups and the varied *cuisines* around the world. The mothers might donate some samples; most parents would be happy to oblige, even if it's not originally manufactured in the home cooking restaurant.

205

We'll get into the real meat and potatoes when the children are about age 10 or 11. They're ready to tackle tough concepts. They should be introduced to the **Knowability principle**. But we'll call it the **Should-a-known-that principle** in this educational curriculum. This principle was known for eons. **Werner Heisenberg** made it into a complex mathematical formulation in 1927. It became known as the **Heisenberg principle**.

We'll have to digress a bit here. Newton's perception of the world was that it existed and could be precisely measured, regardless of the observer. I believe that Einstein felt the same way. Heisenberg postulated that you couldn't measure the location and the velocity of a particle simultaneously with any precision. In trying to precisely observe either the location or the momentum, your very observation altered the other. Then there was the issue about the entity itself. The entity was either a particle or a wave. That just didn't make any sense. The entity could change into either form at the preference of the observer. I think that I now have a better understanding of **shape shifting**. I don't know if it was the Copenhagen interpretation that wave and particle coexisted? Newton was familiar with and used precise measurements. In contrast, Quantum mechanics just offered you probabilities which were forever changing. Not an exact religion! I wonder if *Chaos theory* is just one of the multiple mathematical probability theories?

Werner Heisenberg apparently was clairvoyant and had a *vision* in 1926. He saw himself in Hitler's SS headquarters in 1937 being accused of being a traitor since he was a "white Jew in science." He was blessed with *synesthesia* and saw himself as a particle at the SS headquarters, being moved at some unknown rate of speed towards an unknown location. He saw an equation with the probability that he would be in a concentration camp. He appealed directly, through a friend, to Heinrich Himmler. He was eventually exonerated. It was not long after he had that vision that he understood the vision as God's way of giving mankind the **Uncertainty principle**.

Let me return to the **Should-a-known-that principle**. It is based on observation and critical thinking. Whenever a student fails to observe something, or makes a bad decision based upon unverified "facts," the teacher needs to confront him in a pleasant way. The teacher shows him how to use **critical thinking**. Once the class gets used to this, the class will inevitably respond with, "**I should-a-known-that.**" You know that humans, children not being exempted, are constantly coming to invalid conclusions because they don't **slow** down and think. We all do it all the time. We walk by things all the time, not noticing the obvious. So that teacher gets a chance to teach **critical thinking** as often as she pleases. This **Should-a-known-that principle** is a handy tool in the teacher's locker. For kids to really enjoy doing this, you must convince them that the **Should-a-known-that principle** is really a game. Remember, learning has to be fun. It needs to compete with so many enjoyable distractions.

Our world is also constantly changing. You hear people saying, "the only thing that's certain is that something is going to change." So you can start asking the students to be on the alert for examples of the **rule of persistent variation.** I discussed this with my consultant. He gave me his predictable response, "get rid of it. This section can't be farcical. Can't you ever be serious? You have to convince the reader that this book wasn't just a big waste of his time. You're giving an entirely new meaning to the concept of *good scholarship.*"

Remember that the **Educational Revolution** is greatly facilitated by the availability of new tools. There is the **computer,** the **tablet**, the **cell phone**, the **Kindle**, all of whom bow down and perform the *proskinesis* to their master at the **Internet**. If you're not familiar with the word *proskinesis*, it means getting on your knees and kissing the master's foot.

The schools are already in the process of retooling and placing a lot of computers in the classrooms. Certainly the high-tech industry would come to the aid of the educational industry. The computer, a laptop, the tablet, the Kindle and the cellular could be designed for each school system so that interfacing was easy, and cheap.

We know that the **visual imprint** and the **repetition** of that visual imprint or the repetition of our mental image go a long ways towards finding a nice comfortable place in our long-term memory. If the new educational program is cognizant of that, then repetitive tricks can be built into the teaching system, and hopefully the learning system, over the first eight years.

Learning to read and write is crucial. Book reading is essential. The availability of the Kindle really helps in this area. It is an adequate substitute for having a book in your own hand. But there should be a heavy emphasis on visual imprinting especially by using **DVDs** and downloading from the Internet. There is a ton of stuff out there. Good examples are the travel and cultural DVDs offered by **Rick Steves**. The **BBC** has a lot of available videos offered by **Sir David Attenborough**, the naturalist. That covers a lot of territory with a lot of pictures and information about peoples, cultures, geography, animals, birds and nature in general.

The **BBC** also has available videos concerning *planet earth*, the *ocean* and the *cosmos*. The **Great Courses** have great DVDs on all sorts of areas with great visual imprints. I'm sure that they would be happy to cut and paste and modify some of these works so they are good teaching tools for very young people. And let's not forget **Jacques-Yves Cousteau** who studied the seas, filmed the seas and was a great self taught oceanographer. There is great stuff there, and cut, pasted and modified, it would catch the attention of the average kid. Backing up all these videos would be the teacher, emphasizing the important points, giving some history about the person who put all this together, and encouraging questions. The students and the teacher could become cofounders of *Find the Answers* club. The kids could have a lot of fun looking up the answers. Humanity has to be kept in focus during the process. There is no substitute for a teacher giving direction, correcting things and filling in the missing pieces. Having the kids studying at home on the computer would be just another step towards *dehumanizing humanity*. The concept of "homework" has virtually been extinguished from the memory of the average student. Videos could be sent home and compete with the video games. The school videos could be very entertaining and would lead to some good question and answer interchange at school the next morning.

I would like to reintroduce the concept of *synesthesia* at this point. Don't let me forget about the importance of the parent. Our current educational model thinks in terms of separate informational blocks. American history is one block, geometry is another block, physics is another block and cubism is another. What if we put all this stuff into a **blender?** Interweave the subjects? Are we getting into chaos theory? We're not sure if creativity is inborn or whether it can be developed. Creativity is often associated with the capacity to integrate two or more senses at the same time, or two or more fields of information, to come up with something unique. It's called **blending** or *synesthesia* in this new system of education... might it lead some students to become *sui generis*, i.e. *creative?*

We're not often exposed to a great teacher who is able to unify everything that is happening at one time so that you have a sense of participating in the process, as if you were living it. I took a course on economic history in which the teacher was able to unify everything that was happening at any one time, including the religious, economic, social, financial and political goings-on, and their ramifications. There was a great teacher. I don't know if he appreciated that he was a great motivator. It's really not that hard to blend the various topics that are covered in the classroom if the teacher is herself taught that she should be doing that. How's that for a sentence with grammatical quicksand? That's part of teaching teachers to teach.

Let's not forget the parents. If you make things interesting for the children in the classroom, they will talk about their experiences at home. And their homework, including interesting video assignments, will force the parents to discuss what is going on in the classroom. Perhaps some of the parents will also be the recipients of some education. The teacher should ask the parents, or send home a questionnaire asking what type of work that they do, if they have any hobbies, and what their areas of interests are. That way they could be invited in to talk about their occupation or their area of interest. Remember that the teachers have limited backgrounds and certainly can't be expected to be all things to all people. Nobody knows all things about everything. It's a great way of getting a *superb general education for the teacher*! The more I think about this, the more I want the availability of another life. Then I could have a lot of fun participating in this new school model.

The first thing to do is to decide what the school year is going to be like. The government likes to control everything so let's make it uniform. I propose two models. Both would include vacation time and supervision time while parents are not at home. The first model is the old agricultural model which allows the students to work in the fields during summertime. The school year would comprise 3 three-month semesters. The academic school day would last 6 hours, 5 days week. There would be the availability of supervised sports, games and homework after school hours. An educational movie could be offered. The parents would have the opportunity of caring for their children in whatever way they chose during the summertime. The alternate would be to turn the school into some type of day camp which would be fun for the kids and allow the parents to take the kids out for vacations if they so chose.

The second model is the year-round school. It would be much the same except that the day camp would occur for a week at a time on a monthly basis. During four months of the year, the day camp would last for two weeks, giving the parents a chance for a nice family vacation. But the kids would be safe and the schooling would be solid. The educators could haggle about the exact spacing of time and the goals and experiences of the day camp. It certainly would go a long ways towards solving some of the problems of the working parent and providing safety and education for the kids.

So how do we move ahead with this new model? Remember that we have the computer, DVDs and the Internet. We're going to build a general education model. We don't want to emphasize rote memory, but we want this proffered information to go into long-term memory so that it can be used in **critical thinking** later on. **Critical thinking** is to be constantly in the background. But as the model is being built we must remember that there are three useful tools in imprinting **long-term memory**. It just makes it much easier if you have been born with a great memory. But the three essentials are: **#1** - a visual experience with an audio component, be it speech or music; **#2** - the visual experience being associated with something rather startling, funny or very familiar to us; **#3** – repetition. And the subjects need to be overlapped to allow *synesthesia* to develop if that is possible. Cultures and geography can overlap; geography and animals can overlap, etc.

The "juxtaposition and overlapping" of subjects is the crux to making the learning process interesting so that what is taught will be learned. My father would take me to museums and I would be just bored. Seeing more and more Grecian urns just made it duller and duller, to the dullest. That all changed when I was able to link art to history. I'll give you an example. There are plenty of videos available with which you could cut-and-paste. You can also put colored pictures on the wall. Let's gingerly fuse battles and wars with the weapons of war. The caveman used knives, axes and clubs. The battle of Hastings in 1066 is remembered as the Norman conquest of England. They used clubs, maces, swords and spears. Fast-forward a few years to Agincourt in 1415 when Henry V destroyed the French army when he was vastly outmanned. The current tools of the trade were the lance, the shield, the sword, the mace, the club and the dagger. But what really did the job were the archers who used armor piercing arrowheads which were manufactured in the **Tower of London**. Lots of interesting stories about the **Tower of London**. Lots of history, myths and tall tales.

210

The European cannon showed up in the 14th century and by the 17th century it was pretty well-developed. We see it from then on. We can introduce some famous naval battles to show how they could be used very effectively. The flintlock musket was used by the British soldier from 1722 to 1838. It was called the **Brown Bess.** Both sides used it during the American Revolution. You pull the trigger, the hammer hit the flint, which ignites the black powder, which sends the metal ball flying through a long barrel towards the enemy. However, it took a lot of work to put the black powder in and ram the ball down the barrel of the musket. You're lucky to get three shots off in a minute if you're really good. The Civil War saw the **Enfield** musket-rifle used. Things slowly improved. There are **videos** already available that show how all of this is done.

Colt introduced the percussion revolver in 1836 and **Smith & Wesson** introduce the cartridge revolver in 1856. There is a lot of footage available about the wild West. **Wyatt Earp**'s name comes to mind. The advent of the metal warships in the late 19th century and the early 20th century allowed those enormous guns to propel their bombs miles away. They were extensively used in World War I and World War II. There are a lot of *great war movies* available. The airplane really only came into its own in the early 20th century, just-in-time for those air battles of World War I. Remember the *Red Baron*? The aircraft carrier came later. There is a lot of interesting stuff that can be included.

I can hear you saying, "you shouldn't be showing such violent stuff, and it's only for the boys." So! That's part of history. You can certainly put a lot of material that shows that wars and the killing of people as a terrible thing and there is a lot of BBC stuff having to do with the atrocities in Africa. It is a matter of deciding when it is age-appropriate to include some of that material. Certainly the atomic bomb is another development and the current use of drones is another advancement which allows one to include a lot about science. Not many people really understand how this is done. As you can see you can cut-and-paste a lot of scientific stuff along the way. So you can link the history of wars, the weapons of war, the science of warfare and the cultures that suffer through all of this. You can tie in a lot of ethical stuff here.

And we're certainly not going to exclude the girls. I'm just not going to spend a few paragraphs highlighting the highlights in an area which would be interesting to the girls. But let me say that videos involving the history of ballet and it's great artists and companies could be made very interesting. My daughter and I saw French, American and Russian ballet companies and were amazed to see the differences in the grace, finesse, artistry and differences in the body structure manifested by these culturally diverse companies. I don't care if you don't like ballet. A good teacher pointing out the fundamentals of any industry makes it very interesting. The boys and girls should be exposed to the fashion industry as well as to the cosmetic industry. It's not gender specific if you get into the details of any industry. The mechanical portion of every industry is certainly interesting to the boys. You can always sneak up on any gender if you want to.

I've never been convinced that there is such a gap in the **_gender gap thing_**, and if there is, it's a **_familiarity ignorance gap_**. Once you know something about something, it gets to be interesting. If you're not exposed to something, you probably will think of it as dull and uninteresting. Why are the boys in England, Australia and India so interested in soccer and cricket? Is there something of the gender gap between American and British boys? Exposure to the pastimes of different cultures makes that culture come alive. I just was not sharp enough to see that pulpit being pushed under me.

I should be getting back to the teacher who is supposed to be doing the teaching. She should be interweaving ethical values as she goes along, but she must avoid brainwashing the kids with her own prejudices. We've seen how education has been permeated with a political agenda of liberalism.

No conservative scholar need apply at any of our major universities. Liberalism has been given a bad name. The English Whigs (liberals) of the 18th century felt that the individual was reasonable enough to behave appropriately, free from the control of the government or the church. They believed in the freedom of the individual and that's the principle that the United States was founded on. You've heard of the wolf in the garments of the sheep. Liberalism no longer means conservativism. It means government control with the state making the decisions for the individual. The concept has become one of the welfare state. We certainly do not want our young children exposed to the idea that the state will take care of them. Our revised educational curriculum must emphasize the personal satisfaction that comes from developing one's abilities and having fun doing it at the same time.

Putting this together shouldn't be that hard. I see it as a 5 **stage process.** The **first** thing to do is to fill up the room with teachers who know something about kids and their development. They need to decide at what age children are interested in various subjects, and when they are able to comprehend the complexities in each subject. At this time they need to list the subjects and areas of interests that need to be covered. This is really not very hard to do at this stage. It does get more complicated later on but it is easily achievable with the world of cut-and-paste. It is just tedious and monotonous.

Let's make our own list: **Basics** - arithmetic, reading, writing

My engineer friend says that math should be taught as an *intellectual construct*, whatever that means. Don't bog them down with multiplication and division tables, they can get that from their calculator or from their computer. The fundamentals of weights, measurements, simple concepts having to do with geometry would be covered. Learning the numbers 1 to 100 is fine as well as the letters of the alphabet. Counting by tens and hundreds is fine, and the quick tricks to finding out what a quarter or half of a number is, and learning how to do rough calculations in your head. ..is also good stuff.. these are tools which are always useful. Reading is it's own reward. But these basic skills are fundamental to any child's future so there needs to be a concentrated effort in a pleasant way to develop the skills. It can't be made into a chore or a punishment.

Cultures - the progenitor of great education. There is just a plethora of wonderful stuff. Italian, Peruvian, Chinese, Russian, Middle Eastern and African cultures are so diverse and many of them are so colorful. Current and past cultures can be compared. Under this umbrella we can group: **food, architecture, art-cave paintings-Egyptian pyramids-Greek statues-medieval Christian art-Renaissance full figures-Flemish fine work-cubism-creativity, dancing and music-instruments-performing groups-opera-plays-call and response-country-soul-jazz-musicals-rap, animals, races, religion & Eastern philosophy.**

You can see that if you put all of these components into a blender there is a very good chance that the final product might have some *synesthetic* qualities. The next two subjects can easily blend with all of these subjects and certainly can have a stand alone existence.

Geography
Languages

We're supposed to be a cosmopolitan nation, yet few citizens know a second language. Our military language school has only 10% of the people that they need. It takes at least 10 years to learn a language well enough so that you can sound as if you're part of the culture. What about the espionage issues? I personally think that you could regionalize a required second language and introduce kids to great foreign-language stories and books. Some would go on to learn the language if they got caught up in the culture in the process. They certainly shouldn't be forced to learn it. Whether to require the teaching of a second language is really a political decision. There is a good case to be made since we look upon ourselves as sophisticated global people, who don't speak a second language. The European children learn three or four languages fairly easily. Do you think the European children are just a lot smarter?

By regionalization I mean that different regions of the country could be the assigned different languages. For instance the West Coast could be assigned the job of teaching Japanese and Chinese, the Southwest, Spanish, not the Castilian type but the Mexican type. Pick the location where a foreign language is somewhat endemic, and teach it there. Where are the Germans located? Do they speak French in Louisiana, or just Creole?

A clairvoyant should be consulted to identify the people that will become senators and governors. These kids should be forced to learn a foreign language so that their performance in public office can be improved. And we could also hire a prestidigitator to make it happen. See how we can use critical thinking!

History - History could be taught in a simplified way without rote memorization. Why things occurred might be dull, but history comes alive when the characters and their personal stories come on stage. Many history teachers today have really no basic understanding of the people in the cultures that they gloss over.

Earth sciences - This is the study or physical world and it includes a lot of fascinating observations. People should know a good deal about many of the subjects. Let's quickly put together a list....
Fossils
Geology-rocks-minerals-diamonds-gold-oil-gas

Meteorology-weather, oceanography
Limnology-freshwater habitat
Natural disasters-earthquakes-floods-monsoons-tornadoes-
cyclones-tsunamis
Geographics-people's responses to landscape, climate, soil
and vegetation
Science-ancients-calendars-planets-Newton -nanotechnology-
computer chips
Environmental Impacts on the Individual
Money & banking-making checks and credit cards-stocks-
bonds
Legal-wills-contracts, marriage contracts-divorce
Communications-cave drawings-scribes-printing press-books-
mail-newspapers-radio-television-
computer-Internet-cell phone
Photography-inception mid-19th century-silent movies
-talking movies-cartoons-color-3-D-special
-effects-television-Classics-Three Stooges-
Bugs Bunny
Sports & games
Arts & crafts
Governments-American Constitution-foreign
governments-
Public health services, vaccinations-police
Tools & trades-repair and construction tools-air-conditioning-
plumbing-cooking-carpentry Transportation &
inventions-oxcart-buses-trains-subways
-planes-rockets-electricity

Phase 2 involves a two-person collaboration in each field. One puts together the highlights and basics of each subject and the second person sorts the material at an age appropriate level.

Phase 3 involves the two people in **phase 2** plus two other people, called **third person** and **fourth person**. The **third person** would be in charge of checking for videos, Internet material and printed materials pertinent to the subject. Once the 3 of them reviewed all the material and decided how it should be coordinated, they would then meet with the **fourth person** who is an expert in computer programming and the graphic arts. At this point the subject has been broken down into age-appropriate levels. Enhancing the **memory** by **visualization, familiarity** and **repetition** must be instinctively included in the planning of the material and these videos. The educational technician then puts together a visual and printed outline for each grade. We then move to **phase 4.**

Phase 4 is when critical thinking, morality, good manners, respect and politeness are spliced into the curriculum. A psychologist, a sociologist and a philosopher meet with the people from **phase 1** who understand children well enough so they can put together age appropriate splicing of this material.

Phase 5 is challenging for the coordinators and the cut-and-paste people. Putting the videos together is the first step. There is some negotiating with the people who have the rights to these videos. Then there is the cut-and-pasting. People have to be selected to fill in the material from **phase 3** and **phase 4.** Teaching manuals have to be put together for the teachers at each grade level. They have to be taught how to use videos, games, question and answer periods, parental participation while viewing everything with **critical thinking** and **morality** and **civility.** The colleges are going to have to totally revamp their curriculum. That will become an industry unto itself and add a lot of good paying jobs.

So the colleges are going to have to teach the teachers to teach. The teaching of ethical values is paramount. The teacher has to be building a person of character. We have seen where many students come from homes where the upbringing is been poor. The parents may themselves be bad examples. Nothing should be mysterious. Any professional tends to be secretive about his or her goals. Education should be transparent. The student should know that the goals are #1 - to be a good person, #2 - to be a successful person, #3 - to contribute to the happiness of the kid next to him. He should be rewarded whenever he meets any of these goals. There are many ways of doing that.

The kids will be seeing examples of violence, poverty, famine and war on the television every day. The teacher's job is to reinforce the idea that if you focus on your three goals, that you will go a long ways towards avoiding the human failures seen on the television.

As the children get older they can be shown that the three goals listed above would be leading to be a good citizen. They should be shown examples of great and common men being good citizens. It should be quite clear that a good citizen is an honest person who is responsible for his behavior and his achievement. The second responsibility is part of being involved in the betterment of his social group, his friends and family. The idea that you can be counted on to help somebody must be infused with the expectation that you can expect the same in return. Do no harm to anyone. Kids can come to understand that they can influence others to be good people and improves the whole society. They can appreciate very easily that people who are not doing the right thing should not be supported. Later on they will understand that the welfare state does the exact opposite. Kids just have to be given the tools at the beginning.

The underlying course that you are teaching is **responsibility.** If the student grows up thinking about **critical thinking** and **responsibility** he will make a better citizen. But it should be very clear to the student that he has been taught these two concepts. He should be using these words as commonly as he uses the words **food** and **movies.** We can anticipate some resistance to change such as, "you are dooming the next generation. If you are denying the current group of kids a good general education, they'll be incapable of teaching their kids much at home." I think the term is "poppycock." There will always be parents who are better at imparting information to the kids. The fact that we are imparting **deductive education** automatically makes them better parents.

"And what do you do about those disruptive kids, the mean kids and the dangerous kids who don't have any interests being at school?," comes a very intelligent question which needs to be addressed. The educators have already tried to do something about this. Since these troubled *trolls* and children are graduates of a wobbly culture and/or poor parenting, it is hard for the children to give up their already established patterns. Our proposed curriculum is already involved in doing something about the troubled parenting. The parents are involved, social services are keeping the parents involved, there are some negative consequences for the parents who are doing bad things. The citizenry and the government officials have to be behind this and authorize options. These children need to be kept out of the average school.

The educational system is already spending a lot of money on these kids. They need to be bused to special schools. They need to be involved in something that they show some interest in. By definition they seem to have a strong propensity to compete and *to do unto others that which they would not want to be done unto themselves*.

217

So they should be competing in sports, and severely punished for really bad actions which come naturally to them. They should all be involved in competitive games with the emphasis on being fair and honest. **Fair** and **honest** themes need to be repetitively inculcated. They are still young and you have a chance of getting them to develop a change in their skills sets. Violence and assaultive behaviors can't be tolerated. Corporeal punishment is not tolerated by our society today. So the reward for violent and assaultive behavior should be a form of situational and sensual isolation. Experts can provide various acceptable rewards for bad behavior.

The troubled child needs to be evaluated for native intelligence, level of creativity, and areas of interests. If he is interested in graphic or artistic areas, then he can be moved along in that way. It's quite clear that some research and trial and error will be required to identify how many subjects need to be provided for the students. Then you can hire the teachers who specialize in these areas. You then know how to manipulate the curriculum.

Meanwhile you can be working on developing their **critical thinking skills.** You can develop a lot of **DVDs** which would give good examples of "the ways that the kids are currently thinking and acting," in contrast that with **DVDs** of "the ways that the kids should be acting." If you made them funny they would have more impact. Some of those glitzy **Hollywood movie stars** would probably be willing to donate their time in this venture. Some of those actors are pretty decent people. Or you might choose to cut and paste negative scenes which the students are used to seeing on television all the time. **Social skill building** is a target. I leave it to your imagination as to how to put together **negative visual behaviors, antecedents of those behaviors, consequences, options.** Simply understood **fallacies** are often involved in the **heuristic,** automatic, behavioral responses. Many are really quite funny and then kids wouldn't really be offended, but the impact would be there. With the use of videos you could contrast **critical thinking behaviors** with **primitive behaviors.** Teachers would have to buy into this new style of thinking and teaching.

The optimal thing would be to have the schools for troubled children open seven days a week with an optional *work release program* to study family values on the weekends. After school hours would be filled with fun things. The kids are bused home to sleep. You have to keep them out of their environment. Some decision has to be made if the hard-core troubled student should simply be in a residential program until there is enough improvement for him to be allowed to go home at night. The extreme "liberal" viewpoint that this is punitive needs to be overridden. The alternate to to this or any similar program amounts to an **educational criminal program**. I put this in to stir the ire of well-meaning people who themselves are not using **critical thinking**. They are too emotionally involved to face the facts.

There is someone else who's finding another hole in this damn, oops!, dam. "You're not giving any room for students to be truly educated, to become the great teachers and researchers in academe," is an excellent argument and my back is certainly up against the wall. I see that I have not really explained why there needs to be a revolution in our philosophy of education. This argument is uttered by people who are part of the establishment in the refuge of that mystical ivory tower. They think of themselves as part of the great Greek tradition and welcome the common man into a society of scholars. To them we are the great Roman Empire and worthy of such greatness. Actually our pomposity is rapidly moving us towards being a great third world power. We really can't afford to have college educated citizens who have no jobs and are part of a happy videogame watching welfare state.

As you well know, I don't have a nano of creativity in these tired bones. But I have been consulting, call it plagiarizing, along the way. It's a copycat solution, there is no creativity to it. "You have to know your limits," is another example of **critical thinking**. I'm going to use some evasive action. We already know that less than 1% achieve greatness in any one field. We've been trying to certify everyone worthy of such achievement by granting them the pleasure of a *diplomatic baccalaureate degree*. We have actually been granting a *certificate of attendance* in some sort of social studies program. We can look to France where there is a highly competitive examination which allows talented students to enroll in a free University. So at age thirteen some of our students would sit for such an exam. The student would have had to demonstrate some academic dedication. Then he would have to show an interest in a specific field. You could just rely on a teacher's good judgment and bypass the exam. There could be some initial culling with some basic testing for the intelligence level, how good his memory is and how creative he is. If you don't like the concept of some preliminary culling, then IQ, memory capacity and level of creativity would be measured in the competitive examinations. But the students should not be allowed into these examinations unless he had demonstrated academic dedication.

It's a free school. If he fails to make it at the time of the first cut, or at the second cut, then he is free to do what he has to do to pursue it on his own. My friend is a very strong proponent of the fact that there is a great waste in education. He gave me a long list of successful high school dropouts. I'm just going to pick out a few, names that you will recognize. They are George Carlin, the comedian, Tom Cruise, George Eastman, founder of Kodak, Albert Einstein, George Gershwin, John Travolta, Ansel Adams and Richard Branson. Richard Branson is the founder of the Virgin group, Virgin Records and Virgin Atlantic Airways. He is worth over $4 billion. Some of the creative and/or inventive creatures will find their way regardless of the obstacles.

The focus on having students entered the University is to try to build up a pool of scholars who will keep knowledge alive and growing. The alternate would be that the kids just go to work and as they develop and learn new things that they would put their data into a new informational base where people can go and find it on the World Wide Web. I would propose that we set up an experimental model. The first is that you have the competitive, French like exam, and go to the University specializing in the field. The second track would simply allow the students to go into their area of choice and evolve. At the end of one or two generations the additions to the informational database can be compared. The ease of access to the new material will also have to be evaluated. Will access to the University bring greater scholarship to the world? It would be very interesting, especially if said with a shaky foreign accent.

Since Western society is moving in the direction of a total welfare state, we might streamline and minimize our educational system. Of course we could never abandon testing. So you would have to have some test to be certified as creative/inventive. Then the government could subsidize whatever your interests are and the rest of those lackeys could live comfortably off of your efforts. I wonder if that would derail the **natural order?**

Meanwhile we'll return to the kids when they reach age of 13 and become apprentices. They will now move from being generalists to choosing to be specialists in a field of their choice. If their primary education has been broad enough, they will naturally pick up a few hobbies or areas of interests which they can then refine. With the computer age and the Internet, they can be offered great continuing education courses. They have the option of becoming more interesting people, whom their kids can brag about.

Somewhere around the age of 10 or 11 the teacher should expose the children to current events and to the opposing philosophical and political views of the time. Getting them to read about events and editorial views in both the *New York Times* and *Wall Street Journal* would be a good starting point. The *New Statesman* is an English magazine which is left of center politically. The *New Republic* is also a liberal magazine. The *National Review*, Bill Buckley's magazine, and the *American Spectator* would offer the conservative views. The students would have the opportunity to analyze articles, use their critical thinking and debate amongst themselves. It would be great for them to practice what they should be doing when they become adults.

Around the same age children should be exposed to that list of terms and fallacies listed in the chapter comparing the cultures of the West and the East. Terms like **probability, bias, the first impression, ad hominem (attacking the person, not the issue), pattern recognition, memory distortion, generalization, anticipation** and **critical thinking** are basics that any kid can understand. The teacher can pick out articles in the newspapers and in the magazines that are *very good* examples. If a kid doesn't have a handle on **critical thinking** by the time that he leaves the school, then the schooling has failed. Then we can all use that old standby, it was a *mistake*, not a choice that didn't work out.

You have been watching the pupa or chrysalis transition stage of these young butterflies. They now have fully developed brains equipped with **critical thinking** as they enter the adult stage. It's called **shape shifting**. Surreptitiously they have been exposed to an adult world in the guise of being in *Alice in Wonderland*. Of course we know that many a pupa will never become a butterfly. Many children will fail to take advantage of what is been offered, for whatever reason. We have already been into the forest of genetics, personality structure and their environment.

But the kid is 13 years old and you may feel that he's about to enter the world of *catastrophe.* But you're in error. You're, like me, a product of the mechanistic age. Few know how to write the really complicated software, which is itself analyzed and repaired by something else. You can't even see what is going on... what with lasers and nano items doing their thing. This stuff is not being taught in schools. It's being created and modified as we speak. You'll only find it in the larger engineering companies or in some engineers garage. It's a different age. You'll find rooms that only have computer keyboards which appear to be operated by invisible men. You have to look at all this stuff in a different way. The newer employee can only function with on-the-job training.

So the kid has to be employed and become an apprentice. The lawyers and medical doctors have been in apprentice programs for years. The employers have had a long lead time before all this happens. They know what to expect. And initially it will be quite easy for the government to give them a subsidy for each new employee. The high schools have closed and have been sold. There is a lot of money for the subsidy now. Some industries will find that on-the-job training is the best way to go. Some will find that a combination of work and continued studies is the right mix. Some will find that on-the-job training and subsequent experience is more fruitful, before getting more education. Each industry may have to do the same thing as all of us do in our daily lives. They may have to resort to trial and error.

Let's call this process, *job creating method*, like *method acting* which was a huge success. This solves the current problem that the young people are facing. The "*cognition area of the government and educators*" has written the college educated kids into the "*your highly educated and have no job*" *corral*. The young people start looking for a job after they've been educated. This *job creating method* forces you to find a job at age 13. Private industry certainly nodes with their immediate and short-term needs are.... So you got a job, and you don't have to face a lifetime of debt. Is that an easy solution!?

You're worried about the universities. You fear some domino **effect**. But it may only **affect** the domino without causing it to tumble. I'm not really worried about the universities. They can fend for themselves. The schooling changes at the primary level may actually create a new market for them. With the availability of the Internet, those bright people should be able to find redemption and the revelation of their unanticipated importance in an ever-increasing creative world.

My friend says that we should just eliminate colleges altogether since they just repeat what should've been taught in high school. We can certainly let the current college students finish up and go to grad school if they choose to do that. We could save everybody a lot of money by downsizing the colleges and universities. They would simply offer either tutors and/or courses to the industries who would be referring students for specialized instruction or training. You might even get the former president of Harvard to get on the bandwagon.

We know that empires fade, sometimes they are modified, replaced or plain annihilated. Our educational system should probably be annihilated. That won't happen because of political reasons. The establishment will simply not allow it to happen. But I firmly believe that my engineer friend is on the right path and that this innovation in the educational process would lead to a much more creative and influential nation in the future. The irony about this is that my friend keeps saying that you don't need all of that rote information which you are force-fed in the educational system. Yet this new and improved educational system gives a much broader base of general information and knowledge.

But I would be remiss if I did not conclude with the **unified theory of wisdom.** We have stopped at many places along the road searching for **wisdom.** We have stopped at the cities of **thinking, experience, knowledge** and **natural order.** My friend has concluded that we have spent too much time on the road. We should have stopped at **experience.** I'm glad that I went all the way to the city Don't **natural order.** It has to do with the **Knowability principle.** We have found that **wealth** is the only constant found in the natural order, in that it naturally controls our perceived world. Of course he will say that the perceived world is but an illusion, and that the quantum world is just another illusion.

But let's get back to the **natural order.** So since **wealth** controls everything, one concludes that **wisdom= wealth.** I hate to do this to you, but I must. We all know that real family wealth is dissipated by the third-generation except for the **Rothschilds.** Hence the final equation must be:

Wealth = Wisdom = Rothschilds

My friend's analysis of this was not very complimentary and the words will not be repeated. He decided to contribute something. He fumbled for a while until he found page 161 in Throgmorton Aloysius Malthus' book, *Don't Read this Book Tails from the Red Fox.* He pointed to two pages and said, "put that in your book." I hope that Throgmorton Aloysius Malthus doesn't mind including some of his work in this book. It starts like this:

KNOWLEDGE is POWER
TIME is MONEY
and as every engineer knows,
POWER is WORK over TIME,
So, substituting algebraic equations for these timeworn bits of wisdom, we get:

$$K = P$$
$$T = M$$
$$P = W/T$$

Now we do a few simple substitutions:
Put W/T in for P which yields:

$$K = W/T$$

Put M in for T into the equation which yields:

$$K = W/M$$

Now we've got something...
KNOWLEDGE equals WORK over MONEY
What this means is that:
1. The More You Know, the More Work You Do, and
2. The More You Know, the Less Money You Make.

Solving for **MONEY,** we get:

$$M = W/K$$

or
MONEY equals WORK over KNOWLEDGE.

We see that **MONEY** approaches infinity as **KNOWLEDGE** approaches 0, regardless of the **WORK** done.
What this means is:
The More You Make, the Less You Know.

Solving for **WORK**, we get:

$$W = M\,K$$

WORK equals MONEY times KNOWLEDGE
We see that **WORK** approaches 0 as **KNOWLEDGE** approaches 0

This means that: **"The Stupid Rich do Little or No Work."**

I'm sure that you've been dying to find out what happened to Izzy. I forgot to mention that he went into a psychiatric hospital and received some shock treatments. His depression lifted and he was involved in counseling where he was encouraged to involve himself in something that he was good at. Izzy was good at counting cards so he moved to Las Vegas. He was in his **Mecca.** He made a very good living by playing blackjack. He never got known as a card counter since there are so many casinos in Las Vegas. He made the rounds and always went to the table where there was a new dealer. He only won small sums. He never drew any attention and he always lost a few hands before he cashed out. He bought a small home, collected first editions of detective novels and read 50 books on different topics and became one of the top 1% of the most informed people in the world. You might guess that he read, by accident, an advance copy of this book. He did go on to make some good friends in different fields, but he had the wisdom to stay away from very close relationships. That's about as good as it could get for **Job Lost**.

XI

WEALTH POWER SOCIALISM
NEW WORLD ORDER

It's time for that inevitable synopsis in which a few brief paragraphs "signifying nothing" will end with that inevitable "whimper." We started by documenting that we humans have a not so perfect way of thinking which could be improved by using logical thinking, called **critical thinking**. I think we've managed to have some fun along the way, but our lack of serious thinking has allowed us to be prey to a powerful *subspecies.*

I seem to be always straying off the path into areas that I have very little knowledge. I strayed into the **Wealthies** and the **Socialists** who seem to want to move into something called the **New World Order.** What is that? Reading between the lines it appears to be an organization which would control the political and financial matters of the world, presumably manned by **Plato's** *Philosopher Kings.*

I'm been forced to do some thinking on my own. Is this *organization* supposed to eliminate evil? We have learned that tribal divisions and terrorism can be likened to that *mythical Phoenix. Al Qaeda* and the *jihadist* and the *Taliban* are not going away. Is the **New World Order (NWO)** going to put 50 million soldiers on the ground around the world? Do they need to understand the wisdom of **Genghis Khan** who understood the value of the *scorched earth policy*? Or is the **NWO's** policy one of waiting for the world to become a generic loving entity? So what comes first, dominating and crushing people or waiting for mankind to become kind?

I really find myself in quicksand, and sinking rather fast. At this point I'm grasping at the idea of *fractals.* Science is into that. As soon as you get inside of a secret, you find another secret. It's a lot like a *homunculus.* I think the classic example of that is "the little man inside the head of the little man inside the head of the little man inside the head of the little man, etc." or if you've seen the **Alec Guinness** movie, "*Tinker Tailor Soldier Spy*" you've seen the doll within the doll within the doll within the doll. A **fractal** comes in all definitions, but one of them is that it is a self-similarity, something that is identical at all scales or dimensions. **Benoit Mandelbrot** coined the term in 1975. If you're not a mathematician, it will drive you crazy. I call it *fractalizing*. I'm sure that you feel more comfortable with my *foolicizing*.

We are in a philosophical *no man's land*. Individuals and organizations are asked to or have already made major commitments. Much of the arguments have roots in religion. But let's start somewhere. Scholars tell us that early man looked at the elements which were viewed as gods. Thunder, lightning and storms were caused by **Thor**. Later the qualities, should we say characteristics, of mankind were assigned to certain gods. **Apollo** was the god of light, **Diana**, goddess of nature and the hunt, **Hercules**, god of strength, **Neptune**, god of the Sea, **Athena**, goddess of wisdom, **Sol**, god of the Sun, **Venus**, goddess of love. Pantheism was based on observation.

From what I have learned it would appear that our ancestors were a lot smarter than we are. Our Western religions are based on revelations and hearsay. A lot of our stuff is based upon "*I opine*" this or that. It's built on **wish fulfillment**. Is the **Creator** an *enforcer* or and *observer*? And whose *ideas* should you believe and which ones should you be tolerating or working towards? I'd like some proof that the **NWO** has it right and that we are not just simply watching another *totalitarian organization* being implemented by the *wealthies* and the *socialists*.

We certainly have learned that the secret societies are not that secret and their goals are rather open, and we are being *invited to a banquet* where we are inappropriately garbed. I think I remember something in the Bible where people were invited to come to the table, but were then unceremoniously thrown out. I would certainly hate to have that happen to us guests. The government and the financial institutions seem to be inviting us.

We've managed to discover that our shadow governments are really just puppets controlled by shadow financial institutions which are themselves owned by powerful bankers and a few dozen extremely wealthy people. We have followed the **Khazars** (a mixture of **Jewish** and **Turkish** blood) who married into the wealthy *banking families* of **Italy** known as the Black Nobility. This blending of Southern European and Middle Easterner bloodlines then intermarried with the European aristocracy leading to a domination of the *financial institutions* in Europe.

These powerful *banking families* moved into the United States. The *American plutocrats* joined them creating powerful *international banking institutions* with major impact upon *government institutions*. Many **organizations** have facilitated their efforts, and *not so secret* <u>Secret Societies</u> continue to solidify their positions of influence and power. The *big names*, such as **Rothschild** and **Rockefeller**, number in the dozens. These *big names* and *corporations* and *bankers* are all members of the <u>**Round Table**</u>, the <u>**Royal Institute of International Affairs**</u>, the <u>**Council on Foreign Relations**</u>, the <u>**Bilderberg Group**</u>, the <u>**Club of Rome**</u> and the <u>**Trilateral Commission**</u>. This is really all out in the open.

<u>**American plutocracy**</u> grew out of the opium and slave trading, and we are familiar with the names of **Astor** and **Forbes**. The wealthy are drawn together, so that even names such as **Carnegie** and **Rockefeller** are included within the circle. The **Rockefeller** family now has joined the dynasty of the **Rothschilds**, with a great deal of <u>influence and control over both the financial institutions and the mass</u> media. This is all *verifiable*.

The 20th century has seen an insidious marketing of **Socialism**, which appears to be firmly entrenched in the American culture at both the **governmental** and **educational** levels. A few handfuls of **intellectuals, bankers**, and **politicians** have been powerful **salespeople** for this movement. A few<u> **wealthy men and women**</u> have played significant roles.

The **New World Order** has been a goal of the **socialist intelligentsia**, which parallels a similar goal by the<u> **wealthy financial classes**</u>. Many of the founders of **Socialism** appear to have been truly altruistic with a neurotic zeal. The<u> **wealthy banking families**</u> realize that they can gain more *wealth* and *power* in a less complicated way by concentrating their control over <u>**one entity which controls both the wealth and the peoples of the world**</u>. The **United Nations** and its associated banks and courts can be a useful tool. It was President John Adams who said, "there is a danger from all men. The only Maxim of a free government ought to be to trust no man living with power to endanger the public liberty. Liberty cannot be preserved without general knowledge among people."

We individuals are now ruled by the top down. Our **Founding Fathers** and **Abraham Lincoln** warned us of *despotism*. Its shadow is now upon us. So it is incumbent upon us to awaken to the challenges that the individual must once more undertake. After all it was President Thomas Jefferson who said, "Educated and informed, the whole mass of the people.... They are the only sure reliance for the preservation of our liberty." A *very few colonists* were involved in the **American Revolution**. A *very few* **wealthy men** financing a *very few* **dedicated intellectuals** must commit themselves to an extensive advertising campaign. The message must be plain and simple. We have listed the problems in just a few chapters. They can be concisely documented and addressed through the media and lecture tours.

Problems and Consequences slogans could prove effective with the repetitive visual and auditory cues of **These are the problems**, *these are the consequences, these are the solutions....are you going to take action? Are you willing to make some sacrifices for your children?* That method using *Problems, Consequences, Solutions, Sacrifices, Children* messages could be seen and heard over and over again on the **TV, radio, Internet, cell phones, Facebook, Twitter** and **BILLBOARDS** all over America.

Consider this for a billboard: **Did your Congressman tell you that Social Security is a Ponzi scheme? Is your pension fund also a Ponzi scheme?** We could also use the acronym *SCARE* ... *Socialists & Communists are Real Enemies* as a slogan. As you can see I have no background in propaganda and I certainly couldn't get a job in advertising. But there are many people were very good at this and are available.

The solution is fairly simple. It's important to understand that the middle class is the backbone of a democracy. The government is the enemy. The government power has to be curtailed. Limiting the availability of taxes cuts down on the size of the government and its ability to be the enemy of the people. There is no way to stop the wealthy from becoming wealthy and there is probably little reason to want to do that. If the people are in control of the government and their representatives with the tools to control the government and the financial institutions, then the natural forces of power and wealth can be kept under control. The citizens have to rebel and put citizens, not professional politicians, back in office. If you simplify it in those terms it shouldn't be that hard.

Something needs to be done while old-timers are still around and able to remember what this is all about. This generation is totally indoctrinated with the the socialist movement and has not a clue about its future. They are sacrificing their children.

So that issue has to be tackled. Is the *me generation,* also known as the *quick generation,* to go down in history as the *I didn't see it happen generation* or as the *we squeak a lot generation*? This generation is giving *the pursuit of happiness* a different point of reference. *"I've got it, I'm having fun!"* We all know that there are many very fine and thoughtful people in the current generation. An informational campaign must be directed to these people. So they must have access to the information that we have been discussing, so that they can become converts to the mission of recovering their constitutional rights. Young people, capable of critical thinking should be enlisted to use the modern forms of communication to participate in this mission. They can make movies, go into the *"recovery" apps business,* blog and twitter away, etc.

As I mentioned above, I seem to be in the *homunculus* business, needing to add chapter after chapter as the fractals are endless. I could become the Will and Ariel Durant (*Story of Civilization*) version of critical thinking and maybe write twelve or so volumes. Look at short-term history and you'll find examples of *absolute power being used against the individual* in subtle and not-so-subtle ways. You don't even see it happen.

After the Korean War, there was a period of depression and money was tight. The *big corporations* recognize they had the *absolute power* to delay the payment of their bills from 10 to 120 days. Most people remember when there was such a thing as *customer service.* Many large *corporate stores* now have only people at the cash registers and in the stacking and storage areas. Once upon a time you could make a phone call and have a *company employee* answer the phone and complete a business transaction. *Corporate* learned that they were dealing with *lemmings,* and turned the *lemmings...* customers... into *corporate employees... without pay.* The *lemmings* learned to follow instructions and punch numbers, even dozens of them, to try to get anything done. If that didn't work, they were told to stay on the line and a customer service representative would be happy to assist them. Early on, you would get disconnected after 10 to 30 minutes. *Corporate* stopped that *interminable hold* because the *lemmings* started getting mad. But the *lemmings* never revolted against the basic process, so the *lemmings* simply accepted their new role as *unpaid company employees.* It's really funny how masses of individuals become easy prey to the *prestidigitator.* It's a classic example... you left the barn door open... the horse ran away... you can never get him back.

So what is new on the agenda for a species of *reactive people*, who just does its thing and doesn't worry about the consequences. Suddenly the *social media* is upon us and appears to have some significant influence. *SPECTRE* in the form of a *scary, impulsive, but convincing dude* could make mockery of all critical thinking. Don't go *guffawving* about this potential. It's real. The regulators haven't even started thinking about the possible damage.

So it's time for decisive action. Let's put down a list of problems and goals. The "power of the press" has been replaced by the "*power of the social media.*" So let's use it to help the young people to understand what they are dealing with. It will be crucial to enlist a few of the *wealthy and powerful* who understand the pitfalls of the New World Order. They will have to go into the lists against the *Rockefeller Media* and buy up stations and networks on the Internet and on television and the *new whatever* that is currently being used for communication and propaganda. Intellectuals with good oratorical skills, who are committed to upholding democratic values, would be recruited to go on lecture tours with special attention to the students and faculties of colleges and universities. They should also be prepared to regularly host and speak on talk shows and flood the news media with endless contributions. These *chosen ones* should become household names.

The members of the college *Republican clubs* should be told quite forcefully that a key intent is to return the *middle class* to primacy in the United States. The focus should not be on taxation, but on rebuilding the United States into an independent *Fortress* on its own independent island. The United States must again be self-sufficient and not dependent on globalization and the economies of other nations. A self-sufficient manufacturing industry must be reestablished, and the service economy must never again be the *sine qua non. SCORE (Service Core of Retired Executives)* has been renamed but still works with the *Small Business Administration.* It can be very helpful for the much-needed young entrepreneur. The military-industrial complex needs to remain very strong since the world is not a peaceful place. The *United Nations* needs to be a place of discussion without power over the members who are there just for discussion.

Once that is done **networks of small groups** in every city and town can start pressuring their politicians to make the required

231

changes. It should be made clear that only politicians committed to limiting their terms of office would receive support. They should support **a *new amendment*** to the ***Constitution*** which would limit the time that any one politician could serve in both branches of Congress. This will begin the ***New Amendment*** process that is needed to restore the values that the ***Founding Fathers*** so heroically fought for, *"**that these values not be lost to the tyranny of socialism.**"* To pass a new amendment 75% of the states have to ratify it.

The economy must be returned to one of ***reason*** with an amendment which requires a ***balanced budget.*** The care of the needy must return to being the care ***of the needy***, not a ***dole***, i.e. a redistribution of ***taxes*** to 50% of the citizens. The ***trade deficit*** must be eliminated with the return of ***protectionism*** and the use of ***tariffs.*** That can easily be done by a verbal agreement of, "I only buy as much from you is you buy from me." Suppose you use the ***Utopia*** "labor as currency" formula to decide what is a fair exchange rate? Am I putting the shuck on you? We should withdraw from ***GATT*** and ***NAFTA*** and limit our involvement with the ***IMF*** and ***World Bank.***

If the ***central bank of the nation*** is to be a bank for the nation, then the ***Federal Reserve's*** status as a private bank needs to be changed. It is also clear that the ***banking*** and ***financial*** institutions of the nation need to be tightly monitored since they have demonstrated ***corruption*** at their very core which has led to destabilizing the entire world economy.

There need to be ***new amendments*** curtailing the powers of the ***Presidency*** and the ***Supreme Court.*** The legitimate power of ***Congress*** needs to be written in very clear language so that it can play its proper role. Amendments having to do with ***religion*** and ***education need to*** clearly reflect the wishes of the ***Founding Fathers. Those basic values*** still have their place, to which the ***quick generation*** has had little exposure.

The ***educational system*** needs to be completely reformed, and the citizens need to readdress what ***equality, fairness*** and ***personal responsibility*** really imply.

This fool has learned a good deal during this project. I hope that you have also benefited from this inquiry into critical thinking, which led us into a search for the origin of wealth and power, and then into the impact of **socialism** on American culture. We have uncovered many facts, many of which are true and verifiable. Some are questionable, some are simply entertaining, but at least they have given your **critical thinking** a workout.

The *big names* of the *socialist movement* are all well known. Their goals have been well-known from inception, and repeated by their membership... repeatedly. That is all *verifiable*. W*ealthy American families and bankers* have aligned themselves with these goals. These new *socialist goals* have also been open to the public. It gets repetitious, so I'll only mention a few. They are *government control of the press, of education, of central banks, financial unrest, political instability, free trade and the erosion of religion and the nuclear family.*

It appears that these goals are a *new and improved* version of **American Manifest Destiny.** Many of these goals are manifested in everything that we see today. View any form of media. Is this *cause-and-effect*? Is this a *post hoc fallacy*? My friend would simply say that *it's all an illusion!*

I guess that I have one more question to ask you. In an earthly world which has evolved to contain such dissimilarities, inequalities and passionate hatreds, would you really want to put your fate in the hands of one organization which has no track record?

Please use that **critical thinking** thing that is one of the few tools that we can use. *What do you think*? I hope that you feel empowered to lift the mantle of *good citizenry* from the muddied ground and *go forth and bring glory and prosperity back to the United States of America!*

&

"Now that I have reached the safety of the parapet of wealth and power I am quite secure. This hypothenused ladder will not be used by any followers. Down with the ladder!" Is this what mankind is all about?

I can sense your uncertainty about all of this. It is very hard to live with uncertainty and unpredictability, which of course we are forced to do. Economics comes to mind. *Ceteris paribus* (all things being equal) is continuously used in the world of economics. There are so many variables that things are by definition unpredictable. Hence we can conclude that *economics is the opiate* of the financial world. And certainly Heisenberg must've drawn upon it when he offered the *uncertainty principle.* I marvel that two economists were given the Nobel Prize for stating that psychology influences the stock market. So it is up to you to choose a "watch and wait" attitude or commit yourself to more involvement.

This fool, a jester at the **World Court**, is far from uncovering **wisdom**. We observed the terrible consequences of the nuclear power plant disaster at Chernobyl with a radiation death toll of about 1 million people. Now the fusion of earthquake, tsunami and atomic energy found at Fukushima presents as a disaster with a potential death toll of 10 million people. And we're seeing so many terrorists and ethnic groups killing innocent women and children for selfish and/or altruistic reasons.

I remember that Shakespeare's Coriolanus was described as "*vengeance proud.*" Mankind has never learned the concept of humility. Perhaps mankind is trying to compete with God and the natural forces of Earth....earthquakes, tsunamis and typhoons. Man has become so arrogant that he feels himself to be "so wise." I chuckle ... I have heard that saying since, as they say, "I was knee high to a grasshopper," "the bigger they are, the bigger they fall." We have seen this in our push for globalization and in our "too big" banking institutions.

The magnates of banking had developed a risk-taking principle based upon the past....so-called *reliable* history without factoring in Heisenberg's "**uncertainty principle.**" It's like the young attorney said, "it's the thing that you could never predict which will always cause the problem."

In closing it would be wise to be a bit reflective. We see a few seedlings taking root. Perhaps you could find some stuff by Neil Degrasse Tyson on the Internet which forces us all to be very humble as he clarifies how little we understand about almost everything. He points out that Claudius Ptolemy told everyone that the earth was the center of all celestial bodies. That was 2000 years ago. It was not until the sixteenth century that Nicolaus Copernicus, well educated at the universities of Padua and Bologna, postulated that the sun was the center of the universe and that the earth simply revolved around it. In 1687 Isaac Newton published his famous *Mathematical Principles of Natural Philosophy* which formulated the laws of motion and universal gravitation. He is given credit for establishing **classical mechanics.** That covered the motions of rather large bodies but that was challenged in the twentieth century by **quantum physics** which worked for very small things such as subatomic particles. Einstein helped to reconcile these conflicting views. Now the visionaries are postulating that there are strings from other universes that are allowing us to connect to their universes as particles. Are we to assume that the strings are strong enough for us to be pulled into another universe? Is God in another universe pulling the strings?

So we can conclude that much of what is in this book is pretty trivial. But in our *big thing world* the revolution in technology is capable of creating an entirely different world. In a small or large way, science fiction may be upon us. Only the brightest amongst us will have the capacity to understand and interface with it. Many of us will not be needed. Artificial intelligence has made its debut. The robotization of human functions is just beginning. Astrological physics is really in its infancy. Genetic engineering is or will be modifying viruses, bacteria and humans. It would be naïve not to believe that major decisions will have to be made about the future of humanity. It seems reasonable that the average human being should act to preserve its species. The powerful forces may simply say that it is part of the natural order, that *homo sapiens* should be expected to evolve, and also become extinct like the dinosaur. We know that millions of species die off on a regular basis. We should all think about that.